# Meyerhold

# Meyerhold

The Art of Conscious Theater

Marjorie L. Hoover

University of Massachusetts Press    Amherst 1974

*A resemblance to reality is still supposed to be the chief pre-condition and basis of dramatic art. But what if it could be proved that the very essence of dramatic art is such as to preclude any such resemblance? . . . Where is the resemblance to reality in an auditorium divided in two, one half of which is full of spectators?*

ALEXANDER PUSHKIN,
"On Popular Theater"

# Contents

# List of Illustrations

# Preface

Russian achievement in twentieth-century art, long thought to be the work of but a few—above all, Stravinsky, Stanislavsky, Eisenstein, and Kandinsky—has increasingly become known in its true broad sweep. No one any longer doubts the stature of Stanislavsky's contemporaries in the theater, the directors Vsevolod Meyerhold and Evgenii Vakhtangov. About Meyerhold three basic works have recently appeared in the Soviet Union: recollections about him, here referred to as *Encounters*; his own articles, speeches, and the like, here cited as *Articles*; and a biography by Konstantin Rudnitskii. Further, the publication of Meyerhold's correspondence and an exposition illustrating his productions are planned in the Soviet Union for 1974, the one hundredth anniversary of his birth. In the West only one essential book in English, Edward Braun's *Meyerhold on Theatre,* has thus far been devoted to the great director; it is an anthology of translations from the important works, connected by commentary and summary so as to make the whole career comprehensible. Thus this is the first critical account in English of Meyerhold's entire career as such.

The Library of Congress system of transliteration has been used throughout the book with certain reservations. That is, no ligatures have been used to indicate the rendering of one Russian letter by two Latin ones; thus Iutkevich,

for example, renders Îutkevich throughout. The apostrophe to render the Russian soft sign has been omitted, and the best-known Russian names are referred to in the text in their familiar Western variants, but exact transliteration has been added for the citation of works in Russian both in notes and bibliography. The table of Meyerhold's productions in Appendix I is taken from *Articles*, though abridged to begin with 1905 and supplemented by two slight additions, Meyerhold's collaborations other than directorial and his plans for productions which were not even launched—all in the Soviet period. Identifications of terms are given in the glossary; of people, in the index. Some Russian titles in the bibliography have made necessary the double rendering of a few names, though these are indicated by cross reference. In the rendering of foreign-language titles an effort has been made to strike a just mean between the most usual and the most accurate. The translations in the text are mine unless otherwise indicated.

I wish to acknowledge the privilege of working in several libraries in the West and the Soviet Union, especially those of the All-Russian Theater Society, the Bakhrushin State Theater Museum, the Central State Archive of Literature and Art, and the Leningrad Theater Museum. I wish further to give heartfelt thanks for assistance to specialists: the late Artavazd Aganbekian,

Aleksandr Fevralskii, Marina Ivanova, Jay Leyda, Viacheslav Nechaev, Nikolai Oulianoff, Maia Sitkovetskaia and Maria Valentei. This account is also greatly indebted to the Soviet publications on Meyerhold noted above, the collections cited as *Encounters* and *Articles* and the Rudnitskii biography. Nor would my research have been possible without a Powers Travel Grant from my own college and assistance from the Inter-University Committee on Travel Grants. I am deeply grateful to the director and staff of the University of Massachusetts Press for their cooperation and good advice in publishing my book.

# Frequently Cited Works

Articles      *V. E. Meierkhol'd: Stat'i, pis'ma, rechi, besedy,* 2 vols. (Moscow, 1968)

Desiat let      A. V. Fevral'skii, *Desiat' let teatra Meierkhol'da* (Moscow, 1931)

Encounters      *Vstrechi s Meierkhol'dom* (Moscow, 1967)

Iutkevich      Sergei Iutkevich, *Kontrapunkt rezhissera* (Moscow, 1960)

Komissarzhevskaia      *Vera Fedorovna Komissarzhevskaia: Pis'ma aktrisy, vospominaniia o nei, materialy* (Leningrad and Moscow, 1964)

Rudnitskii      K. Rudnitskii, *Rezhisser Meierkhol'd* (Moscow, 1969)

Volkov      N. Volkov, *Meierkhol'd,* 2 vols. (Moscow and Leningrad, 1929)

werkausgabe      Bertolt Brecht, *Gesammelte Werke,* 20 vols., werkausgabe edition suhrkamp (Frankfurt, 1967)

# Introduction

In an age such as ours with its overwhelming sense of change new gods are sought. Stanislavsky and the method are no longer invoked in the American theater as frequently as Bertolt Brecht and Antonin Artaud or Jerzy Grotowski and Vsevolod Meyerhold. Though these new names we worship all await clearer definition, a little knowledge of the last, Meyerhold, is finally becoming available. And with each further revelation Meyerhold again amazes by his relevance to our time. Though Meyerhold has been called the Picasso of the theater for the protean changeability of his innovations during his long career as director (1902–38), he nevertheless remained faithful to one principle throughout, and it is this underlying principle of his work which, above all, brings it close to us. Whereas Stanislavsky sought the truth of reality in the theater, Meyerhold denied imitation as the goal of modern art. Rather, he conceived of art as a law unto itself, creating its own truth, not imitating a truth lodged elsewhere. Not that Meyerhold believed in art for art's sake; instead, he insisted on including the audience in theater art as its fourth dimension.

To achieve communication with the audience he used older and more naive means than those established as the convention of his time; so he broke the confines of the then customary peepbox stage. He revived devices of folk theater and circus as well as those of other times and places, such as the *commedia dell'arte* or the Oriental theater. He tried not only old devices but also new ones, experimenting with music and movement, cinema and light. Thus he achieved firsts in the use of many devices which have since become an inevitable part of modern practice; for example, he had been staging without a curtain long before 1917. Above all, he tried to make the actor a trained and conscious artist, rather than one hypnotizing and hypnotized by feeling. In order to put the actor's physique at his disposal as an instrument for communication, he insisted that he remain outside and show, as well as inside and be, the role. To the same end he trained the actor in body movements, which after 1917 he renamed "biomechanics" in the fashion of our twentieth-century love affair with technology. He put a sense of music into productions not just for timing but also for ironic commentary. He conceived stage space in three dimensions and by 1932 had begun construction of a theater building on principles like those of Walter Gropius's "total theater." [1] A decade before, he realized constructivist designs on stage. Known as "a director's director," he was teaching courses in directing by the time of the Revolution. The political revolution went hand in hand for him with his artistic revolution; so it was Meyerhold who after 1917 first proclaimed the political theater in Russia.

The innovations Meyerhold achieved, especially in the early Soviet years under the double aegis of political and artistic revolution, reverberated even in the West, though the Meyerhold Theater never toured America, as did Stanislavsky's Moscow Art Theater, nor was Meyerhold's book *On Theater* (1913) translated, as was Aleksandr Tairov's into German. The great productions Meyerhold staged during his prerevolutionary decade as director at the Imperial Theaters were never shown abroad as the splendor of Russian opera and ballet was revealed in Sergei Diaghilev's Paris seasons beginning in 1907. Nor did he produce the canon of an international author's work, as Stanislavsky did Chekhov's, though he created Vladimir Mayakovsky in the theater and with rare intuition for new talent drew into collaboration such artists as Kazimir Malevich and such musicians as Dmitrii Shostakovich. Indeed Meyerhold's ideas reached the West largely through the work of others who had been associated with him, Mikhail Fokine, Tairov, Fedor Komissarzhevsky; or through his pupils and associates in his workshop, Sergei Eisenstein, Nikolai Okhlopkov, Sergei Tretiakov; or through those who paid tribute to him, Evgenii Vakhtangov, Iurii Liubimov, Jerzy Grotowski.

When his own pronouncements were finally translated into English,[2] for all their innovative impact they were also puzzling and, in part, misleading. This was perhaps because the first texts were excerpts only and perhaps because, though written between 1907 and 1912, they were taken out of historical context as universal truth applicable to theater art today. For Meyerhold's name was intentionally buried during the considerable period of Stalinism. When his credo became questionable to the new realism pervasive in the thirties, early errors and late failures were cited against him, until under Stalinism he suffered both physical repression and artistic annihilation. Only some quarter century later has a broad spectrum of Meyerhold's pronouncements become available in English, through Edward Braun's anthology *Meyerhold on Theatre* (1968), while in the Soviet Union at least three basic publications have appeared,[3] with more promised.

Indeed it is no anachronism to rediscover Meyerhold now a half century after his first reverberation in the West during the early Soviet period.[4] Certainly some of his work has aged with its time and now seems as quaint as an old Chaplin movie or the unrealized constructivist tower designed by Vladimir Tatlin as a monument to the Third International. Admittedly, in his 1907 plan for change at the theater of Vera Komissarzhevskaia, he himself called outmoded a couple of his symbolist productions of Maeterlinck. Nevertheless, a career of such innovative genius as his deserves to be viewed whole in the perspective of criticism and history. For Meyerhold's consistent principle of art in its own right, not as imitation, is relevant to our age, and the rich inventiveness of his practice, inasfar as it has been reconstructed,[5] makes his work a prime source of creative ideas for the theater today. As that gifted Russian theater director Vakhtangov is said to have remarked, "The ideas for staging which Meyerhold dreams up but does not always exhaust completely would suffice other directors for innumerable productions." [6]

# Vsevolod Emilevich Meyerhold (1874-1940): Chronological Table of his Life

1874    Born Karl Theodor Kasimir Meyerhold, eighth child of a German citizen and well-to-do distillery owner in Penza (a provincial capital south of Moscow having some cultural life and literary associations with the romantic Mikhail Lermontov and the satirist Mikhail Saltykov-Shchedrin).

1892    Began acting in amateur theatricals, first in a comic role in Aleksandr Griboedov's *Woe from Wit,* for which he was also assistant director. His Riga-born mother, though not of wealthy origin, brought a heritage of Western culture; she allowed him constant use of her subscription box at the local theater and provided steady exposure to music which led to his later auditioning in violin at the Moscow Conservatory. In Penza he not only saw famous actors on tour in such classic roles as Hamlet but also met them in his own house, thanks to the soirées given by his father. The decline of his family's fortunes, confirmed as bankruptcy upon the father's death in 1892, caused Meyerhold to turn with professional seriousness to the theater as a means of earning his living.

1895    Though upon graduation from gymnasium Meyerhold first read law for a year at Moscow University, his interest remained with the theater, where he spent most evenings in the capital. He returned summers to act again in Penza with a provincial company. He had there an experience decisive for his view of the actor's art, when he empathized with the hero all too completely during a dramatic reading of "Monologue of a Madman," by Aleksei Apukhtin; as he wrote in a letter quoted by his biographer, Nikolai Volkov, "I lived every line. In a word, I thought I was insane!" Volkov commented: "This crisis after the recital of 'The Madman,' which came from re-living every line, later caused Meyerhold to oppose the naturalistic method for actors of

experiencing [the role]"
(Volkov, 1:41–42).
That same year of his ma-
jority Meyerhold opted for
Russian citizenship and
conversion to the Russian
Orthodox faith. Though
both decisions brought
him practical advantage—
naturalization, the avoidance of military service in
Germany; and conversion,
the right to marry Olga
Mikhailovna Munt the fol-
lowing year in the Ortho-
dox church—Meyerhold
was primarily moved by
the ideal consideration of
being Russian born and
bred. Accordingly, he
took upon conversion the
Christian name of his fa-
vorite Russian writer,
Vsevolod Garshin.

1896   Transferred after one year
at law school to the Mos-
cow Philharmonia as a
second-year acting stu-
dent.

1898   Graduated from the Moscow Philharmonia with
the gold medal for the best
actor, together with Olga
Knipper, later Chekhov's
wife, who received the
gold medal for the best

actress. Both were invited
by their teacher Vladimir
Nemirovich-Danchenko
to join the new Moscow
Art Theater, which Ne-
mirovich was then in the
process of founding with
Konstantin Stanislavsky
(fig. 0.1).

1898–1902   As a member of the original company of the Mos-
cow Art Theater played
some eighteen roles, in-
cluding Treplev, the
young hero of Chekhov's
Sea Gull, the play which
made the new theater's
reputation and gave it the
emblem it still uses. Also
played Tusenbach in
Three Sisters (fig. 0.2).
Was not, however, invited
to become a shareholder
when the company was re-
formed in 1902.

1902   Travelled to Italy.

1902–4   Left the Moscow Art Theater to direct, as well as
act, in a cooperative of
young actors, staging some
170 plays in two years, the
first year spent in Kherson,
the second in Tiflis.

1905   Invited to direct in Stanislavsky's own personally

*Figure 0.1.  Young Meyerhold*

*Figure 0.2.  The young Meyerhold of the Moscow Art Theater period, who impressed Chekhov as bookish and intellectual*

financed Theater Studio of 1905 with the experimental aim of finding ways to project the new symbolist works, "to stage the unreal." [1] Meyerhold's two productions for the Theater Studio of 1905, Maurice Maeterlinck's *Death of Tintagiles* and Gerhart Hauptmann's *Schluck and Jau*, were shown in dress rehearsal but never opened, both because Stanislavsky did not approve them and because the Revolution of 1905 caused Moscow theaters to close temporarily. The account which Meyerhold wrote of the Theater Studio, the first major article of the many he wrote, was published in an anthology of opinion, *Theater: A Book about New Theater* (1908), and was also included in Meyerhold's collected articles, *On Theater* (1913).

1905–6   Spent half of the theater season among the literary élite of Saint Petersburg, Andrei Belyi, Alexander Blok, Georgii Chulkov, and Viacheslav Ivanov, who welcomed in Meyer-

hold the practical man of the theater capable of carrying out their new ideas of theater.
Completed the theater season back again in the provinces with his former actors' cooperative.

1906–7   Recalled to Saint Petersburg as director for the actress-manager Vera Komissarzhevskaia, who was about to launch her own company. Meyerhold's most important productions for her theater, each of which represented a new departure, were Ibsen's *Hedda Gabler,* Maeterlinck's *Sister Beatrice* (Carl Vollmoeller's version of the same material, *The Miracle,* is more familiar in English), Alexander Blok's *Farce* (*Balaganchik*), Leonid Andreev's *Life of Man,* Frank Wedekind's *Awakening of Spring,* and Stanislav Przybyszewski's *Eternal Fairy Tale.*

1907   On one of several trips abroad during his life saw productions by Max Reinhardt in Berlin. Was replaced as director by Komissarzhevskaia's brother Fedor before termination of contract.

1908–18   Appointed director for both opera and drama at the Imperial Theaters, Saint Petersburg. Among his notable dramatic productions of the decade were Molière's *Don Juan* (1910) and Lermontov's *Masquerade* (1917); among the operas were Gluck's *Orpheus and Eurydice* (1911) and Richard Strauss's *Electra* (1913).

Equally important were the unofficial experimental productions which Meyerhold signed with the pseudonym Dr. Dapertutto (after a tale by E. T. A. Hoffmann, the German romantic master of the grotesque). Meyerhold himself singled out particularly *Columbine's Scarf* (1910), a musical pantomime after Arthur Schnitzler, and Alexander Blok's *Farce* as representing, along with *Don Juan,* turning points in his consciousness. That he staged *Farce* three times is symptomatic of his persistent experimentation in summer theater and various studio and cabaret ventures. Among the locations for the latter, all in Saint Petersburg, were Lukomore (Crescent Bay), a small club theater (1908); the Liteinyi Theater, where Meyerhold's play after Hermann Bang, *The Lady from the Box* (1909) and his translation via German of the Kabuki *Terakoya* (1909) were staged, though not by him; the Tower Theater, the apartment of Viacheslav Ivanov (1910); the House of Interludes, a pantomime group using the stage of the Nobles' Assembly (1910 and 1911) (fig. 0.3); *Love for Three Oranges,* actually the Meyerhold Studio, at Tenishevskoe high school (1914 and 1915); the Comedians' Cellar (1916).

1910   Travelled to Greece (fig. 0.4).

1912   Collaborated with the summer theater group, Cooperative of Actors, Writers, Artists and Mu-

*Figure 0.3. Poster for the House of Interludes, dated 1910 and signed by the artist, N. Remi [Nikolai Vladimirovich Remizov]*

sicians, in Terioki, Finland (now Zelenogorsk, USSR), where he directed with Blok's advice August Strindberg and *commedia dell'arte* in adaptations by Vladimir N. Solovev.

1913    Published his collected articles, *On Theater*. Directed Gabriele D'Annunzio's *Pisanella* in Paris for Ida Rubinstein.

1914–16    After instructing in various classes and schools for almost a decade, conducted his own studio.

Edited the magazine *Love for Three Oranges,* a literary and theater journal, and also his studio organ, of which nine numbers appeared. Coauthored in the magazine the scenario *Love for Three Oranges* (1914), after Carlo Gozzi, and the melodrama *Under Fire* (1914).

1915    Directed the film *The Picture of Dorian Gray,* after Oscar Wilde, in which he played the part of Lord Henry, and also *The Strong Man,* after Stani-

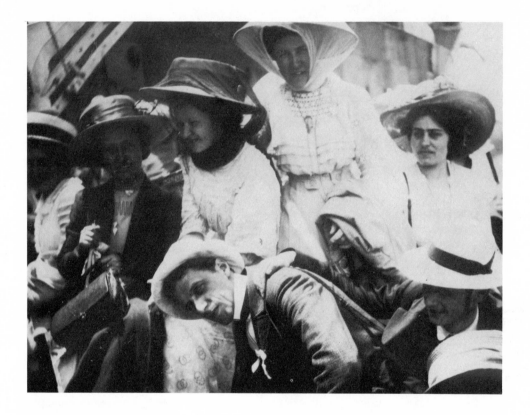

*Figure 0.4. Achilles among the maidens: Meyerhold on the steamer to Greece in 1910*

slav Przybyszewski, in which he played the poet Gursky; both films have been lost.

1917    Beginning with the February Revolution, active in various associations of theater people; after October worked for the Theater Division, of which he then became head in Petrograd (1918–19).

1918    Joined the Communist Party; produced outside the established Petrograd theaters Vladimir Mayakovsky's *Mystery-Bouffe* in honor of the first anniversary of the October Revolution.

1919    Published *Alinur,* fairy-tale play in three acts with a prologue and epilogue. Began editing various theater bulletins and periodicals, an activity continuing for several years. While recuperating from fatigue in the south, arrested by the Whites. After liberation by the Reds, directed the municipal theater at Novorossiisk.

1920–21   Returned to Moscow to head the Theater Division of Narkompros (the People's Commissariat of Enlightenment); promulgated the slogan "Put the October Revolution into the Theater."
Opened the new Theater RSFSR I with his production of Emile Verhaeren's *Dawns.*

1921    Organized the first courses in directing in his own theater workshop, where he taught "biomechanics," a science of movement and technique for stage communication, to such future directors as Sergei Eisenstein and Nikolai Okhlopkov and to such actors as Igor Ilinskii and Mariia Babanova. In his first workshop production, Fernand Crommelynck's *Magnanimous Cuckold,* he used biomechanics and embodied "constructivism" in the sets as well, which were designed as apparatus for acting. Trained in his workshop Zinaida Esenina-Raikh, who became his second wife and the leading actress in his theater (fig. 0.5).

*Figure 0.5. Meyerhold and*
*Zinaida Raikh in the early twenties*

1922    Lectured on biomechanics and published statements on it, one in his review of Aleksandr Tairov's book *Notes of a Director* (1921), the other in a pamphlet which he co-authored, *The Set Roles of the Actor's Art (Amplua aktera).*

1922–24    Headed the Theater of the Revolution, where he directed two notable productions, the classic *A Profitable Post (Dokhodnoe mesto),* by Aleksandr Ostrovsky, and a new play, Aleksei Faiko's *Lake Liul.*

1923    Spearheaded the new movement in art, constructivism, with its leaders Vladimir Tatlin, Liubov Popova, Aleksandr Rodchenko, and Varvara Stepanova, whose work was explicated in Mayakovsky's magazine *Lef.*
Staged the adaptation with interludes by Sergei Tretiakov of a play by Marcel Martinet, as the antiwar epic *Earth Rampant,* which travelled and was shown to thousands

as a mass spectacle. Celebrated in the Bolshoi Theater five-year jubilee as Soviet director.

1923–38   Directed at his own Meyerhold Theater notable productions (fig. 0.6), including Ostrovsky's *Forest* (1924), Gogol's *Inspector General* (1926), and Alexandre Dumas fils's *Camille* (1934). After *Mystery-Bouffe* and its revival (1921), staged the other major plays of Mayakovsky: *The Bedbug* (1929) and *The Bathhouse* (1930). Produced the Soviet authors Nikolai Erdman (*Mandate*, 1925), Tretiakov (*Roar China,* 1926), Vsevolod Vishnevskii (*The Last Decisive Battle,* 1931), and Iurii Olesha (*A List of Assets,* 1931).

1928   Appeared in the motion picture *The White Eagle* as the senator.

1930   Published the pamphlet *Reconstruction of the Theater.*
Took the Meyerhold Theater on its only tour to the West, though with

a repertory of plays all four or more years old: to Berlin in April and to Paris in May.

1932   Moved to temporary theater in order to permit construction on former site of new building planned as "total theater"; building not completed as Meyerhold Theater, though eventually finished with changed plans as Tschaikovsky Concert Hall, Mayakovsky Square, Moscow.

1930–38   Subjected to increasing criticism under Stalinism. Some plays, though long rehearsed, not allowed to open; Tretiakov's *I Want a Child* (1927–30) and Erdman's *Suicide* (1932) fell in this category.

1931–39   Directed for other theaters and media: for the Pushkin Theater, Leningrad, revivals of Aleksandr Sukhovo-Kobylin's *Death of Tarelkin,* Molière's *Don Juan,* and two revivals of Lermontov's *Masquerade* (1933 and 1938); a radio version of Pushkin's *Stone Guest*

*Figure 0.6. Meyerhold at his director's lectern*

(1934); and for the Malyi Opera Theater, Leningrad, Tschaikovsky's *Queen of Spades* (1935).

**1938** The Meyerhold Theater closed on 8 January by government order.

**1938–39** Appointed director by Stanislavsky and, after Stanislavsky's death, chief director of the Stanislavsky Opera Theater, Moscow. There he completed Verdi's *Rigoletto,*

the opera Stanislavsky left unfinished, while Serafima Birman completed for Meyerhold the staging of Prokofiev's *Semen Kotko.*

**1939** Arrested on June 20.

**1940** Died in custody on 2 February in a manner still unknown.

**1955** Rehabilitated as having been illegally victimized under Stalinism.

# Chapter 1: The New Theater

The remarkable renewal of the theater toward the turn of the last century is usually thought of as the inception of a new realism: the Duke of Meiningen's players placed increased demands upon representation and historical accuracy, while at the same time, with unprecedented frankness, such dramatists as Ibsen and Gerhart Hauptmann made live issues of hitherto unmentionable social ills. Yet close upon the new realism, or even intermingled with it, as in plays by Ibsen and Hauptmann, there arose a nonrealist or symbolist art. Thus almost simultaneously with the Théâtre Libre of André Antoine, which depicted a "slice of life," the poetic theater of A. M. Lugné-Pöe had its debut. And Otto Brahm, who pioneered the "new naturalism" of Hauptmann in the Berlin Freie Bühne, also first sponsored the lyric symbolism of the young Hugo von Hofmannsthal and the psychological dream plays of Arthur Schnitzler.

Stanislavsky, too, should not be labelled merely the champion of realism. True, his Moscow Art Theater had opened with Aleksei K. Tolstoy's *Czar Fedor Ioannovich* (1898), a production remarkable for the historical trappings which Stanislavsky had secured on an "expedition" for that purpose. But Chekhov's *Sea Gull,* which made a name for the new company, is distinctive instead for its lyricism and its symbolist quality, despite a concretely realistic setting. Though Chekhov is

unthinkable without this outward show of realism, surely Maurice Maeterlinck, to whom the Moscow Art Theater turned in the early 1900s, or Shakespeare, whose *Hamlet* Stanislavsky called Gordon Craig to design in 1911, are not realistic in the naturalistic sense, but are, rather, poetic dramatists. Clearly, from the start the new impulse in theater around 1900 also moved away from realism.

It was to Vladimir Nemirovich-Danchenko, his teacher in the Moscow Philharmonia, that Meyerhold owed his first acquaintance with Chekhov, the representative of "new theater." Meyerhold's fellow pupil, Olga Knipper-Chekhov, recalled that Nemirovich paid more attention to literature than to his teaching: "[He] was just then finishing his play *The Price of Life* and did not often favor us with his extremely interesting lessons" (*Encounters,* p. 26). When Nemirovich's play was awarded a literary prize, he proposed to share it with Chekhov for his play *The Sea Gull,* which had failed at the Imperial Alexandrinskii Theater, despite the excellence of the actress Vera Komissarzhevskaia. Nemirovich infected his pupils with his enthusiasm for the play, and they were soon carrying copies of it about with them, reading and discussing it in their free time. With their teacher they took seriously the notion implicit in *The Sea Gull* that a new theater was needed, the very "new forms" demanded by Treplev in the first act of the play; they too sought a deeper interpretation of character and meaning than is possible through the routine declamation of dramatic speeches. To realize the dream of the new theater Nemirovich and Stanislavsky soon thereafter founded the Moscow Art Theater, and Nemirovich invited the gold medalists of his Philharmonia class, Meyerhold and Knipper, to join it. The year after graduation, Knipper and Meyerhold played leading roles in the new theater's epoch-making production of *The Sea Gull* (fig. 1.1).

The innovations introduced by the founders of the new theater seemed at first only the result of strictly applying the methods of the Meiningen company, which had presented its ultrarealistic drama in Moscow in 1885 and 1890. Stanislavsky, who had undertaken expeditions to Rostov-Iaroslavskii and other cities with a medieval past for Aleksei K. Tolstoy's play, and to Venice for the *Othello* he had staged with his own former company, planned similarly exact naturalistic details for *The Sea Gull*. Meyerhold told in his article on new theater, published in an anthology of 1907, of Chekhov's coming to an Art Theater rehearsal: "One of the actors told Chekhov, who had come for the second time to a rehearsal of *The Sea Gull*

[11 September 1898] at the Moscow Art Theater, that backstage in *The Sea Gull* frogs would croak, locusts call, and dogs howl. 'What for?' asked Chekhov in a tone of displeasure. 'It'll be real,' the actor answered. 'Real!' Chekhov repeated with a laugh and added after a moment: 'The theater is art. Kramskoi [a portrait painter famous for his realistic likenesses] did a genre painting in which the faces are splendidly rendered. What if we were to cut out the nose as it is drawn on one of the faces and stick in a live nose? The nose would be 'real' and the picture spoiled' " (*Articles*, 1:120).

So the Art Theater directors were obliged to move on from realism. The new theater, as they exemplified it with Chekhov's play, became a theater of mood and of implicit psychological depths which the audience had in imagination to fill in. As Chekhov wrote to Meyerhold a year later, when advising him on his role as Johannes Vockerat in Hauptmann's *Lonely Lives:* "Modern people are nervous, yes—but who sees us gesticulating and tearing our hair on the street?"[1] So Chekhov urged Meyerhold to let the "sub-text," the unspoken depths, remain implicit. Nevertheless, Nikolai Efros in his history of the Moscow Art Theater called Meyerhold's interpretation of the similar role of Treplev in *The Sea Gull* "neurasthenic," rather than deeply suggestive. And it was Stanis-

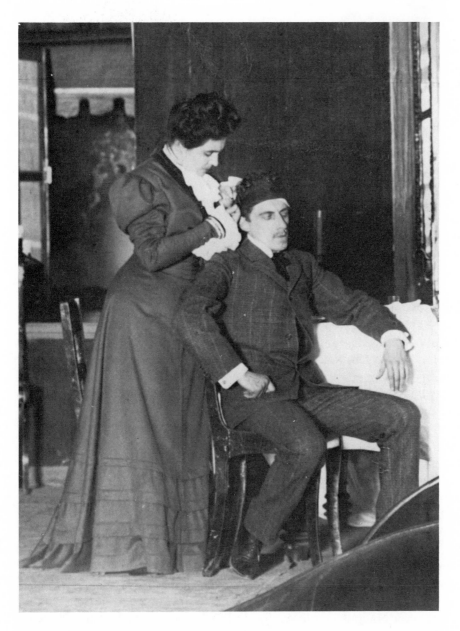

*Figure 1.1.* The Sea Gull: *Arkadina (Knipper) bandaging the head of her son Treplev (Meyerhold) after his unsuccessful first attempt at suicide in act 3*

lavsky's advice, not Chekhov's, that Meyerhold followed in making Hauptmann's Vockerat almost a pathological figure, rather than a poetic victim of misunderstanding. So the Moscow Art Theater twice opted for outward show; indeed the theater generally leaned toward realism rather than lyricism.

Still, Meyerhold apparently left the Moscow Art Theater in 1902 more for practical and personal reasons than for differences of principle with its artistic tendencies. First, he was not made a charter member of the company and chose to resign before the charter was inaugurated that year. Secondly, his gifts as an actor were proving less than they had at first promised, and by this time he was getting fewer, not more, leading roles. Finally, his keen literary perception caused him at least once to disapprove the theater's choice of a play as departing from its own set goals.[2] Yet his own earliest work showed his debt to his former teachers and directors to outweigh his differences with them. Indeed, the repertory of the actors' group which he thereafter codirected, and in which he acted, closely followed that of the Art Theater and revealed no clearly defined goals of his own. Meyerhold launched his first season in Kherson with several repeats from the Art Theater: plays by Chekhov, Hauptmann, Ibsen, Gorky, and Nemirovich-Danchenko. Of course the great number of plays

staged—often a new one every other day—mainly demonstrated the ruthless frequency with which one new bill must follow the other in a repertory system. Moreover, Meyerhold obviously tried to produce the latest works of contemporary drama. He not only brought the new Chekhov play, *The Cherry Orchard* (1904), to Tiflis, where his company went the next year, but also presented Hauptmann's *succès de scandale, Before Dawn,* in his own translation from the German. The immense repertory of these early years also included other new writers like Maeterlinck and Schnitzler.

Yet at least one play staged with the actors' cooperative reflected more than just the young director's beginnings with the Art Theater and his sensitive awareness of the latest literary fashion. This was *The Acrobats* (1903), by Franz von Schönthan, again in a translation from the German by Meyerhold himself. The director's notes for this play represent the earliest written evidence of a Meyerhold production, according to Konstantin Rudnitskii's recent study. In his notes for this sentimental "vehicle," the director went beyond the re-creation of a milieu (the circus) with Art Theater exactitude to add some touches recognizably his own. First, Meyerhold, as the old clown beyond his successful years, was seen between two audiences, the actual theater audience and the imaginary circus audience. Then, as he listened for applause which did not come, he stood far forward, almost directly addressing the real audience, like the melancholy Pierrot of Alexander Blok's *Farce,* whom Meyerhold was later to play. "At that moment on the stage of a provincial theater in Kherson the unsure hand of a beginner at directing touched upon a theme which was to be one of the most important in great art of the twentieth century," and Rudnitskii cites not only Blok, Picasso, and Stravinsky, but also Chaplin, Jean-Louis Barrault, Ingmar Bergman, and Frederico Fellini, who show "the confrontation of a simple and naive art with the highly complex life of our time" (Rudnitskii, p. 34). Surely the essence of this theme lies less in the melancholy and the simple-mindedness of the lonely clown figure than in the confrontation as such, the breaking of illusion to show the human being within the circus costume, holding up the mirror of consciousness, or rather of self-consciousness, which makes us human. In this the device resembles the play within the play or the actor's direct address to the audience—both artistic devices which break the frame of realism.

Still it was not formalistic devices as such but a new literature, a new matter, not a new manner, which compelled the departure from realism.

A decade after his success with Meiningenism, Stanislavsky himself, the master of the real on stage, founded a first studio, the Theater Studio of 1905, to seek means of "realizing" symbolism, "to stage the unreal" and called Meyerhold back to direct in it. The plays which Meyerhold actually mounted in the Theater Studio were Maeterlinck's *Death of Tintagiles* and Hauptmann's *Schluck and Jau,* though the list of plays planned for production included many more by Ibsen, Hauptmann, Knut Hamsun, Hofmannsthal, Stanislav Przybyszewski, the Russians Valerii Briusov and Viacheslav Ivanov, Calderón de la Barca in Balmont's translation, and, interestingly, Emile Verhaeren's *Dawns* (though Meyerhold actually mounted the last only much later, after the Revolution). In his article of 1907, republished in his book *On Theater* (1913), Meyerhold formulated the Theater Studio's reason for being: "The Moscow Art Theater has achieved virtuosity in the presentation of the naturalness and simplicity of life. But plays have appeared which demand new methods in staging and acting." (*Articles,* 1:106).

To develop such "new methods" was the purpose of the Theater Studio. The first step in departing from the usual practice of the Moscow Art Theater was to scrap the scale model of the set. The designer for the Hauptmann play, Nikolai Ulianov, went immediately to work on stage to render "the age of the powdered wig" in large strokes only. Without the Moscow Art Theater's museumlike detail, the set for the first scene of *Schluck and Jau* merely suggested castle gates of exaggerated dimensions with a bronze Cupid on top.

This lordly background was meant as contrast to the two drunken fellows of the title. In Hauptmann's play these characters become the victims of a practical joke: seized after a drinking bout, they are put to bed drunk and are duped upon awakening into the belief that they are noble lords. Therefore the luxury of their surroundings and the delicate colors of the courtier's dress were magnified so as to emphasize the uncouthness of the two ridiculous fellows. Meyerhold described the enhancement, or "stylization," of nature in the third scene: "As a backdrop, blue sky with lamb's wool clouds. On the horizon bright red roses the whole length of the stage. Crinolines, white wigs, the costumes of the characters harmonizing with the colors of the set so that together they make one artistic whole, a symphony in mother of pearl" (*Articles,* 1:109). Another device to enhance the ironic contrast was that of multiple uniformity: the scene offered, not a crowd of differentiated individuals, as Meiningen's troupe would have done, but instead a bevy of court ladies, dressed alike and seated in a straight

line across the forestage with the heroine in the center, each in an identical bower, all embroidering on the same broad ribbon. "And all together to the beat of a distant eighteenth-century duet, accompanied by harpsichord and harp. Rhythmically musical: movements, lines, gestures, words, colors of set and costumes" (ibid., 1:110). Meyerhold noted that canvas flats were used "without attemping to make the audience forget that it was in the theater" (ibid.). From the time of this first opportunity to realize new possibilities, Meyerhold worked from hypotheses that governed all his directing: first, the nonrealistic tenet that theater is art, not life; and second, the new aesthetic demand that all the elements of theater art must be composed into one rhythmic whole.

Similarly, when the Maeterlinck play came to production, the two designers, Nikolai Sapunov and Sergei Sudeikin, working from a sketch by the director, began without preliminaries to paint flats and arrange lighting on stage. In Meyerhold's view this preliminary work resulted, first, in "a method of disposing the human figures on the stage by bas-reliefs and frescoes" —that is, "pictorialism"; secondly, in "a means of revealing [the characters'] interior monologue through the music of plastic motion"—that is, "biomechanics"; and, thirdly, in "the opportunity to try out in practice the aesthetic, not the 'logical' accentuation" —that is, the substitution of a musical for a conversational tone in the lines (*Articles,* 1:112). Evidently the musical background of *The Death of Tintagiles,* composed by Ilia Sats, included an a cappella choir designed to express not only the howling of the wind but also the characters' inner monologue. As if to contradict the melodrama of this background, the actors trained in the Moscow Art Theater tended nevertheless to speak in conversational tones.

Rudnitskii's study publishes for the first time passages from the director's notebook for *Tintagiles,* showing that in the fourth act Meyerhold placed the three serving maids in a row in front of the central white column and made of their separate speeches a single chorus: "They all speak simultaneously." Rudnitskii interprets Meyerhold's reason for their unison: "He envisions the theater at that time as a kind of temple in which the actors are priests, servers of the cult, and the audience the believers" (Rudnitskii, p. 54). To this end, no doubt, Meyerhold noted the following points of principle for the actors:

1. *Experience of the form, and not experience of single psychological emotions.*
2. *A smile for all.*
3. *Never tremolo!*
4. *Read the lines as if there were hidden in every phrase a profound belief in an all-powerful force.*
5. *Firmness of tone, since blurring will make it sound fashionably "modern."*
6. *Motionless theater.*
7. *Don't drag out the end of words. The sound should fall into a great depth. It should be clearly defined and not tremble in the air.*
8. *Like a piano. That's the reason for no vibration.*
9. *No speaking in a rapid patter. Epic calm.*
10. *Madonna-like movements.*
(*Quoted in Rudnitskii, p. 55.*)

(Does the last point imply merely a preconceived notion of religious pictures, or did Meyerhold show his actors certain paintings, as he is later known to have done?)

Rudnitskii observes the director's concern for the spoken word evident in most of these principles and further quotes the rhythm of sound which Meyerhold carefully designed for the end of *Tintagiles:*

*The laughter of the serving maids, and then*
*the cry of Tintagiles,*
*again the laughter of the serving maids,*
*the laughter of the serving maids,*
*the cry of Tintagiles,*
*a brief pause,*

„Жизнь Человѣка". Танцы на балу.

*Figure 1.2. "Dances at the ball" in Leonid Andreev's* Life of Man *at Komissarzhevskaia's theater (1907): a caricature sketch doubtless by P. Troianovskii*

*the sound of Tintagiles' body falling,*
*a brief pause,*
*the triumphant laughter of the serving*
*    maids. (Rudnitskii, p. 56.)*

By "motionless theater" Meyerhold obviously did not mean a theater without motion, but only one without the chance and fleeting movements of everyday reality. He worked out significant ritual gestures in slow tempo, carefully harmonized with the set and the musical background, a kind of rhythmic bas-relief. Central to the director's notebooks were sketches by which Meyerhold fixed the actors' harmonious poses in relation to each other for each of their speeches. A similar "rhythmic bas-relief" recurred in Meyerhold's production of Leonid An-

dreev's *Life of Man,* which, unlike *Tintagiles,* actually opened a year later at Komissarzhevskaia's theater (Saint Petersburg, 1907) (fig. 1.2).

Though early rehearsals of *Tintagiles* were enthusiastically hailed by everyone, including Stanislavsky and Gorky, the dress rehearsal in October did not succeed in uniting all the elements of production. Rudnitskii quotes from Ulianov's memoirs (*Moi Vstrechi,* Moscow, 1952), which describe the dress rehearsal of *Tintagiles:*

*Half-darkness on stage. Only people's silhouettes are visible. The set is flat without wings, hung almost at the front edge of the stage. This is new, and also new is the actors' rhythmic speech as it carries from the stage. Slowly the action*

*develops; it seems as if time were
standing still. Suddenly a shout from
Stanislavsky: "Light!" A tremor is
felt in the theater, noise, confusion.
Sudeikin and Sapunov jump up from
their places, crying objection. Stanislavsky's voice: "The audience can't
take darkness on stage for long, it goes
against psychology, they must see the
actors' faces!" Sudeikin and Sapunov:
"But the set is made for half-darkness,
it loses all artistic meaning in the light!"
Again there is silence, with only the
beat of the actors' measured speech.
But no sooner have they turned on the
light than the whole set is ruined. The
various elements disintegrate, the set
and the figures fall apart. (Rudnitskii,
p. 62.)*

It was not possible to rework the
Theater Studio shows, for soon after-
ward the First Russian Revolution temporarily closed Moscow theaters, and
the Art Theater decided suddenly to
depart on tour for Germany. Meyerhold
could have remained with the company; indeed, his role of Treplev in
*The Sea Gull* was again offered him.
But he was now aware of his calling as
a director and of his stand against psychologism. Stanislavsky kept trying
to produce the symbolists effectively, as
in Maeterlinck's *Blue Bird* (1908),
still in the repertory of the Art Theater
today, or in the *Hamlet* designed by
Gordon Craig (1911). However, his

system aimed chiefly at representing
through actors that psychology in the
name of which he broke up the Theater
Studio dress rehearsal.

Though Meyerhold did not show the
Theater Studio plays publicly, he went
on to apply their methods, notably in
productions for Vera Komissarzhevskaia. Certain innovations, such as the
"multiple uniformity" and the oversize
objects used in *Schluck and Jau*, he
restored to use in the theater tradition.
With such others as "pictorialism," the
bas-relief on the narrow-strip stage used
in Maeterlinck's *Sister Beatrice* with
Komissarzhevskaia the following year,
he had tremendous success for a long
time (figs. 1.3–1.4). Meyerhold's
groupings are perhaps reminiscent less
of altar paintings, such as those by
Hans Memling which he showed his
actors, than of the bas-reliefs of medieval cathedrals (fig. 1.5). Still others
were successful from the start, like the
technique of speaking lines in a rhythmic monotone (which Meyerhold reused in Ibsen's *Hedda Gabler* with
Komissarzhevskaia), or the melodramatic communication of emotion
through background choral music. Unfortunately, several of these early
methods, though soon abandoned, per-
sisted in the popular image of Meyerhold which came under attack. As late
as 1920 Stanislavsky saw "the former
Meyerhold of mysticism and Maeterlinckism" in contrast to his own ideal of

*Figures 1.3–1.4.  Costume sketches by Sergei Sudeikin for* Sister Beatrice *(1906)*

"the New Theater (my dream)." [3]
And it was the Meyerhold of pictorialism which Tairov continued to rail
against in *Das entfesselte Theater*
(1923).

Yet even before Meyerhold could
give his Theater Studio methods a public showing at the theater of Komissarzhevskaia, he was beginning to ab-
sorb quite different ideas from the
intellectuals he met in Petersburg,
where he went after Christmas in 1905.
With the partiality of hindsight, one of
their number, Andrei Belyi, assigned
to himself an all too leading role and
to Meyerhold an all too conscious des-
tiny in their meeting:

*At his [Georgii Chulkov's] house I ran
into V. E. Meyerhold, who had just
broken with the Art Theater and turned
up in Petersburg. Of course, since my
school days I had known the latter as
an actor playing with great talent in
[Chekhov's] Sea Gull, The Three Sisters, and [Hauptmann's] Lonely Lives,
and I had just visited in Moscow his
studio for young people located on
Povarsky Street. . . . Meyerhold broke
abruptly and irrevocably with the theater which had previously been the
most avant-garde [The Moscow Art
Theater] and consciously took sides
with the "radicals." For the first time
the serious theater came over to the
symbolists. . . . In my recollection V. E.
comes alive. . . . He is too dry, too*

*thin, unusually tall and angular. . . .
At first it seemed to me that of all the
senses his "nose"—smell—predominated. . . . Later I realized he is just as
sensitive to sight, to touch, to taste,
and the truly dominant sense in his
inner ear.*[4]

Belyi went on to the results of this
first encounter: "With Chulkov we had
already had conversations about the
new theater, and V. I. Ivanov had
shown that for the time the new theater
was still a theater of improvisations.
Soon thereafter I took Ivanov to see
Blok to discuss such a theater; Ivanov
then took Chulkov to see Blok, who got
the latter in touch with Meyerhold.—
Soon we were talking seriously about
the new theater: it came into being a
year later, the Vera Komissarzhevskaia
Theater with Meyerhold as director." [5]

Among the Petersburg circle which
Meyerhold met at the Wednesday at-
homes of Viacheslav Ivanov in his
"tower" apartment were, besides Belyi,
Blok, and Chulkov, Valerii Briusov,
Aleksei Remizov, Fedor Sologub, and
Mstislav Dobuzhinskii. They thought
of establishing a theater, *Fakely* (The
Torches), which would resurrect the
ancient Greek theater of Dionysus.
This is not to be confused with N. N.
Bashkevich's "Theater of Dionysus"
(1906), which aimed at "synthetic"
theater but marred its effects with
amateurish background music, colored

*Figure 1.5.  The death of Sister Beatrice, mourned by her sister nuns in a "pictorial" grouping from act 3 of Maeterlinck's* Sister Beatrice

stage lighting, action veiled behind a scrim, an audience enlisted as worshippers in the temple, and wreaths of flowers distributed at the door. Rather, the Wednesday circle adopted its host's unattainable goal: the classical scholar Ivanov hoped to recreate a theater in which audience and actors alike would participate as in a religious mystery.

Immediately upon arriving in Petersburg Meyerhold read a report on the theater of Dionysus—"The Technique of Theater"—at a symposium of the Wednesday circle in which Ivanov and Chulkov also participated. Though the Torches Theater project was still less fully realized than the Theater Studio, the contact with it evidently meant much to Meyerhold. For when he left Petersburg to spend the second half of the season with his former actors' cooperative he wrote, "This year I lost the first half of the season because I didn't act. Or it seemed so. But it only seemed so from without. When I got on the train to begin the new [half-] season, I involuntarily looked back and realized how much the past season had given me. This year something new was born within me which will . . . bear fruit" (Volkov, 1:221).

What Meyerhold meant by "something new" is clear from the article he contributed to the anthology on new theater *Teatr: Kniga o novom teatre* (Theater: A Book about New Theater) published in Saint Petersburg in 1908. This collection of articles by such diverse advocates of new theater as Anatolii Lunacharsky and Alexander Benois, along with habitués of the Wednesday circle, was dedicated to Stanislavsky, and Stanislavsky's Theater Studio of 1905 was the point of departure of Meyerhold's contribution, later republished as the first major article of his own book *On Theater* (1913). In his more than fifty pages of discussion entitled "The Theater: Its History and Technique," Meyerhold broke with Meiningenism and naturalism. Instead of theater as imitation, he proposed Viacheslav Ivanov's principle of theater as *uslovnyi,* an action in which both actors and audience participate. The total representation of naturalism was renounced in favor of suggestions offered by set design and acting to an audience moved to imaginative completion of such a partial statement (*nedoskazanie*). And Meyerhold quoted Briusov's article "Unnecessary Truth" (1902), from the *World of Art* magazine, in which the conscious renunciation of total realism was advocated. He might well have cited Pushkin, as he often did later, in the thirties, for Pushkin too called attention to the audience, before whom the actors create "an agreed-upon semblance of reality [*uslovnoe pravdopodobie*]." Meyerhold further quoted Briusov's notion that the actor performs before an audience by means of his own body, speech, mimicry, and gestures. Unfortunately, Meyerhold found such means wholly lacking in the Art Theater actors with whom he worked in the Theater Studio of 1905, and indeed he was able to inculcate such performing skills in them only later through his system of "biomechanics." No wonder the aim of the symbolists—that the actor in understatement reveal his soul to the audience—took over the meaning of nonrealism (*uslovnost*), which has become synonymous with a period in the literature of the theater, as in the plays of Maeterlinck, Ibsen, and Verhaeren.

In the Petersburg Theater of Komissarzhevskaia, in which Meyerhold accepted an invitation to direct in 1906–7, his new ideas came at last to fruition. Komissarzhevskaia, who was herself seeking new plays and new ways, settled on Meyerhold as director probably on the strength of his plans for the Theater Studio, as well as the recommendations of Stanislavsky and the Torches Theater idealists. Valentina Verigina, one of the two actresses Meyerhold took with him from the cooperative when he joined Komissarzhevskaia in August 1906, described the meeting at which the director was introduced to his new theater and addressed his troupe:

*The young director declared war on all too faithful realism, on theater routine.*

*. . . Among other things, Meyerhold said that we were perhaps not destined to realize the new theater and we would perhaps fall in the fight, but over our bodies, as over a bridge, others would march on toward the theater of the future. This did not frighten us young actors, but even inspired us. To me at the time, though, it seemed most astonishing that Komissarzhevskaia's eyes shone at this. She, after all, was at the height of her fame! And yet she was caught up in the new trend in art and was fearlessly entering on the path of experimentation.* (Komissarzhevskaia, p. 263.)

Verigina conceded, however, that Komissarzhevskaia took the risk quite as much from necessity as from love of experimentation: "Komissarzhevskaia accepted Meyerhold's ideas with her usual enthusiasm, but the sixth sense of a great actress also told her that to play Maeterlinck's *Sister Beatrice* in realistic tones was impossible" (ibid., p. 264).

Actually Komissarzhevskaia first took an exactly opposite risk: she played Hedda Gabler in Meyerhold's symbolist production of Ibsen's realistic play. They began their collaboration on a tour, from the proceeds of which she meant to pay for the opening of her new theater. V. Khvostov, the theater carpenter, recalled a detail typical of the remodeling done on the theater building in Ofitserskaia (now Decembrists')

Street, Saint Petersburg: the new entre-
preneurs cancelled advertising and with
it advertising income when they abolished the usual curtain covered with
commercials and replaced it with Leon
Bakst's beautiful painted curtain
"Elysium" (*Komissarzhevskaia,* p.
256). In addition, the program for the
new theater was redesigned.

The new theater opened on 10
November 1906 with Meyerhold's re-
markably original production of *Hedda,*
created around the leading actress herself. Meyerhold made of Komissar-
zhevskaia-Hedda a goddess against a
background of golden autumn. He
wrote of a walk into the hills in Kovno,
Lithuania, during the tour: "Gold reverberated, gold tremoloed, gold in-
toxicated, the gold of dying autumn.
We did not want to take the beaten
paths. We scrambled over the steep
edges of the ravine, over abysses.
Ahead of us Hedda Gabler, behind her
Thea, further Lövborg, and after them
the one (I), who means to pour the
souls of these characters into one
harmony against a background of
golden autumn. In [autumn's] dying cry
the voice of luminous Milda [love-
goddess of Lithuanian mythology]"
(Volkov, 1:258).

Disregarding Ibsen's stage directions,
which call for a living room furnished
in dark colors in the style of the eighties,
Meyerhold asked the designer Sapunov
for an impression of golden autumn

instead. He had just read Georg Fuchs's
*Die Schaubühne der Zukunft* (1906),
which exposed the falsehood of the
realistic convention, a falsehood seen,
for example, in the incongruous perspective of the actor's body against
realistically painted flats. To avoid this
apparent deception, Meyerhold opened
the stage only some eleven feet in
depth and asked the designer for only
"color accompaniments" as background. Petr Iartsev, an assistant director of the theater, described the colors:
"The walls were blue, and so was the
sky, which was seen through a great
window entwined with ivy; a tapestry
which filled the whole wall was gold,
the straw-like color of gold" (ibid.,
1:263). The daytime sky seen through
the window as bright blue in acts 1,
2, and 3 became a night sky with cold
stars in act 4. Besides blue and straw
gold, there was white in the set, the
white fur of Hedda's all-enveloping
chair, the white grand piano, white
chrysanthemums in vases, a white chest
in which Hedda hid Lövborg's manu-
script. The costumes too had their
color leitmotif: Hedda's green blue was
to express coldness against the background of golden autumn.

On so shallow a stage, motion had
to be carefully planned. Each character
was given a basic pose comparable to
the gestus of Brecht: Brack was a faun
crouching at the pedestal, while
Hedda sat enthroned like a goddess.

The closeness of actors and audience resulting from the shallow stage was used to enhance effects of facial expression and voice: "This frees the actor from the incidental realistic detail of the stage apparatus which weighs him down. This lends the mimicry of the actor the capacity for more subtle expression. This helps the actor's voice to render finer nuances, heightens the audience's receptiveness and, so to speak, destroys the dividing line between actors and audience" (*Articles,* 1:237). This dividing line in European theater buildings, frequently dating back to the nineteenth century, often consists of a formidably large orchestra pit; as a result, even first-row orchestra seats are sometimes tens of feet from the stage. All too rare even today is the arena stage, with its proximity of actor and audience, such as Meyerhold planned in the thirties for the new Meyerhold Theater, unfortunately never completed. Meyerhold's notes continue: "The poses, movements and gestures of the actors are transformed into the very means of expression and are subject to the laws of rhythm. The poses, movements and gestures derive from the word with its inherent property of expression, and the words in turn are the culmination of the plastic work of art" (ibid.).

Yet the first scene between Lövborg and Hedda was to consist of words recited in a monotone quite without movement: "During all of this scene Lövborg and Hedda sit side by side—tense, frozen—and look straight ahead. Their exchange of lines, quiet, passionate, falls rhythmically from lips which are felt to be dry and cold. Two glasses are in front of them and the punch flame burns (in Ibsen this is Norwegian 'cold punch'). Not once in the course of the whole scene do they change the direction of their gaze and their motionless poses. Only at the words, 'So there is in you too a thirst for life,' does Lövborg make a quick gesture toward Hedda. But at this the scene breaks off" (*Articles,* 1:242). And Iartsev's description makes clear that real people could never have carried on a conversation like this: "The listener hears in this a dialogue meant for the audience. The whole time the audience sees before it the faces of Hedda and Lövborg, and reads in them the two characters' most subtle feelings. In the rhythm of the monotonously falling words and behind the actual dialogue, an inner hidden dialogue comes out, the presentiments and emotions which are not expressed in words" (ibid.).

One critic of the production, Chulkov, Meyerhold's acquaintance from the Ivanov circle, rushed to Ibsen's defense: Meyerhold had disregarded the author's stage directions and taken it upon himself to find his own key idea for the play. Another critic, Alek-

sandr Kugel, who was to remain Meyerhold's constant loyal opposition even
as late as the twenties, struck a blow
for psychological realism, arguing that
a Hedda so transplanted out of her
bourgeois habitat into such "an imperial orangery" need never yearn for
escape. That, for all its talented effort,
the production did not communicate
the subsurface meaning is clear from
the general negative reaction of the
critics. The failure was attributed
chiefly to the nonrealism of Meyerhold's production, in which it was said
he had wasted the gifts of a great actress. Only Verigina advanced the
notion that, instead, Komissarzhevskaia
was inadequate to Meyerhold's conception of Hedda. The younger actress
sufficiently overcame her clearly heartfelt admiration for Komissarzhevskaia
to admit:

*Komissarzhevskaia did not make a
success of the part. She could not con-
jure up the image of the 'ice maiden'....
Her weak hands, soft weary motions,
melancholy tone of voice did not suit
the image of Ibsen's heroine. Everything seemed soft, hesitant. The scene
with Brack was thrown away. Komissarzhevskaia did not communicate
Hedda's ironic coquetry; the essential
shade of malice was lacking. Bravich,
though a fine actor, couldn't play
Brack. Meyerhold wanted the dialogue
between Brack and Hedda to be like a*
*duel with sparks flying, yet in some of
Brack's speeches there was a hint of
whining. (Komissarzhevskaia, p. 266.)*

If the actors did not quite live up to
Meyerhold's demands upon them,
surely the public too was not quite
ready for this first daring experiment of
Meyerhold's, of which at least one
critic, Iurii Beliaev, saw the far-reaching implications: "The experiment with
*Hedda Gabler* astonishes by its daring.
The director has completely scrapped
the realism of the play and done a symbolic stylization of Ibsen. Chiefly for
such treatment (of a classic) he has
been punished. . . . [Yet] once launched
in the world, this idea has taken on a
mysterious life of its own and has somehow stimulated the imagination. So
people have been asking: 'Won't Ostrovsky or Gogol be given symbolic
treatment next?' And indeed why not
try to symbolize *The Storm* or *The
Inspector General?*" (Volkov, 1:267).
Meyerhold was to realize both Beliaev's
apparently fantastic proposals, with his
production of *The Storm* ten years
later and his symbolic *Inspector General*—perhaps the greatest classic production of his whole career—twenty
years later. Today in the English-
speaking world we may ask with
Brecht (or Peter Brook), "Why not
treat Marlowe or *King Lear* just as
freely?" Though the treatment suitable
for contemporary sensibility is surely

not that of pure symbolism, still Meyerhold's once daring principle is universally recognized today, namely, the director's right, even duty, to make a classic fresh and exciting for a modern audience.

Certainly the experience Meyerhold gained from his attempt at a symbolic staging of *Hedda* bore fruit in the great success he achieved with Maeterlinck's *Sister Beatrice* (1906). Was it because *Sister Beatrice,* a symbolist work to start with, required no adaptation to symbolism? Meyerhold again used the shallow stage, on which he arranged pictorial groupings, this time after known works by Hans Memling and others. The same critics who had opposed *Hedda* were enthusiastic about *Beatrice.* The poet Alexander Blok wrote of "a sense of miracle," and continued: "We felt at the performance of *Sister Beatrice* an excitement of love, a rush of wings, the joy of the future, which filled the theater." [6]

Not *Sister Beatrice* but Blok's own play *Farce* (*Balaganchik*) was the true miracle for Meyerhold. It contained the elements essential to much of Meyerhold's later work: the traditional theater devices of satire and irony embodied in *commedia dell'arte* characters and the sense, derived from the ironic German romantics, of breaking the illusion of theater. *Farce* must have seemed, further, the antidote to the exaltation of *Sister Beatrice* (with which it shared

a bill during the theater's Moscow tour). This one-act verse play, which Chulkov had coaxed out of its author originally for the Torches Theater, was staged instead at the Komissarzhevskaia theater, so that at least once the Ivanov circle's dream of "new theater" was there realized. Radically different from the "Maeterlinckism" and mysticism, from the pictorialism and the "mystery" cult of *Hedda* and *Beatrice,* it combined irony—exemplified in such a comedy as Ludwig Tieck's *Puss-in-Boots* (1798)—with the earlier naive tradition of theater art. Thus Blok's Author-character, like Tieck's, was jerked back by the seat of his pants to prevent his interfering in the action of the play; Blok himself even wrote Meyerhold (22 December 1906) to ask that the ironic gesture be emphasized by making the hand that did the pulling clearly visible as it emerged between the curtains (Volkov, 1:279).

The most conspicuous butts of Blok's irony in *Farce* are the five mystics, whom Meyerhold seated solemnly in a row at a table facing the audience as close downstage as possible. Their multiple uniformity was underlined by their mechanically similar attitude: all alike "they so drop their heads that suddenly busts without heads or hands remain. . . . The actors' hands were thrust into round openings in cardboard busts, and the actors only leaned their heads against the collars painted on the card-

*Figure 1.6. The mystics in Nikolai Sapunov's design for Blok's* Farce *(1906); right, Pierrot, played by Meyerhold*

board" (*Articles,* 1:228). This same device by which Blok and Meyerhold ridiculed the mystics as cardboard men is again used today in John Reed's *Ten Days that Shook the World* at the Theater on the Taganka, only now the targets of ridicule are United States senators at a congressional hearing, dressed in uniform mortarboards and academic gowns. Indeed, multiple uniformity as Meyerhold used it in *Farce* to satirize the mystics has proved seminal in theater practice ever since. Not only have directors repeated it, as did Meyerhold

himself in multiplying the number of figures who simultaneously, rather than successively, offer bribes in *The Inspector General,* but writers also have frequently employed the device, as with Jean Giraudoux's couple of capitalists in *The Madwoman of Chaillot* (1945) or Peter Handke's four Kaspars in his play of that name (1968) (fig. 1.6).

But not just characters were mocked in Meyerhold's production of *Farce;* the theater itself was exposed as the makeshift that it is. With the opposite intent Stanislavsky had once had a house, real to the last detail, built on stage and was downcast to hear from the lips of a child that it nevertheless remained "theater" because no real house would ever be built inside a house. Meyerhold, on the contrary, placed the small theater for Blok's play on stage with the express purpose of showing up the machinery of illusion; the prompter's box, the wheels and ropes for raising the curtain were all exposed. And in the end the properties for Pierrot's monologue, a bench and a stone Cupid, were even hoisted in full view, leaving the main character, Meyerhold-Pierrot, alone on an empty stage to address the audience.

Of course, such unusual moments presented difficulties for staging, as Chulkov himself pointed out, and it is no wonder that another critic, Sergei Auslender, praised the newness of Meyerhold's solutions: "Everything in a new manner, everything unusual: the tender languorous music by [Mikhail] Kuzmin, Blok's sprung rhythms, Sapunov's sets and costumes; Harlequin's tambourine has a ring of victory, terrible alluring masks flicker by, and oh my! the white Pierrot. He is not in the least like those familiar, consciously sweet, whining Pierrots. All in acute angles with a muted voice, whispering words of not earthly sorrow, he's simultaneously full of barbs and insight, tender and impudent. This is how Meyerhold played Pierrot and played him unforgettably" (Volkov, 1:280). Just

such a union of opposites was, of course, what Meyerhold later understood by "the grotesque." He defined it with Harlequin as his example in "Balagan" (Farce), the final major article of his book *On Theater*: "This chameleonlike quality hidden under the actor's changing mask gives the theater a fascinating play of light and shadow. . . . The mask allows the audience to see not only a given Harlequin but all the Harlequins he can ever remember" (*Articles*, 1:219).

If such features as the deep stage, irony, and impudent *commedia dell'arte* sharply differentiate Blok's *Farce* from Meyerhold's preceding productions, so did his next and last show of the season, Leonid Andreev's *Life of Man* (1907), differ from all the rest of his productions for Komissarzhevskaia. The stage was once more opened in depth to its back wall, though not in order to show every rope and pulley. The purpose was rather to show gray, distant depths to give a sense of unreality. Weak light from a single source on a few selected furnishings of exaggerated proportions was meant to create the effect of the author's stage direction: "Everything as in a dream. Like a distant transparent echo there will pass before you the life of man" (*Articles*, 1:252). From complete darkness, silhouettes gradually emerged. "The main source of stage effects in this play was light," Nikolai Volkov's biography of

Meyerhold comments (Volkov, 1:285). Indeed, light was perhaps the final new device which Meyerhold successfully exploited in his work for the Theater of Komissarzhevskaia.

Certainly light was the major device used in the first show of the new 1907–8 season, Frank Wedekind's *Awakening of Spring*, though the manner again was new: all eighteen tableaux were ready in advance on stage to be brought by light to the audience's attention, one after another, as needed. Sergei Auslender wrote in the magazine *Zolotoe runo* (The Golden Fleece): "In the midst of the most complete darkness suddenly one corner is lighted up: a bed, a chair. The brief scene is soon over. Again darkness for a moment and then a forest clearing high above stage level" (Volkov, 1:324). But, however fruitful such area lighting later proved to be, this production employing it was not entirely successful.

The next play of Meyerhold's second season with Komissarzhevskaia, Maeterlinck's *Pelleas and Melisande* (1907), was a resounding failure; still it was remarkable for the use of yet another new device, perhaps the most important of all Meyerhold's innovations for Komissarzhevskaia. This was the theater-in-the-round, or arena stage. Meyerhold had first urged it for Fedor Sologub's *Gift of the Wise Bees* in letters to Komissarzhevskaia and her brother Fedor about the new season.

But the Komissarzhevskys all too easily renounced the idea when they learned that the law did not permit it; Meyerhold replied with some bitterness: "About producing *Gift* in the round: I think we've got to work on it just as I'm working to get permission for *The Awakening of Spring* [forbidden at first on moral grounds by the censor]. After all, here in Russia they always begin by saying it's forbidden" (Volkov, 1:308). However, permission for arena staging was not granted, and *Gift* was not produced. Still Meyerhold would not give up his device altogether, for *Pelleas and Melisande* was done with a "round" placed in the middle of the stage, not in the auditorium. Such a half measure could not, of course, succeed, since it did not achieve the close audience contact which is the very essence of arena staging. Nor could an idea originally meant for another play be successfully transferred to this one. Doubtless, though, the ineffectiveness of this device —indeed, of any one device—can hardly explain the failure of *Pelleas and Melisande*, which was unsuccessful not just for single reasons but because of a subtle change in the time itself. Clearly, it was no longer fashionable to realize *uslovnost* as static bas-relief and symbolic stare.

The failure of *Pelleas and Melisande* occasioned a crisis in the Theater of Komissarzhevskaia, which even the success of Meyerhold's last production there, Sologub's *Victory of Death* (1907), could not avert. Volkov observed that there were favorable notices for *Victory* from all the critics, including those usually hostile to Meyerhold. He quoted the remarks of a friend, Chulkov: "The sets, simplified after the principle of *uslovnost*, were very pleasing: a broad staircase the width of the stage, massive columns, and quiet severe colors in the general background left the audience free to combine its visual impressions with those of the classic exact style of the tragedy itself. Stage grouping was beautiful and intelligent, the whole production well composed" (Volkov, 1:345). The critic saw particularly in the last scene an element of "modern" theater: "Apparently the author wanted at this moment to cross the fateful gap—'destroy the proscenium dividing line.' And this would have been possible not only visually but also through the action, by continuing the stairs from the stage into the auditorium and ending the tragedy amid the audience. But of course today, given the conditions of our culture, it is impossible to carry this out" (ibid., 1:346). Despite general acclaim for *The Victory of Death*, three days after its premiere and two days before the first anniversary of the theater's opening Meyerhold received a letter of dismissal from Komissarzhevskaia herself.

Personal reasons were in part the cause of Meyerhold's dismissal. Komissarzhevskaia had raised funds for the enterprise in order to have "her own theater," yet among the four outstanding successes in the first year she had played in only one, *Sister Beatrice*, and the others, *Farce, The Life of Man*, and *The Victory of Death*, had been cast without her. Also, her brother aspired to direct, but might hope to do so only by displacing Meyerhold. Beyond all personal considerations, however, differences of principle were at stake. Chulkov, in the Torches anthology he edited, pointed out the first principle to which Meyerhold steadfastly adhered: "[It is] the great merit of V. E. Meyerhold, that he has firmly and consistently carried out in his productions the principle of *uslovnyi* theater. Admittedly the principle was not always successfully applied, but it is undeniable that elements of artistic creativity were always to be found in the dangerous experiments which V. E. Meyerhold undertook" (Volkov, 1:350). Komissarzhevskaia, however, had acquired her reputation through realism at a time before even the first great realistic director, Stanislavsky, was firmly established.

Besides *uslovnost* as opposed to realism, Meyerhold also represented the new age of the director's precedence over the actor (figs. 1.7–1.8). Both friend and foe, Chulkov and Meyerhold's arch opponent, Aleksandr Kugel, placed Meyerhold together with Stanislavsky in the "director's theater." Chul-

*Figures 1.7–1.8. Meyerhold as dictatorial director, whip in hand, in caricatures by P. Troianovskii (ca. 1908); figure 1.8, "pictorial" groupings from* Sister Beatrice, *shows Meyerhold at lower right*

kov likened the two directors in greatness, acclaiming both as creators of a theater with its own artistic coherence, where before there had been only actors leading their own troupes, in the manner of Komissarzhevskaia. In the hands of so strong a director, Komissarzhevskaia felt her talent subjected to an alien will.

She was to resist the principle of the director's predominance again with Meyerhold's successor. A. L. Zheliabuzhskii, who played opposite her in Gabriele D'Annunzio's *Francesca da Rimini* the next year under the direction of Nikolai Evreinov, said that she protested as too "realistic" the occasion when the director had a severed head in a bloodied sack flung at her feet. Evreinov, who kept this detail, insisted rather that it was "theatrical" (*Komissarzhevskaia,* p. 278). If Komissarzhevskaia objected to extremes of realism and stylization alike, what cause did she espouse? Lunacharsky, from the hindsight of 1930, doubtless best explained her principles:

*If later after solemnly proclaiming realism as her artistic credo, Komissarzhevskaia went over to stylization along with Meyerhold in the era of the "new theater" and there created figures such as Sister Beatrice—still no break really occurred in her understanding of artistic truth. Komissarzhevskaia only tried to learn a new theater language, new methods, so to speak; she tried to use between herself and the audience new conductors, but along these conductors was to flow the same electric energy of psychologism.* Sister Beatrice *was interesting not for its new forms of expression (which were, all the same, interesting), but because through these new forms it was possible to communicate with such extraordinary acuteness the humility and ecstasy of Beatrice. (Ibid., p. 184.)*

More pertinent than estimates by others of Meyerhold's success and failure at the Theater of Komissarzhevskaia is surely his own view of his accomplishment there. Above all, his view helps clarify the vexed terms *new theater, uslovnost,* and *theatrical.* Meyerhold's own view emerges first from notes which he prepared for his report at a meeting of the theater's artistic directors a month before his unexpected dismissal. According to Volkov's account, Meyerhold intended to praise the theater, first, for having a "true repertory"; secondly, for its rhythm in both language and movement; thirdly, for its experimentation and its search for "new forms," in which he thought it had found the right way, though without yet reaching its goal; and, fourthly, for being a theater of strong personalities on stage, an actors' theater. Meyerhold intended then to urge the creation of a drama school and a summer theater and to ask for confidence in himself as director, particularly in his aim of "simplicity." He wanted finally to analyze past productions and suggest future plans. "The future of the Theater lay, according to Meyerhold, in tragedy, rhythm, and immobility in the sense of simple and strict expression" (Volkov, 1:340).

However, Meyerhold never gave his report as planned but had, instead, to answer Komissarzhevskaia's opening charge that her theater was headed for disaster if it continued on its present path. In reply, Meyerhold admitted that the manner of *Pelleas and Melisande* must be abandoned. He too now saw it as the end of an era which he himself had launched in the Theater Studio with *The Death of Tintagiles*. Now this style of the "decorative panel," or "*uslovnyi* decorative theater*," as he also called it, would have to yield to "sculptured staging," which would give play to the actor's three-dimensional body (Volkov, 1:342). In answer to the criticism that he "pressured" the actor and wanted to make him a mere puppet, he admitted the first charge but denied the second: he did not view the puppet as the end goal of acting style or consider puppet theater desirable, although he did require that the actor realize the director's aim; that is, he openly admitted his belief in the "director's theater." Blok, however, in a first report on the Komissarzhevskaia theater, charged that not Meyerhold but Stanislavsky "holds the actors in an iron hand. . . . Meyerhold's

methods are completely different. . . . He gives the actors general guidelines, works out a general plan, and then, loosening the reins, throws the individuals to the caprice of the stage like a flare of sparks." [7]

It is not surprising that Meyerhold set *The Death of Tintagiles* and *Pelleas and Melisande* as, respectively, the beginning and end of a style. Later in the initial article of *On Theater*, which he first gave as a lecture after his dismissal and then published in the avant-garde anthology *A Book about New Theater* (1907), he rightly saw his work as one whole from the Theater Studio to the Theater of Komissarzhevskaia, as if the projects of Stanislavsky's earlier venture had been realized in the laboratory provided by Komissarzhevskaia. In this sense the whole sweep of Meyerhold's effort began even before Stanislavsky's charge to the Theater Studio: "The time has come to stage the unreal"; it began with Chekhov's advice to Meyerhold at the Moscow Art Theater not to play Johannes Vockerat, in Hauptmann's *Lonely Lives*, with nervous gestures: "One must express suffering as it is expressed in life, not with one's legs and arms, but by a tone, a glance, not by gesticulation, but with grace." Chekhov's advice could explain the immobility of Meyerhold's *Hedda*, in which Komissarzhevskaia and her partner Bravich recited their lines in rhythmic monotones, gazing straight ahead without movement, leaving the passionate emotion behind the words to be filled in by the audience. Indeed, Chekhov's admonition may have provided the first basis for the audience participation which Meyerhold postulated in one form or another throughout his career.

Again in the first article of *On Theater* Meyerhold cited Chekhov's criticism of the excess of naturalistic detail planned for *The Sea Gull*, to which Chekhov preferred the economy of art as the quintessence of life. His demand echoed in Meyerhold's description of "stylizing" Gerhart Hauptmann's comedy in the Theater Studio: "Work on the third play, *Schluck and Jau*, taught us to show on stage only the most important things, the 'quintessence of life,' as Chekhov said; it showed us the difference between the reproduction on stage of a style and the stylization of the stage set" (*Articles,* 1:112). Not only the stage set but the characterization too should not be overburdened with detail; it should give only the essentials: "The naturalistic theater teaches the actor to express everything without fail with definitive clarity and outline; it never allows allusive acting, intentional understatement. This explains why the acting in the naturalistic theater is so frequently overdone" (ibid., 1:115).

Meyerhold remarked naturalism's overemphasis of face and makeup: "Obviously the naturalistic theater regards the face as the actor's major means of expression and, in consequence, disregards all other means. The naturalistic theater does not know the beauty of sculpture, does not make its actors train their bodies, does not realize that physical education must be a basic subject of theater training if they dream of producing *Antigone* and *Julius Caesar*—plays which belong, thanks to their music, to a quite other theater. So one remembers many character faces of virtuoso make-up, but never poses or rhythmic movements" (*Articles,* 1:114). Such criticism thus early foreshadowed some of Meyerhold's postrevolutionary innovations: his abandonment of makeup, his biomechanics for the physical training of actors, and his return to earlier theater traditions. Though he was to repudiate "the beauty of sculpture"—indeed, beauty altogether just after the Revolution—still Meyerhold, much more than Stanislavsky, would again make the actor whole, an integrated moving person.

In *Pelleas and Melisande* the "simplicity" Meyerhold demanded—stylization in the set and understatement in the characterization—apparently went so far that the audience, far from using its imagination to complete the picture, was provoked to laughter instead. As Verigina described it, the discrepancy between what was implied and what was shown proved too great: Pelleas invites Melisande, " 'Sit down under this willow: the sun never penetrates its foli-

age.' But not only was there no dense foliage, there was not even a semblance of leaves. 'It is dark under this tree,' adds Pelleas, and the audience cannot help laughing despite its respect for Komissarzhevskaia" (*Komissarzhevskaia*, p. 271). In addition, Meyerhold adopted for this play Maeterlinck's requirement that his plays be acted without continuous motion, with a marionettelike quality. At that point, then, "new theater" and *uslovnyi* theater coincided in meaning with "immobile" and symbolist theater.

However, Meyerhold soon began to replace immobility with the "sculptured" use of the body in three-dimensional space. After the success of *Sister Beatrice* with its static pictorial groupings against a decorative panel far forward on only a narrow strip, Meyerhold opened the stage in depth so that the actor might convey meaning with his whole body moving in space. In the first article of *On Theater* Meyerhold wrote:

*Richard Wagner expresses inner dialogue with the help of the orchestra. . . . Just as in the musical drama the phrase sung by the singer is not a sufficiently strong means of expressing inner dialogue, so in the drama the word. . . . Just as Wagner makes the orchestra tell of psychological experience, so I make sculptured movements tell of them. After all, though, sculptured movement was an indispensable means of expres-*

*sion in earlier theater too. Salvini [Tommaso Salvini (1829–1951)] in* Othello *or* Hamlet *always impressed us by his sculptured gestures. Sculptured movement is not new, though I don't mean the kind of sculptured movement which is carefully coordinated with the words. I mean sculptured movement "not coordinated with the words." What does this imply? Two people are carrying on a conversation about the weather, about art, about apartments. From their conversation about subjects having nothing to do with their relationship a third person observing them . . . can accurately determine who they are, whether friends, enemies, or lovers. . . . Gestures, poses, glances, silence determine the truth of mutual relationships between people. Words don't tell all. Thus a clear design [risunok] of movements is essential on stage so as to communicate with the perceptive observer, that is the audience, so as to provide it with the material which the two people conversing gave the third person observing them, the material which will let the audience guess the characters' psychological experience. Words for the ear, sculptured movement for the eyes. (Articles, 1:134–35.)*

Nikolai Gorchakov quoted the witticism of Mme. Teffi (pseudonym of Nadezhda Lokhvitskaia) that Meyerhold produced "something halfway between metaphysics and ballet,"[8] though her comment more justly applies to the beautiful movement later cultivated by Tairov, who got his start with Meyerhold at the Komissarzhevskaia theater. Meyerhold himself was to direct his Soviet system of movement away from mysticism and beauty; surely his "biomechanics" came closer to meaningful demonstration as Brecht analogically explained it in 1938: "The eye witness of a traffic accident demonstrates to a crowd, which has gathered, how the accident happened . . . —the main thing is that the demonstrator shows what the driver or the victim or both did in such a way that the bystanders can form an opinion about the accident" (*werkausgabe,* 16:546).

Like Nietzsche and his Russian exponent, the classical scholar Viacheslav Ivanov, Meyerhold saw the origin of theater in the cult of Dionysus and the spirit of music and movement. In this view of theater as audience participation in a cult, the proscenium stage, which divides actors from audience, is a late phenomenon. Its advent in the Baroque period changed the nature of theater by presenting spectacles to be watched passively, as in a frame. The Moscow Art Theater, with its photographic reproduction of reality, thus became a last step in the long development toward the picture-frame stage and the small intimate theater.

In opposition to this trend, however, certain avant-garde directors, among whom Meyerhold named specifically Stanislavsky, Gordon Craig, Max Reinhardt, and himself, sought to create the *uslovnyi* theater which would return the theater to large audiences and again embrace the whole gamut of dramatic literature. Meyerhold defined this new-old departure: "The *uslovnyi* theater will free the actor from a painted background, creating three-dimensional space for him and putting sculptured depth at his disposal. Thanks to *uslovnyi* technical methods, the complicated apparatus of theater must collapse; the production is taken back to such simplicity that an actor can come out upon a space and play his scenes there, free from the set and properties devised for the proscenium stage and from all surroundings, whatever they may be" (*Articles,* 1:140–41). Movement is thus the precondition of *uslovnyi* theater, which in turn demands the active participation of the audience, at least in fantasy. In fact the word *uslovnyi*, meaning literally "conditional," or "conventional," is predicated on "the willing suspension of disbelief." Here Meyerhold added the programmatic passage which he had already used in his earlier article on Max Reinhardt and which he attributed to Leonid Andreev in a letter to him, now lost: "The *uslovnyi* theater is such that the spectator does not forget even for a moment that he has before him an actor who is acting, and the actor, that he has before him an audience, beneath his feet a stage and round about him a stage set" (ibid., 1:141–42).

Though *uslovnyi* refers to a convention of theater, or a form of theater, Meyerhold at first identified it in this early article with content, with the "new theater" and the then new literature: "The new theater will emerge from literature. . . . Not only the dramatists act as prompters [of the new] by creating examples of a new form requiring new techniques, but also the critics, by rejecting the old forms" (*Articles,* 1:123). Just as the Moscow Art Theater grew out of the need for new ways of staging Chekhov, so the Theater Studio was to fill the need for new ways of staging Maeterlinck. And the "new theater" was to find new means of producing, besides Maeterlinck, the Russian dramatists of the Ivanov circle: Viacheslav Ivanov himself, Aleksei Remizov, Mikhail Kuzmin, Alexander Blok, Fedor Sologub, Andrei Belyi, and Vladimir Solovev, among the better known. Today Maeterlinck is outmoded and the Russians forgotten, at least as dramatists. And unfortunately the term *uslovnyi* is so linked with the outmoded work of these turn-of-the-century dramatists that it has lost its usefulness as a designation of form or technique apart from content.[9]

One period piece, however, Blok's *Farce,* launched the new theater in a direction still valid today. In the preface to his book *On Theater* Meyerhold declared, "The first impulse toward determining the path my art was to take came . . . from the happy improvising of plans for the wonderful *Farce* by Blok" (*Articles,* 1:103). And, together with Molière's *Don Juan* and *Columbine's Scarf,* after Schnitzler (both 1910), Blok's play in its epiphany gave Meyerhold his awareness of the two basic problems of his whole career, the "forestage" (thrust or apron stage) and the "mask," as he called them in the preface to *On Theater.* The concept of the apron stage means direct contact with the audience and the renewal of theater technique associated with arena staging. The concept of the mask relates to the dichotomy between the actor and his role, his skill in "showing" the character he plays; this concept is best known today under Brecht's term *alienation.* The two ideas together—apron stage, or arena staging, and the mask, or alienation—amount to what is today understood by "theatricalism," as opposed to realism.

Though Meyerhold thus came to theatricalism in both theory and practice so early that his name has become synonymous with it, he did not at this point use the word. Rather, Nikolai Evreinov, his successor as director in the Theater of Komissarzhevskaia, claimed the discovery of theatricalism. From the hindsight of 1927 he wrote in *The Theater in Life:* "V. E. Meyerhold paid no attention to theatricality and believed that 'the new theater should grow out of literature.' Mr. Meyerhold changed his mind and began to extol theatricality only after my 'Justification of Theatricality' had appeared." [10] However, Evreinov understood by "theatricality" not theatricalism but a total view of life. He held the "pretend" instinct to be basic in children, savages, and human nature generally, and, using examples both from sexual and criminal pathology and from normal conduct, he tried to prove that "all the world's a stage" and life is total theatricality.

The "Justification" on which he based his claim did indeed appear early (1908), but only in a newspaper, *Utro*. His book *The Theater as Such,* which came out in the same year as Meyerhold's *On Theater* (1913), revealed a different slant in its subtitle: *A Justification of Theatricality in the Sense of the Positive Basis of Theater Art in Life*. True, Evreinov included in the book at least one observation which made him an early and important theatricalist, though, interestingly, like Meyerhold, he used in this sense the word *uslovnyi,* not *theatrical:* "The theater in my opinion never was, indeed never could be anything but *uslovnyi*. . . . Everything in art is *uslovnyi* inasmuch as one thing stands for another. Between artist and spectator a wordless contract is concluded. . . . 'This canvas is not canvas; rather I willingly assume it to be the sky.' " [11] Evreinov's example clearly illustrates the meaning of *uslovnyi* as "agreed upon," a contract or artistic convention accepted by actor and audience alike. Evreinov further insisted on theater as an art in its own right: "The theater is not a temple, a school, a mirror, a tribunal, a lecture platform, but only a theater." [12] Again, he disapproved linking *uslovnyi* with outmoded symbolism and went on to cite Meyerhold's own admission after *Pelleas and Melisande* that Maeterlinckism had run its course.

Certainly the 1907–8 and 1911–12 seasons of Evreinov's Starinnyi Teatr (Archaic Theater), with its program of medieval and then Renaissance plays, helped to provide others with new content taken from traditional sources. However, Evreinov's own directorship with Komissarzhevskaia was terminated with the closing of her theater that same year, and his "monodramas" in his later cabaret, The Crooked Mirror, remained isolated phenomena, as did the cabaret itself. His emigration after 1917 greatly limited his further career in the theater. Granting Evreinov's merit in furthering twentieth-century theatricalism, still his achievement is even quantitatively not comparable with that of Meyerhold.

Evreinov had rightly noted Meyerhold's change of direction, a change strikingly evident in the contrast between the first and the last articles of the book *On Theater*. The first derived from Meyerhold's period of experimentation in the Theater Studio and the Theater of Komissarzhevskaia. Though at one point in the article he identified the new theater with Maeterlinckism, at another he denied its commitment to any one content and defined it as a concept in form. In so doing he showed his awareness of the wealth of the theater tradition as a source of stylistic possibilities:

*One says "uslovnyi theater" not at all as one says "Ancient Greek Theater" or "the theater of medieval mystery plays," "the Renaissance theater" or "the theater of Shakespeare." . . . All these designations, beginning with "the Ancient Greek" and ending with "Ibsen's theater" denote ideas of a literary style. . . . The works of Shakespeare's time and of the Ancient Greek theater were originally uslovnyi, though Julius Caesar and Antigone can be staged—but need not be—realistically in the Meiningen style. [Here Meyerhold, of course, thought of the Julius Caesar at the Moscow Art Theater, for which Stanislavsky had done archaeological research.] The Drama of Life (Knut Hamsun) and Hedda Gabler can be treated for just the same reasons either way. [Here Meyerhold obviously referred to his own uslovnyi Hedda for Komissarzhevskaia.] (Articles, 1:163–64.)*

Meyerhold then filled in the meaning of *uslovnyi* as form, not content: it pre-supposes an audience to complete in imagination what is merely suggested by the production. It presupposes the art, not the reality, of the stage, which, like all great art, can give an even stronger feeling of life than reality.

While the first article of *On Theater* thus offered an open field of formal possibilities, "Balagan," or "Farce," the last article of 1912, specified one formal possibility, the Italian *commedia dell'arte* or the cabotinage of French theater in Molière's time. As though Blok's ridicule of the mystics in *Farce* had driven out the solemnity of symbolism and as though *commedia* characters and antics had replaced it, Meyerhold in "Balagan" no longer argued for "the new theater" but for the "theater of masks." He inveighed against the "decadent" vagueness of the symbolists and advocated laughter above all. He recommended the example not of the ancient Greeks but of the seventeenth-century Spaniards and Italians, from whom he urged borrowing "antics peculiar to the theater."

Meyerhold acknowledged taking at least one naive device from Evreinov's Starinnyi Theater, the wooden horse in the medieval farce of *Robin and Marion*, which he reused in Evgenii Znosko-Borovskii's *Transformed Prince* (1910). Working no longer with Maeterlinck's sense of naiveté but with E. T. A. Hoffmann's, he there deliberately exposed the illusion: to show the shock and transformation of the prince at the news of his father's death, stage assistants, like Japanese *kurambo,* bound a white beard on him. This device recalls the soldiers in Brecht's *Man is Man,* who plunge their faces in white chalk to show the pallor of fear. Here the parallel with Brecht and the later Soviet Meyerhold ends, however, for the goal Meyerhold urged upon the theater in "Balagan" was to amuse, not teach. He still advocated depth, but in the sense of contrast, the juxtaposition of the gay and the terrible, under the slogan of the "grotesque," which he derived as much from the irony of the German romantics as from the Italians. Between the first and last articles of his book, then, Meyerhold filled the concept of *uslovnyi* theater with a wholly new program, not so much of literature as of formal devices and possibilities, which he owed to Blok's play, as he said, and surely also to the many impulses of his time toward greater awareness of theater history.

Still, *uslovnyi* has come in the end to mean not abstractly a condition of theater or a formal concept (that is, the nonobservance of the realistic convention), but instead, concretely, the symbolist era in theater history. Unfortunately, symbolist plays like those of Maeterlinck and Andreev are no longer of interest in their single-minded pathos. But the basic formal principle used in producing them, most often called "theatricalism," is certainly rele-

vant today. Of course, the word "theatrical" is also loosely used in the sense of "dramatically effective," as Evreinov meant it when speaking of the severed head flung at the feet of Komissarzhevskaia in *Francesca da Rimini.* Evreinov gave it a further and private meaning by urging the total "theatricalization of life." Nevertheless, the term today has the useful meaning of a quality of theater art in its own right which need not adhere to the realistic convention. In Meyerhold's practice during the early experiments of the Theater Studio of 1905, this meant resorting to rhythmic speech and movement and "stylized" groupings, all reminiscent of earlier theater. At Komissarzhevskaia's theater he transcended the dividing line between actors and audience with Blok's *Farce,* breaking the illusion as in the *commedia* or the plays of Ludwig Tieck, and he taught the actor again to use his whole body, not just his face and hands, and to work even on a bare stage. He also developed such new devices as the area lighting of *The Awakening of Spring.* Perhaps his greatest success, however, the "pictorialism" of *Sister Beatrice,* remained inevitably linked to the symbolist age. But above all, Meyerhold's first two years in the capital (1905–7) found him representing the new force of the strong creative director; as such he experimented early with a rich variety of ideas which together amount to liberation of theater art in this century.

# Chapter 2: Petersburg Productions (1908-18)

Compared to Stanislavsky's straightforward career, Meyerhold appeared to pursue one tangential flight after another. Perhaps the most unexpected departure from a seemingly logical course of development occurred in 1908 when he became a director at the Imperial Theaters of Saint Petersburg, a position in which he remained until its termination after the Revolution of 1917. How are we to understand the appointment of so radical a proponent of new theater to the prime theatrical stronghold of the establishment? Meyerhold had just exposed his radicalism on a theoretical level in his article for the 1907 anthology on theater and on a practical level by his productions for Komissarzhevskaia's theater. In particular, his insistence on the major role of the director as creative artist set him apart from the directors at the Imperial Theaters, most of whom were still mere prompters or arrangers of footlights. Only in Moscow had Stanislavsky shown how one might direct a uniquely conceived production in the dramatic theater; Savva Mamontov had demonstrated the process of unified operatic creation in his own opera house there; and a set designer at the Moscow Bolshoi, Aleksandr Golovin, had begun in 1900 to realize set, costumes, and properties as a single conception, with his designs for Arsenii Koreshchenko's opera *The Ice Palace* (1900).

To Golovin is often ascribed the initiative for Meyerhold's imperial appointment, perhaps because Meyerhold himself thus mentioned it in the unfinished biographical data he set down in 1921: "Thanks to the energetic wish of the artist A. Golovin, I was appointed, despite great obstacles, to the staff of the Imperial theaters" (*Articles*, 1:313). However, Golovin gave Vladimir Teliakovskii, chief administrator of the Imperial Theaters, responsibility for the appointment; Teliakovskii, while clearly recognizing the appointment of so radical an innovator as Meyerhold for the paradox it was, admitted the fact: "I became interested in him when I heard unflattering opinions of him on all sides. When everyone attacks a man, he must be of some importance. You can't expect much of a man whom everyone praises." [1]

Meyerhold had not only, in general, to carry the day for the new age of the director in the theater but also, in particular, to make his peace with senior actors, pillars of the imperial establishment. He succeeded quite well in realizing unified works of art through constant collaboration with Golovin and often also with the ballet master Mikhail Fokine, but achieving cooperation with older actors was more difficult. At least one of the leading actors, Iurii Iurev, was immediately persuaded to work with Meyerhold on physical movement, especially for the leading roles he played in both of Meyerhold's outstanding imperial productions, Molière's *Don Juan* (1910) and Lermontov's *Masquerade* (1917). To accommodate another star of the Aleksandrinskii company, Konstantin Varlamov, Meyerhold created special conditions in the staging of *Don Juan*. He had two prompters in period costumes, each with a huge book of the play, seat themselves on stage, creating thereby a piquant illusion and also solving Varlamov-Sganarelle's difficulties with memorization. Even the great actress Mariia Savina finally came to collaborate with Meyerhold (on Zinaida Gippius's *Green Ring*), though not until 1915, the year of her death. Unfortunately, another great performer, Vladimir Davydov, remained obdurately hostile. And equally unfortunately, the main obstacle to innovation, the inherent conservatism of so representative and subsidized an institution itself, was insuperable. Meyerhold therefore carried on experiments outside the establishment in various private and cabaret ventures in which he worked, after 1910, under the pseudonym of Dr. Dapertutto.

Meyerhold's debut at the Aleksandrinskii in the double capacity of director and actor in Knut Hamsun's *At the Imperial Gates* (1908) was not very successful. The play had only eight performances, and thereafter Meyerhold the actor almost disappeared from view. Temporarily the director too seemed to withdraw into stocktaking, or perhaps it was just that the slower pace of work within the establishment gave him the opportunity to read widely, write articles, and even give courses, such as an acting course at K. I. Daneman's conservatory of music or a course in collaboration with Mikhail Gnesin on the musical reading of verse, which formed the nucleus of a later Meyerhold studio. He even was able to join an archeological study tour of Greece (1910), and he continued independently to Italy, where he tried to meet Gordon Craig, though in vain; at least he saw Craig's Arena Goldoni.

Though the number of productions actually realized diminished greatly—Rudnitskii compares fifteen a season for Komissarzhevskaia to one or two a season at the Imperial Theaters—there was no diminution in Meyerhold's efforts to further the new theater. Work was begun together with Mikhail Fokine, Leon Bakst, and the composer Aleksandr Glazunov on a production of Oscar Wilde's *Salomé* (1909), which was, however, forbidden by the censor. Together with the designer Mikhail Dobuzhinskii short pieces were put on representing a wide spread of interests, *Petrushka* (folk farce), *Fall of the House of Usher,* after Poe (the Gothic macabre), and Sologub's *Honor and Revenge* (symbolism). Dobuzhinskii, who successively represented in his long eclectic career almost every important trend of Russian stage design, realized for *Petrushka* a setting in the vein of pseudonaiveté; three years later this folk subject became in Stravinsky's musical setting a classic of Russian ballet (fig. 2.1). Unfortunately, the cabaret Lukomore (Magic Bay), at which the three experimental productions by Meyerhold were staged, for all the wealth of literary allusion in its name to Pushkin and Chekhov, soon became impoverished. In another cabaret venture two seasons later, The House of Interludes, the name of Dr. Dapertutto acquired resonance with the highly significant musical pantomime *Columbine's Scarf* (1910).

In the same year, 1910, Meyerhold achieved his first resounding success with Molière's *Don Juan* at the Aleksandrinskii. Not only did he and Golovin create a uniquely conceived whole, but Meyerhold burst through the fourth wall of the realistic convention and made the whole auditorium one. He in this respect departed from the practice of Molière, who had used a proscenium stage. Indeed, the reestablished unity of actors and audience was accomplished not just by abolishing the curtain: even the Moscow Art Theater had done *Antigone* in its first season (1898) without one, and, years before, Meyerhold himself had staged Ibsen's *Ghosts* in Poltava without a curtain (1906) and had used full light in the auditorium for his second production of *Farce* in Minsk

(1907), both with the actors' cooperative. But in *Don Juan,* for the first time, these devices became part of an important single conception.

The stage built out over the orchestra pit concentrated attention on the actor alone, standing outside the proscenium frame in close contact with the audience, in a further Meyerhold innovation. Even the negative criticism of a rival director, the designer Alexander Benois, which branded the production as "a folk farce in ornate dress [*nariadnyi balagan*]," conceded to Meyerhold "the great merit of having taught Russian actors to walk, move their arms and legs, and make an about-face" (quoted in Rudnitskii, p. 137). Golovin so splendidly executed Meyerhold's idea of recreating the golden age of Versailles with "ornate" costumes, tapestry backgrounds, mirrors, and chandeliers—in the auditorium as well as on stage—that the production inaugurated in Russian theaters a new epoch of the designer, in which Benois participated. The little Arabs, the target of Benois's deprecatory title "Ballet at the Imperial Dramatic Theater," were further described in Iurii Beliaev's favorable review: "Livried Arab boys run about like black kittens, do somersaults on the soft rug, burn incense, ring a silver bell, light wax candles [fig. 2.2]. A mysterious Gobelin tapestry opens, revealing picture after picture in the fantastic adventure of *Don Juan*" (quoted in

*Figure 2.1. Mikhail Dobuzhinskii's setting for the folk farce* Petrushka, *staged by Meyerhold at the Lukomore Cabaret (1908)*

*Figure 2.2. Golovin's costume
sketch for a "little Moor," or
stage assistant, in Molière's*
Don Juan *(1910)*

of a piece: a fairy tale, an amusing bag
of tricks," whereas Konstantin Derzhavin, historian of the Aleksandrinskii
Theater, called it two decades later
(1932), "one of the most overwhelming events in the history of the European
theater" (quoted in Rudnitskii, p.
139).

Indeed, the principles of innovation
which Meyerhold put into practice in
this exemplary production recur in ever
new applications: Sganarelle sharing
confidences with the audience developed as the actor's address often directed at the public today. Or, again,
the livried boys have become, as Meyerhold later called them, the "stage assistants [*slugi prostseniuma*]" whose function it is both to serve the stage illusion,
supplying needed properties and facil-
itating scene change, and at the same
time teasingly to test its credibility.

Unity of conception also animated
Meyerhold's collaboration with the ballet master, Mikhail Fokine, with whom
Golovin and he realized what was perhaps their greatest opera production,
Gluck's *Orpheus and Eurydice* (1911).
From then on, the movement, rhythm,
and music essential to opera and ballet
became as much part of Meyerhold's
constant purpose as the realization of a
total stage picture through the deco-
rator's art. Meyerhold's exposition of
his ideas on opera went beyond his
debut production of Wagner's *Tristan
and Isolde* (1909), to which he devoted

Rudnitskii, p. 136). Of course it was
only a month later that the last-minute
errand of a similar little Arab page
closed the curtain with a musical flour-
ish on the première of *Rosenkavalier*
(1911) in Dresden (for which Reinhardt served as an adviser). In Benois's
words, Meyerhold's *Don Juan* was "all

an article in the book *On Theater*. He showed his preoccupation also with Japanese Noh theater: "In Japanese Noh the actor had to be also a dancer" (*Articles*, 1:148). Again in the *Tristan and Isolde* essay Meyerhold struck a blow against realist psychology in opera, pointing out that opera is un-realistic in its basic convention: people sing instead of talking. So the opera singer must base his acting not on events and psychology—that is, not on the libretto—but on the musical score. Like other critics Meyerhold called Fedor Chaliapin the ideal opera performer but, unlike others, not because of his much-praised realistic acting. Instead, Meyerhold wrote that with Chaliapin, "thanks to the pantomime and move-ments of the actor, ruled by the musical design, the illusory becomes real, the expression which hovered in time is materialized in space" (ibid.). Thus, for Meyerhold, Chaliapin's greatness consisted in giving shape to musical form.

The following season (1909–10), Meyerhold carried the attack on histor-icism and naturalism into the field of opera with Wagner and Adolphe Appia as allies. He produced *Tristan and Isolde* and wrote an essay on it. Despite Wagner's categorical rejection of histor-ical subjects in favor of myths, Wag-nerian operas were always staged historically, with a plethora of helmets and shields, as Meyerhold said, against

"the boring, not in the least mystic or mysterious, and colorless background of a historicism which invites the audi-ence to deduce in what country and *in what year* of what century the action takes place. . . . Wasn't it for this rea-son, as Wagner's intimates report, that he would go up to his friends at per-formances in Bayreuth and cover their eyes with his hands so that they might more fully give themselves up to the magic of the pure symphonic music?" (*Articles*, 1:158; Meyerhold's italics).

So Meyerhold advocated sweeping away the clutter of Meiningenism from the operatic stage, as he had swept it from the dramatic stage. Far from shut-ting out visual impressions, though, he demanded an atmospheric effect, such as only the best artists of stage design could achieve: "You can overcharge a huge stage with all possible details and still not make it believable that this is a ship. Oh what a difficult task it is to represent on stage the deck of a ship in motion! . . . 'To express a great deal with very little—this is the essential thing. . . . The Japanese draw a single twig in blossom and this is a whole spring. We draw a whole spring without making even a twig!' " [2] The "twig" principle of Oriental art was later pre-empted for film by Eisenstein, doubtless from his teacher Meyerhold.

Once Meyerhold had cleared the stage, he faced the problem of what to do with it. (Peter Brook puts the same

question with the very title of his 1968
book, *The Empty Space*.) In Meyerhold's formulation we discern the beginnings of constructivism: "The greatest difficulty is the stage floor, its flat
surface. As a sculptor shapes clay, the
director must break up the great ex-
panse of stage floor into compactly designed surfaces varying in height.
Broken lines" (*Articles,* 1:155). In the
center of the stage was to be the actor,
and he had to be moved forward toward
the audience, who would thus see him
not only in close-up but also in the
round. Meyerhold cited the Greek and
Shakespearean theaters and the circus.
To achieve proximity in a conventional
theater one needed to abolish the curtain and build the apron forward over
the orchestra pit.

Placing the actor in the center of
attention would make him the work of
art. "Mastery for the actor of naturalistic drama consists in observing life
and translating his observations into his
creative work. . . . The actor of musical
drama must grasp the essence of the
musical score and translate all the sub-
tleties of the orchestral design into the
language of plastic design" (*Articles,*
1:148). This, Meyerhold thought,
would require a masterful flexibility of
the body, and he asked: "Where does
the human body achieve its highest development in flexibility for stage purposes, flexibility through its expressive-

ness?" He underlined the answer: *"In
the dance"* (ibid.). Yet he recommended that pantomimic expression be
sparingly used, declaring music to be
the added means of expression: "Besides the flexibility which makes an
opera singer into a dancer in his movements, still another peculiarity distinguishes the actor of musical drama from
the actor of word drama. When some
recollection causes the dramatic actor
suffering, he reveals it to the audience
by his mimicry. In musical drama the
music can communicate this suffering
to the audience. So the operatic artist
must postulate economy of gesture as a
principle, for his gesture is needed only
to complete what the score omits or the
orchestra begins but leaves unfinished"
(ibid., 1:149).

Meyerhold's recommendations to the
nondramatic actor were, of course,
put into practice with his own productions of opera and ballet in Saint
Petersburg. These included one ballet,
the *Jota Aragonesa,* which he produced for Fokine with Golovin's
designs in 1916. Again, in the Soviet
period, his theories might have borne
fruit as markedly in opera as in the
theater if he had continued the work
of his last years in Stanislavsky's opera
studio, but this work was unfortunately
cut short by his arrest in 1939. As it
is, however, Meyerhold's contact with
opera and ballet is primarily interesting

for the lessons he drew from it for the "drama of the word," as he called the dramatic theater.

Though the battle of his first decade as a director was waged against plays that were better read than acted— "library drama [*literaturshchina*]"— Meyerhold fought not against literature but for the restoration of spectacle and action, as they are best found, together with the word, in the theater of other times and places. He cannot be branded an enemy of the word. True, his advocacy of movement and music— not in opposition but in addition to the word—did carry him to extremes, especially in the later revolutionary period with the acrobatics of *The Death of Tarelkin* (1922) or with the added Wagnerian dimension of music in *Bubus the Teacher* (1924). Still, even those two shows, in which the use of movement and music was, doubtless, too radically experimental, prepared the way for later major productions like *The Forest* (1924) and *The Inspector General* (1926).

If Meyerhold's work in opera was most important as a corollary to his dramatic productions, yet certain of his ideas represented a genuine contribution to operatic theater as such. How obviously right he was to insist that the operatic singer be an actor and be able to move like a dancer as well. More controversial was his insistence

that the role of Orpheus be sung by a man, not a woman, and his choice partly for this reason of the second, not the earlier, version of Gluck's *Orpheus and Eurydice* for his production of 1911. Finally, in his staging of Gluck's opera he strove to make one whole of the conventionally separate elements, singers, ballet dancers, and chorus. The ballet master Fokine recalled how he was at first asked to stage only the dances and with what enthusiasm he conceived the scene in Hades, which began with hundreds of bodies lying motionless in tormented poses and then crawling over the cliffs and each other.

*When this was transferred to the stage, Meyerhold asked me to instruct the choir and all the participants in this. I was glad to do so. . . . It has always shocked me the way the ballet enters in an opera. It always seems that in the midst of one troupe, the singers, another troupe appears for a time, the dancers, and without any connection whatever between these two elements. I joyfully undertook this, my first assignment to carry out in an opera my principle of the unity of all participants in a scene. Of course no one in the audience could tell where the ballet begins and the chorus ends. The dance of the furies and shades then emerged naturally from this whole sculptured mass. The chorus too became enthusiastic. I remember that when I noticed some ladies of the chorus having to sing in improbably inconvenient and unwonted poses, lying almost upside down on the cliffs or kneeling in the most improbable embraces, I went up to them to ease their position, but they asked me not to change anything, saying they could manage.*[3]

After describing the other scenes, which he also conceived as a union of soloists, chorus, and dancers, Fokine added that he received equal credit with Meyerhold as director of the opera. He could explain the short run of *Orpheus and Eurydice* only as the result of wholly extraneous circumstances, first his own sojourn abroad with Diaghilev during the next two seasons, so that he could not rehearse the dances, then Gluck's German nationality, which prevented the opera's performance during the war years 1914–17, and finally the lack of a notation system for nonclassical movement, so that no record of the dances was available when in 1923 a repeat performance was proposed for Fokine's twenty-fifth anniversary as ballet master.

It is interesting that Meyerhold's association with the dance occurred in the time of Fokine, who helped liberate ballet from strictly classical forms. Meyerhold would later observe that he himself differed from Aleksandr Tairov in that

his own biomechanics did not consist of prettified ballet movements but included angular, folk, and expressive movements, the basis of so-called modern dance. According to Fokine, the modern Renaissance of the dance stems from this period in Russian ballet and from Isadora Duncan, not from the Germans.

*Twenty-five years ago the Russian ballet saw most clearly the problem of how to unite virtuosity and mastery of the dance with naturalness and expression in movement. I dare maintain that the problem was solved, and it was proved that ballet can be the art which expresses in movements of the body all the variations of being human. . . . Angular movements are not a new discovery of the German dance. Whole ballets were staged in Russia thirty years ago on the basis of angular movements* (Egyptian Nights, *and* Judith). *The same style was realized both in the drama by V. Meyerhold and in the opera by F. Chaliapin (in the role of Holofernes). After the ballet* Petrushka *was produced [1911], in which all the tragedy was communicated in angular movements, the ballet masters Nizhinskii, Massine, Mme. Nizhinskii, and Balanchine did almost all their ballets with angular movements. Both the initiative and the best achievements in this do not belong to the Germans.*[4]

The dance Meyerhold recommended to

actors and the assorted movements of biomechanics in which he later trained them were certainly in this "angular" and natural style, not the classical style.

Though traces of Meyerhold's early period were recognizable in his Soviet period, chiefly as a continuous trend in physical movements, the splendor of his imperial artistic settings, achieved in cooperation with the World-of-Art painter Golovin, were later starkly contradicted. The lush elegance and decorative style of his collaboration with Golovin, an associate more constant and important to his productions than Fokine, was actively repudiated by the Meyerhold of the early Soviet years. Golovin's colorful painted flats and curtains and the elegant costumes familiar to the world from his productions for Diaghilev's Paris seasons of *Boris Godunov* and *The Fire Bird*, as well as from Meyerhold's *Don Juan, Storm*, and *Masquerade*, seem indeed a paradoxical component in the work of a director who featured the actor and discounted the illusion. So it seems only logical that Meyerhold later abandoned both painted backgrounds and painted curtains. Not that he abandoned Golovin personally, for he still invited Golovin in 1924 to design costumes for Griboedov's *Woe from Wit* at the Theater of the Revolution, for which Viktor Shestakov was to do a constructivist set. However, Golovin refused: "If I worked only with you then even the

constructivist method wouldn't prevent the execution of this assignment. But in the collaboration you suggest, we shall not achieve unity; also it's hard to communicate in letters." [5]

Golovin rightly saw that the unity of conception on which his whole work in the theater depended was unthinkable in the combination of a constructivist set with his typically decorative costumes. It is true that Meyerhold did successfully combine in *Camille* (1934) an elegance of costumes and properties with the schematism of a partly constructivist set. And from the very beginning he used Golovin's painted backgrounds, as in *Don Juan*, not to create illusions but to further his constant play with illusion. He demonstrated in this way that it is not necessary to abandon all background and bare the stage in order to practice play with illusion. Indeed, even in the early period Meyerhold had it both ways: in *Don Juan* at the Aleksandrinskii Theater with Golovin's elaborate flats and carefully designed costumes and makeup he played with the theater illusion quite as much as in his production of Dmitrii Merezhkovskii's *Paul I* (1910) in a private apartment with neither stage nor set.

Just how painted flats, apparently so much a part of illusionistic theater, served Meyerhold in his aim of breaking the illusion is apparent in his treatment of Lermontov's *Masquerade*. Not only in *Don Juan*, as we have seen, but also in *Masquerade* Meyerhold added an apron stage, built out over the orchestra pit, bringing the actor far forward into close contact with his audience. "Molière is the first among the master dramatists of the *Roi soleil* who tries to bring the action forward from the depth and middle distance onto the stage apron to its very edge," wrote Meyerhold (*Articles*, 1:193), and he pointed out the parallel with the ancient Greek and Shakespearean theaters, where the actor was not just a part of perspectival illusion. Rather, "the actor with his gestures, his mimicry, his plastic movements, his voice was the unique bearer of all the dramatist's meaning" (ibid.). Therefore Meyerhold freed the actor from the frame or portals of the baroque proscenium stage. "Like a circus arena, ringed about on all sides by spectators, the stage apron comes close to the audience so that the dust of the wings does not obscure a single gesture, not a single movement, not a single grimace of the actor. . . . The atmosphere of this space, not confined between the columns of the wings, and the light, poured on this dust-free atmosphere, surround only the flexible figures of the actors—everything about them is created as if to emphasize the play of bright light both from the candles on stage and in the auditorium, which is not plunged in darkness during the course of the whole performance" (ibid., 1:194–95).

How then could painted flats aid and abet such a directorial conception? The actress Elizaveta Timé explained how Meyerhold brought the author's meaning home to the audience in *Masquerade:*

*The dimensions of our theater and its stage [in the Aleksandrinskii Theater, today the Academic Pushkin Theater, Leningrad, some thirty feet still separate first-row orchestra seats from actors downstage], the rhythmic and syntactic complexity of Lermontov's youthful verse—all this caused Meyerhold and Golovin to try an experiment, unheard of till then: they brought the action close to the audience by moving forward a stage platform into the very auditorium on the apron and making doors for the actors' exits in a specially built wooden portal. This portal almost merged with the auditorium and the box seats on the side, and from the apron two little half-circular stairs with gilded railing led down into the orchestra. The playing area in all scenes but two was seemingly impossible, unheard-of in its lack of depth—after all, the painted drop representing the wall of the room was at the level of the second wing! Improbable, new, unthinkable! Yet the result was splendid: the verse had resonance from close by without one's straining for it, because it was easily audible, and at the same time the stage appeared as large as usual. That is, a kind of optical illusion had been achieved.*[6]

So, though Meyerhold never got the "total theater" which was still being built for him when his career was terminated, he nevertheless achieved the proximity almost of theater-in-the-round by a device he had used ten years before with an exactly opposite aim: to show the actor in pictorial perspective against a painted flat!

Dr. Dapertutto found it much easier when he produced two scenes of Merezhkovskii's *Paul I* that same year (1910) in a private house. Sergei Auslender wrote:

*This was a strange show. There was no stage, no set, and, properly speaking, no audience. Casually a certain number of guests, friends or partial acquaintances, gathered in a large room, disposing themselves on old-fashioned sofas and armchairs. Then suddenly the lights were extinguished. When they came on again, in place of the yellow screens which no one had particularly noticed at only one end of the room, there now lay Alexander I in a thoughtful pose on a small sofa, one hand outflung, in which he held a volume of Rousseau; seated beside him was Psyche-Elizabeth, quietly touching the strings of a harp. Of course it was soon evident that Elizabeth was the quite well-known actress Musina, Alexander was Golubev, and Paul, who soon appeared, Ozarovskii. Yet the first impression remained of a kind of genuineness which it is impossible to achieve on stage and which lent a special beauty to this production devised by Meyerhold. (Volkov, 2:88.)*

Later with the same aim of genuineness Meyerhold drove army trucks and motorcycles into the theater and onto the stage in *Earth Rampant* (1923). Rudnitskii cites as "historic" (p. 129) what he takes to be the earliest example of introducing properties from the audience's midst: a ladder needed for Calderón's *Adoration of the Cross* (1910) at the Tower Theater was brought in by an actor entering from the audience, simply because there was no other way. Paradoxically then, along with genuineness, complete awareness of theater as such was also Meyerhold's aim. Both aims, taken together, amounted to a titillating back-and-forth play with the illusion of reality.

Not all the devices by which Meyerhold created, manipulated, or dispelled illusion in the theater have proved equally durable. The painted flats of optical illusion at the Imperial Theaters were swept away during the Soviet years. The little Arabs who did chores on stage during the action of *Don Juan* are rarely employed in modern practice, though visible-invisible property men recurred after the Revolution under the direction of Meyerhold's pupil Nikolai Okhlopkov in Nikolai Pogodin's *Aristocrats*. The use of the apron and the arena stage, however, with the resulting immediacy of contact between actors and audience, have become common-places of theater today. And, especially, Meyerhold's use of bright light to reveal the stage devices as illusory was adopted and promulgated by Brecht as a means of freeing the audience from "the hypnosis of theater" (*werkausgabe,* 17:1011).

If taking the actors out on the apron resulted in bringing the word closer to the audience, the opposite result of eliminating the word altogether was also achieved in the pantomimes or half pantomimes that Meyerhold staged in his early period. The most important of these was the adaptation of *Columbine's Scarf*, after Arthur Schnitzler, which, along with *Farce* and *Don Juan*, Meyerhold himself considered decisive in his career. *Scarf*, as the only pantomime among the three crucial plays, remains unusual as an art form in its own right today.

Evidently Meyerhold found pantomime an important weapon in his reaction against the established theater. "To make a dramatist out of the literary man writing for the stage, it would be a good thing to force him to do a few pantomimes," Meyerhold counseled in "Balagan," his last major article in *On Theater* (*Articles,* 1:211). Yet to Meyerhold *Columbine's Scarf* meant not just compensatory training to fill a lack but also the successful realization of his

theories of the grotesque. True, in an interview for *Rampa i zhizn* (The Stage and Life, Moscow, 1911), he was to call the grotesque merely a new method for the recovery of true theater as opposed to library drama, and he would again name *Scarf* and Blok's *Farce* as examples of such true theater. But in Meyerhold's definition the grotesque also meant play with mood, the quick transformation of audience sensibility. Meyerhold employed various means to this end: movement and elements of dance, rhythm and quick tempo, farce. In his article "Balagan" he traced the ancestry of the grotesque back to precedents in the tradition: the medieval mystery play with the break in mood represented by the comic interlude, Shakespearean tragedy with its transitions to folk clowning, and the *commedia* with the dual mask of Harlequin, now fool, now devil. Such alternation and contrast come closest to romantic irony, that technique of hovering between two extremes without falling prey to either which Blok as well as the German romantics admired. So it was no accident that the adaptation from the German *Columbine's Scarf* was descended quite as much from the German romantic E. T. A. Hoffman as from the *commedia dell'arte*.

Elements of the "grotesque," as Meyerhold used the term, are often found at the beginning of a Hoffman tale, when upon the sunny horizon of the most ordinary scene a sinister presence all at once obtrudes. So in *Columbine's Scarf,* at the ball to celebrate the engagement of Columbine and Harlequin, the guests look with benevolent amusement at Pierrot and Columbine, the one pair that is not dancing. Suddenly, however, amusement turns to horror when a chance blow in the heat of the dance grazes the motionless couple so that they fall apart and are seen to be dead. Pierrot has poisoned himself for love of Columbine, and she has been so haunted by his death that she has finally kept their promise of joint suicide. Meanwhile, the true villain of the piece, the eccentric orchestra leader, both diabolic and ridiculous with his upturned pigtail à la Hoffman, drives the originally gay waltz to ever more excessive rhythm and cacophonous distortion.

Volkov described, besides the foolish-frightening image of the orchestra director, other *duratskie rozhi* (ugly fools' faces) created to Meyerhold's order by the designer Sapunov, with whom Meyerhold had collaborated in the Theater Studio of 1905 and on Blok's pivotal *Farce.* Though Sapunov died young in a boating accident in 1912 while working with Meyerhold at the Terioki summer theater, Volkov thought that the sense of irony and the grotesque which they had in common never left Meyerhold. Volkov even insisted that "when Meyerhold staged Nikolai Erdman's *Mandate* in the spring of 1925 he admitted to conceiving Barbie Guliachkin as one of Sapunov's petty bourgeois" (Volkov, 2: 238). The same spirit of the grotesque or, literally, the horribly funny, animated the *svinye ryla* (pig snouts) of the officials in Gogol's *Inspector General,* undoubtedly one of Meyerhold's major productions of the Soviet years.

Such a sense of double meaning, sinister or even diabolic, beyond the obvious everyday surface of life is, of course, the very essence of symbolism, and Meyerhold, whose work so often alluded to such duality, is sometimes thought never to have escaped his symbolist beginnings. His production of Sologub's *Hostages of Life* (1916) at the Aleksandrinskii Theater was praised for its communication of symbolic meaning with a wholly realistic setting, just as today Harold Pinter's symbolic plays move toward overwhelming revelation from such casual occurrences as the milkman's delivery of milk or the arrival of relatives with suitcases in hand. Though such contrast between the realistically ordinary and the sublime is the prevalent form of the grotesque in black comedy and in the plays of Kafka, Beckett, Pinter, or Edward Bond, the mocking humor, even irreverence, of these writers does not belie the true seriousness of their intent: Bond's *Early Morning* (1968), which shows the hero as a mere head, ridiculously emerging between the skirts of Florence Nightingale, is a serious play about love and man's inhumanity to man. Perhaps, indeed, all art except the most *terre à terre* naturalism is symbolic, and to call Meyerhold's work allusive to more than surface meaning should not imply that he remained stranded in the symbolism of his youth. Instead, like Picasso, he moved from one manner to another, from symbolist affectation of naiveté through romantic irony to ebullient satire.

In the five years between the first and last articles of his book *On Theater* Meyerhold grew from the pictorialism of his Maeterlinck productions to the dynamic farce of his *Don Juan*. Rudnitskii lists the possibilities Meyerhold realized from a single scenario, Vladimir N. Solovev's *Harlequin, the Marriage Broker*. Two of them were described by Meyerhold in the remarks on his productions appended to *On Theater*. One production given in the hall of the Nobles' Assembly (1911) represented with its approximation of the original *commedia* style a return to the naive playfulness of the tradition. Another, performed at the home of Sologub, had its actors, dressed in modern evening clothes, don masks representing single attributes of character; the evening dress suggested the sophistication, the masks the ambiguity of modern life. Rudnitskii also sees in this variant interpretation the precedent for the "parade" in Vakhtangov's famous produc-

tion of Carlo Gozzi's *Princess Turandot* (1922). Meyerhold's third production (1912) of Solovev's scenario, at the summer theater in Terioki, was excessively mannered and manipulated, according to Rudnitskii, and suggested chiefly the theme of deceit on which Meyerhold was soon to concentrate in his production of Lermontov's *Masquerade*. Besides Solovev's *commedia,* Calderón's *The Constant Prince* was repeated at Terioki. Blok, a faithful spectator of the summer theater, found that this somber version of Calderón effectively communicated the quality of Catholic mysticism.

Though Blok by his enthusiasm persuaded Meyerhold to stage Strindberg's *Crimes and Crimes* at Terioki, the poet himself no longer entrusted his own work to Meyerhold and the company he referred to as "modernists." The word *moderne*, which means "art nouveau" or "Jugendstil," a period in art that is again in favor in the West, still connotes condemnation to the Soviet critic Rudnitskii, who brands as "moderne" Meyerhold's Paris production of D'Annunzio's *Pisanella* (1913) with Ida Rubinstein. Undoubtedly, this was an enormously tasteless and expensive failure which Meyerhold perpetrated for a wealthy woman with the ambition but not the talent to become an actress. Still, *Pisanella* was interesting for Meyerhold's development if only because it brought him to Paris for several weeks at the time of Diaghilev's Paris seasons and caused him to meet Guillaume Apollinaire. No actual connection between Meyerhold's efforts to "stage the unreal" and the surrealism which Apollinaire fathered can, of course, be established, yet undoubtedly the two men shared interests, the *commedia*, the new spirit in art and, if not exactly the new theater, the circus; they honored this last interest on a tour of Paris they took together by visiting the Cirque Médrano (fig. 2.3).[7] During his Paris stay Meyerhold also saw the splendor of Diaghilev's opera and ballet, and he explored the city for material that would be useful in *Masquerade*.

The production of Lermontov's romantic verse tragedy, which after some five years of preparation Meyerhold finally premiered in the first days of the February Revolution, was not only his most luxurious (and ironically so at such a moment) but also his most durable, for it continued in the repertory of Soviet Leningrad and, as redirected by Meyerhold in 1933 and 1938, lasted even into World War II. First planned in 1911 to celebrate the one hundredth anniversary of Lermontov's birth in 1814, the production was overlong in preparation partly because of Meyerhold's and Golovin's research in the libraries and archives of Petersburg and in the antique shops of Paris, where they sought materials during Diaghilev's 1913 season. Not that they in-

tended historical exactitude in the manner of Meiningen. They aimed rather at romantic splendor masking the passion and demonism which Meyerhold proposed as central to the play (figs. 2.4–2.5). With this as his key idea, Meyerhold read Byron and, of course, all available material on Lermontov. Out of his research he evolved a significantly new conception of the hero. Arbenin is often taken as not only the hero but also primarily the "raisonneur" of the play. Meyerhold instead made him all passionate hero, a reflection of the author himself and even, like the protagonist Pechorin of Lermontov's novel, a "hero of our time." When conceived as "raisonneur," Arbenin comes close to Chatskii, the hero and critic of czarist society in Aleksandr Griboedov's satiric play *Woe from Wit,* and of course it is especially the aspect of social criticism which Meyerhold emphasized in his Soviet productions of classics by Griboedov and Gogol. But in his 1917 *Masquerade,* while stressing social satire, he looked beyond it to the human meaning in Lermontov's play. His model was that other tragedy of jealousy, Shakespeare's *Othello.*

Meyerhold explicated *Masquerade* in his second revival of his own production in 1938 (having touched on the same key idea quite as unmistakably in the material he gave to the press before the 1917 premiere): "The central figure appears in the third part.

*Figure 2.3.  Apollinaire and Meyerhold as they saw Paris together in 1913*

This is the Masked Man. We have seen him for but a brief moment at the ball of Scene 2. But even then we sensed how important a part he was to play in the fate of the Arbenins. The Masked Man brings down his prey only after his helpers (Shprikh and Kazarin) have sufficiently prepared it for the kill" (*Articles,* 1:303). Meyerhold's conception made the usually disparate elements of Lermontov's play fall into place. For the czarist censor had forced Lermontov to add the role of the Masked Man so as to punish Arbenin for the murder of his wife and point the moral that crime does not pay. By viewing the Masked Man not as the instrument of God's justice, however, but as an incorporation of the demonic principle, Meyerhold restored Arbenin to his rightful place as a romantic hero. Just as Othello remains a hero if Iago is considered guilty of Desdemona's murder, so Meyerhold made the lesser demons Shprikh and Kazarin guilty of feeding the fire of Arbenin's jealousy; Arbenin had then to receive his true punishment for Nina's death not from external justice but from within himself, in the suffering of his final madness.

Meyerhold's division of the play into three parts derived less from technical considerations than from his key idea—his intention, as he said, to bring out "the superb dramatic architecture of Lermontov's play" (*Articles,* 1:303). The first of the three parts showed the

inception of Arbenin's jealousy; the second, his exchanges with the prince and the baroness whereby the hand of the Masked Man was felt in the machinations of the lesser intriguers. Finally, in the third part, the conflict between Arbenin and Nina reached its climax at the ball and concluded with their tragic end. The technical problem of brief scenes in swift succession was solved by painted curtains, before which some of the action took place far forward on the stage apron, the effect heightened by this use of optical illusion in which a small area appeared large. So Meyerhold created a small and intimate space for the bedroom scene in which Nina, like Desdemona, dies by her husband's hand. Only twice was the enormous stage of the Aleksandrinskii fully opened in depth: in the masquerade scene of the first part and the ball scene of the third. Especially in these two scenes the music commissioned of Aleksandr Glazunov was to serve the purpose of fourth-dimensional commentary, as in opera: a function that Meyerhold tried, not always successfully, to give it in the theater. The satanic waltz at the masquerade (today Aram Khachaturian's music replaces Glazunov's) emphasized the contrast between the superficial gaiety and the demonic meaning. And at the final ball Nina's song brought out, instead, the quite different contrast between her true purity and the corruption

*Figure 2.4. Costume design by Golovin for Nina in* Masquerade *(1917)*

*Figure 2.5. Costume design by Golovin for the Masked Man in* Masquerade

*Figure 2.6.  The climactic ball scene in* Masquerade *at which Nina sings her song; Golovin's set shows the use of the full stage for this, as for the masquerade scene.*

of society. Golovin's set design showed Meyerhold's use of the whole stage in this scene, as in the masquerade scene (fig. 2.6).

Nor were music and space Meyerhold's only means for underlining what he considered the play's basic demonism: the dance and the pantomimed encounters of the masquers further conveyed the dynamism and satanic meaning he intended. None of the devices employed in *Masquerade* was particularly new or radical, but all together made this production the culmination of Meyerhold's prerevolutionary career.

# Chapter 3: The Meyerhold Method

## Before the Revolution: The Meyerhold Studio (1913–18)

Although "the method" is indelibly associated with Stanislavsky, he himself would doubtless have disclaimed any method in the sense of a rigidly codified system. He was still attempting to put his system on paper at the time of his death. The very titles of his finished volumes, *The Actor Prepares* (1948), which first appeared in English, and *Creating a Role* (1961), point to Stanislavsky's central concern with the actor's creation of his part through his experience of it. Early in his career Stanislavsky believed that "psychologism" and the ability to convey a real-life sense of character depended on the actor's ability to cut himself off from the audience and concentrate almost mystically on reliving the events on stage.

Of course, Meyerhold both began and ended with Stanislavsky, and he often expressed gratitude to his teacher —more heartfelt at some times than at others. Sometimes the difference between their theories of acting seems merely academic; at others they seem at opposite poles from one another. In the early twenties one might assume that the two directors would have offered diametrically opposed solutions to the problem of communicat-

ing experience on stage: Meyerhold at this time espoused the notion of the American psychologist, William James: run and you will feel fear; and Stanislavsky might have been expected to teach actors first to experience the feeling, which must then lead naturally to running. But according to Boris Zakhava, who trained in both systems, Stanislavsky too was teaching his pupils not to act their feelings; rather, he never wearied of repeating to them, "Act physically and be sure: the feeling will come of itself," and further, " 'The life of the human body' is the way to 'the life of the human psyche.' " [1] Also contrary to expectation, Zakhava concludes that Meyerhold was not against feeling on stage; indeed, accomplished actor that Meyerhold was, he himself in demonstrating his system invariably made feeling credible. Stanislavsky and he were therefore not at odds, Zakhava maintains, about the end; each simply tried different means of attaining it. Perhaps Zakhava owes this synthesis of the two directors' views to his study with Vakhtangov, who was strongly drawn to both. In the last analysis, Meyerhold's chief resemblance to Stanislavsky was doubtless the failure wholly to systematize his method. For though Stanislavsky had finally set down a great deal of his thinking, he never published a handbook as such, and Meyerhold left very little written material of instruction.

Yet, according to Volkov, Meyerhold taught throughout his professional life, beginning with the very start of his career (1902) as a director in the provinces. Doubtless the need felt in the Theater Studio of 1905 for actors capable of more than realistic acting led to Meyerhold's giving the course which for the first time he called "my Studio": "During the season of 1908/09 in my Petersburg Studio in a course given for Studio pupils [the composer Mikhail] Gnesin laid the foundation for his theory of 'musical reading in the drama.' Applying Gnesin's method, the Studio pupils performed excerpts from Sophocles' *Antigone* and Euripides' *Phoenissae*" (*Articles,* 1:245). Though Meyerhold mentioned his "Studio," and a course was given by Gnesin at Meyerhold's invitation, another in diction, and one by Meyerhold in movement, all at Meyerhold's apartment, no real studio apparently existed at this early date of Meyerhold's first season at the Imperial Theaters.[2] Meyerhold himself taught theater elsewhere.

The Meyerhold Studio as such was founded in 1913. By then Meyerhold was quite aware of his goal. As always throughout his long career, he opposed the naturalistic reproduction of reality. But if the negative pole on which he turned his back was clearly discernible, the positive one toward which he directed his efforts was less clear. For Meyerhold was, above all, a practical

man of the theater who learned by doing, and his major theoretical work, his book *On Theater* (1913), contained not argued exposition of a system but occasional articles on his own practice and that of such others as Reinhardt and Craig, with a chronological table and descriptions of his productions (1905–12). Rudnitskii reproves Meyerhold for being by no means a great theoretician of the theater. The first article of the book, "On the History and Technique of New Theater," previously published in 1908, was actually an account of Meyerhold's work for the Theater Studio and for Komissarzhevskaia, as well as an exposition of ideas for "the new theater." As Rudnitskii comments, "It wordily defends ideas of symbolist 'motionless theater' at a time when Meyerhold had abandoned these ideas" (Rudnitskii, p. 113).

Rudnitskii's criticism gives less than its due to this earliest capital pronouncement by Meyerhold. True, as Rudnitskii says, Meyerhold did weigh down his article with numerous quotations from Briusov, Viacheslav Ivanov, and Maeterlinck; yet he also cited the great authority from whom his kind of theater had its being: he quoted Chekhov's remark, at the *Sea Gull* rehearsal of 1898, that the theater is art, not reality. Here too he enunciated the positive principles of theater as art, not imitation, thus setting forth the essence of theatrical convention

(*uslovnyi teatr*): "The theatrical theater is such that 'the audience does not
for one moment forget that the actor
it sees is acting, and the actor does
not for one moment forget that he has
before him a theater, beneath his feet
a stage and at his back a set'" (*Articles,*
1:141–42)—though again Meyerhold
attributed so basic a formulation to
another, the playwright Leonid Andreev, who, said Meyerhold, had written it in a letter to him.

With so large an overall purpose
Meyerhold cannot be labeled with any
single "ism." Even before his dismissal
by Komissarzhevskaia he had urged
that a dimension of depth be added to
the flat pictorialism with which he had
experimented. This may have been the
"intuition" which Rudnitskii claims for
him, but it was an intuition hardly susceptible to systemization.

Nevertheless, Meyerhold devoted
considerable effort to formulating systematic means of realizing in practice
the basic principle expounded in his
first article. With the opening of the
Meyerhold Studio the same year as the
publication of his book, the by then
mature director broke through the
fourth wall of the peepbox stage with
*Don Juan.* He effectively used rhythm
and musical timing in *Columbine's
Scarf,* and he sought to create the double
mood of the grotesque. Since the production of *Farce,* the *commedia dell'arte* interested him not only as a weapon

against psychologism or the problem
play but also as a way of achieving total
performance for the actor, involving his
whole physical self as instrument, and
greater involvement for the audience.
He not only argued theoretically in his
book for these achievements of his
practice, but also helped perpetuate
them through his teaching. The three
courses given in the first year of the
Meyerhold Studio (1913–14) were
"The *Commedia dell'Arte*" by Vladimir
N. Solovev, "Musical Reading" by
Gnesin, and "Movement on Stage" by
Meyerhold himself.

The announcement and descriptions
of the studio courses appeared in the
magazine *Love for Three Oranges; or,
Dr. Dapertutto's Magazine* (1914–16),
for which Meyerhold was both editor
and a major contributor. So as not to
involve in the venture his own position
as director in the Imperial Dramatic
and Opera Theaters of Saint Petersburg
(1908–17), Meyerhold edited the magazine under the pseudonym which he
also used for his cabaret and private productions. The nickname Dr. Dapertutto
(Dr. Everywhere), after the magician
of E. T. A. Hoffmann's tale *Adventures
of New Year's Eve,* was given him by
Mikhail Kuzmin, poet and composer
for *Farce.* The founding of *Dr. Dapertutto's Magazine* has been described by
the actress Verigina (*Encounters,* p.
59). Studio teachers and some experienced acting pupils, dining in the

autumn of 1913 at a small *shashlyk* restaurant, decided to start a periodical expressing the studio's aims. Among them they collected a hundred rubles for the purpose. One actress, Liubov Dmitrevna Blok, contributed more than money; she enlisted her husband, Alexander Blok, as poetry editor. So each of the nine numbers of the magazine (published from January 1914 until two months before the February Revolution) included a poetry section in which some of Blok's own poems, including the Carmen cycle and the well-known "Voice from the Choir," received their first publication, along with poems by Vladimir Piast, Sologub, Gippius, and others.

Each number also included articles, some by Meyerhold himself, on subjects of concern, as well as a play considered exemplary for the new theater. From the exemplary play published in the first number, Carlo Gozzi's scenario *Love for Three Oranges* (1761), adapted by Meyerhold, Konstantin Vogak, and Solovev, the magazine got its name. The first play was the only one of the sort actually brought to the stage. Meyerhold urged it upon Sergei Prokofiev, who took the first issue of the magazine with him to America in 1918; there in 1921, in Chicago, Prokofiev premiered his opera *Love for Three Oranges*. Golovin made *Love for Three Oranges* the subject of his charming cover in colors, which, beginning with number

one of 1915, replaced Iurii Bondi's abstract cover design (figs. 3.1–3.2). Finally, each number of the magazine contained news and criticism of the theater and books, and all but the three numbers issued during vacation contained studio announcements and course descriptions, so that the periodical became compulsory reading for studio participants. Besides editing each issue and contributing one play which he coauthored and several articles, Meyerhold himself, according to the Soviet theater historian Aleksandr Fevralskii, surely wrote the studio announcements for his own course.

The first issue of the magazine announced for a later issue an article by Gnesin explaining his theory of musical reading. Though the article never appeared, four pages of illustrative material pertaining to it were published in number one. This material consisted of poems from classic Russian literature shown with the note values, though without the melody, given in settings by well-known composers. For example, Gnesin showed how the rhythm of Pushkin's poem "To the Shores of a Distant Home" was transcribed by notes in the setting by Aleksandr Borodin. The half-page description of Gnesin's course in the same issue promised instruction in rhythmic reading and in transcription: "Verse is transcribed in the notes of music" (no. 1 [1914], p. 60). From such transcription the actress who had originally played in the excerpts from Greek dramatists for the so-called Studio of 1908 could reproduce her role in 1913–14. So transcription in notes served as a permanent record of a performance. It also solved problems of choral recitation, as a Meyerhold pupil (1908–9), Anna Geints, has testified.[3] However, Aleksei Gripich, another studio pupil, who later became a Soviet director and a teacher of dramatic art, complains in *Encounters* that Gnesin's method produced a chanting artificiality of voice and required of the student an otherwise unnecessary ability to read notes. Still, Gnesin continued to teach in both Meyerhold's studio and his Soviet workshop after the Revolution. Doubtless the continuity of such instruction in music attests to Meyerhold's insistence that rhythm and timing are basic to theater art; in the Soviet period he verified what he called the "chronometrage" of a production, and he used music to fix tempi in rehearsal, even though none was to be played in performance.

A further reason for Meyerhold's interest in Gnesin's system was revealed in his polemic with Jurii Eichenwald, summarized in the magazine: Meyerhold answered Eichenwald, who claimed that the theater was merely ancillary to literature, by arguing that the theater was an art in its own right and that a work of art was truly created in the theater. Gnesin's transcription provided a means of at least partially recording it. Though systems of dance notation have been devised, of which Rudolf von Laban's is probably the most comprehensive, even now there is still no means of fully recording a theater performance, despite cinema, television, and the phonograph, and still no copyright exists for actors and directors. Meyerhold, who jealously defended the creativity of theater art, was interested in every means of transcribing it.

The *commedia dell'arte* featured in the magazine's title was the subject of the second course, given by Solovev, codirector with Meyerhold of the studio. Solovev's lectures on the *commedia* were published serially, beginning in the first number of the magazine (the first lecture having been delivered as the inaugural speech at the opening of the studio). They treated the movements and gestures proper to the principal masks or stock characters of the *commedia,* the "parade" or introduction of characters to the audience, such ready-made situations as "the night scene," "the city," and "the duel," with their geometric blocking, and finally the ploys of slapstick and acrobatics, the so-called antics proper to the theater. As practice material for the course, "interludes" were used—clowning or acrobatic entertainment customary between acts of a medieval play or

*Figure 3.1. Iurii Bondi's cover used for the first five numbers, all in 1914, of* Love for Three Oranges

*Figure 3.2.  Aleksandr Golovin's cover, which, beginning with the first issue of 1915, was used for the last four numbers of* Love for Three Oranges *(1915 and 1916)*

*commedia.* In addition, plays were staged: Pierre de Chamblain de Marivaux's *Harlequin Refined by Love,* Cervantes' *Cave of Salamanca,* and Solovev's own *Harlequin the Marriage Broker.*

If Gnesin's course used Greek tragedy and Solovev's used Italian comedy, Meyerhold's course, "Movement on Stage," was evidently dedicated to both. And his article "Balagan," written about this time, made tragicomedy a final achievement of theater art. Since no lectures for Meyerhold's course were published in the magazine, the article in his book and the course announcements in the magazine must serve as evidence of what Meyerhold taught at the time. In the article he opposed the library or problem play consisting wholly of ideological discussion. Instead he proposed action and prescribed pantomime as "a good antidote to the superfluity of words" (*Articles,* 1:211), both for actors who have forgotten how to move and for playwrights who have forgotten action in the theater. He refused to accept as art the actor's effort to be the character and, foreshadowing Brecht's notion of "alienation," demanded rather that the actor show the character according to the laws of the actor's art. But unlike Brecht, who substituted reason for the emotion he opposed, Meyerhold compounded emotion with reason. He cited the Dionysian celebrant, who was certainly ruled by feeling, yet for whom "the ritual dedicated to the god of wine has pre-established meters and rhythms and certain prescribed methods of movement and gesture. Here the actor's reasoning did not obstruct his temperament" (ibid., 1:217). Finally, Meyerhold recommended the contrast inherent in the "grotesque," that is, an oscillation between the tragic and comic as in Goya's drawings, the tales of Hoffmann, or Blok's *Farce.*

Though his course was called "Movement on Stage" and exercises in pantomime were assigned, still Meyerhold also emphasized the seemingly motionless element of *risunok* (outline), that is, the actor's attitude or pose, and even his consciousness of his attitude or pose. In his first course announcement Meyerhold gave the topic, "The actor as artist and his concern to live in the form of his pose or attitude. . . . Why the study of primitive painting leads to the only true understanding of what pose or attitude on stage means" (no. 1 [1914], p. 62). Brecht too recommended that the actor adopt a fundamental pose, best found not in life but in art. For in art the task of shaping the raw material of reality has already been accomplished. So the program of Brecht's theater for his play *The Caucasian Chalk Circle* [1954] reproduced Breughel's painting "Mad Meg" as the model for the heroine Grusche's fundamental pose.[4]

Brecht's richly ambiguous term *gestus* seems partly synonymous with Meyerhold's *pose* in the one meaning of attitude or gesture which summarily conveys character; for instance, the servility of the tutor in Brecht's play of that name (1950) is completely rendered by his attitude of humbly bowing, hat in hand. In the other meaning of fable, gestus denotes the whole action of a play: the tutor's bow also epitomizes the action of *The Tutor,* the nonhero's sacrifice of himself to those he serves.

Meyerhold similarly had his pupils render whole plays of Shakespeare in the summary action of a pantomime exercise. For example, the course announcement in the second number of the magazine described the visit of the Italian futurist Filippo Tommaso Marinetti to a lesson of the "grotesque" group (i.e., hitherto inexperienced actors trained solely in the Meyerhold method): "As a theme for improvisation he [Marinetti] suggested 'Othello' to the group which had just shown him 'Cleopatra' [three actors and four property men]. Without leaving the stage, the students agreed in a three-minute conference on the basic steps of the tragedy; then they acted out their scene, rendering in no more than three minutes the essence of Shakespeare's tragedy" (no. 2 [1914], p. 63). Gripich, the Iago of the scene, recalls "how I knelt to pick up the handkerchief

Desdemona had lost, followed Desdemona with my eyes and looked again at the handkerchief, and how I then waved the handkerchief before Othello, who seized it" (*Encounters,* p. 127).

Meyerhold was reproached with neglecting the literary text of his plays. The charge referred not only to such pantomime exercises but also to theoretical passages taken out of context from his book, such as: "Words in the theater are mere decorations on the canvas of movement" (*Articles,* 1:212). Actually, in the larger context of studio training, his pupils repeated in the second year the previously pantomimed scenes from Shakespeare, only this time adding the words, which had to be spoken with greater regard for metrics and rhythm than Stanislavsky required. Meyerhold himself later admitted that in the heat of his early struggle against the conventional theater he had sometimes used extreme methods intended as "a battering ram against naturalism" (ibid., 2:497). He emphasized pantomime without words only in order to deemphasize the wordy preachment of the conventional discussion play.

But he did not use negative weapons alone. His justification of his studio course in the third number of the magazine amounted to a positive declaration of freedom from the naturalistic peepbox stage; the actor was postulated as central to theater, which was described as occurring—the modern word *happening* seems close at hand—whenever an actor appeared before an audience:

*Movement is the most powerful means of creating theater on stage. . . . Strip the theater of the play, costumes for the actor, the stage, the set and theater building, leaving only the actor and the movements in which he has been trained—and you will still have theater: the actor will communicate his thoughts and motives to the audience by his movements, gestures, and grimaces. As a theater for the actor any space will serve: without the help of a builder the actor can himself arrange his theater where and how it suits him, and as fast as his skill permits. (No. 4–5 [1914], p. 94.)*

In defining essential theater almost metaphysically as "the actor and the movements in which he has been trained," Meyerhold drew an extreme theoretical conclusion. In practice he included in his course the material elements of production of which he himself showed such mastery, especially in his work then in progress, Lermontov's *Masquerade* (1917). But his reduction of theater to its essential nucleus with the axiom "strip the theater" prepared the way for the "poor theater" of Jerzy Grotowski half a century later.[5]

A demonstration of studio exercises was given in the school auditorium of the Tenishevskoe high school on the evening of 12 February 1915 with the "parade" at eight o'clock. Neither of the two Meyerholds represented in Boris Grigorev's portrait of the time (1916)—neither the imperial director in tall hat and tail coat nor Dr. Dapertutto, the magician-innovator—but rather a third, unfamiliar Meyerhold, the school principal and teacher, sat near the piano, launching each number on the program by a hammer blow on two pendant bells. All of the numbers were pantomimes except Cervantes' interlude *The Cave of Salamanca,* in Ostrovsky's translation. Each demonstrated a different theater tradition, in accord with Meyerhold's recommendation: "The actor of the new theater must establish an entire canon of technical devices such as he will discover by studying principles of acting in truly theatrical eras of the past" (no. 4–5 [1914], p. 96). The aim of the demonstration, to show studio exercises as the raw material, not as finished performances of dramatic art, was much misunderstood, though Meyerhold had explained: "We do not try to re-create earlier forms of theater (the exact reproduction of an earlier period is the business of Evreinov's 'Starinnyi' Theater). This is the difference between reproducing the past and freely rebuilding a new theater based on study of the past and selection from it" (ibid.).

More illuminating than the program published in the issue before the demonstration (no. 6–7 [1914], pp. 105–15) is the selection of criticism from the press published in the issue thereafter. The *Petrograd Gazette* of 13 February had described the demonstration evening thus:

*Seats were arranged in a half circle with a center and two side aisles through which in the course of the evening players entered, sometimes running or even carrying each other on their shoulders [figs. 3.3–3.6]. There was no stage in the accepted sense; in its place was a quite high platform with a white silk curtain closing off a narrow entrance in the middle. In front of the platform was a forestage carpeted in a semi-circle with navy-blue cloth. The players jumped constantly from stage to forestage and back, performed clown's tricks or did resounding falls, crawled, climbed under the platform, or even feigned to pull out each other's teeth. All this either at unusually high speed or with the slow stateliness of a funeral march (Hamlet, the madness of Ophelia) to the accompaniment on the piano of classical music by Mozart and Rameau or the improvisation of the pianist." (No. 1–2–3 [1915], pp. 148–49.)*

Like the costumes devised by Adolphe Appia for the demonstrations of Emile Jaques-Dalcroze which drew international attention in the years just before World War I, a uniform exercise garment was worn in the Meyerhold Studio demonstration, wine red with gold for men and dark blue with colored belts for women (figs. 3.7–3.8).

It was a mistake to regard the studio exercises as finished theater, for the pupils had had no other opportunity for professional performance. The studio unfortunately had no connection with a theater, such as existed later between Meyerhold's Soviet workshop and the Meyerhold Theater; it did stage one production at the Tenishevskoe high school, of Blok's two one-act plays *The Unknown Lady* and *Farce,* but was denied credit for it. The plays ran for seven performances, from 7 to 11 April 1914. In an explicit statement in his magazine, Meyerhold assigned responsibility for the production to the editorial board, perhaps because this early in the studio's history pupils wholly trained in his method were still beginners not yet ready for leading roles. These were played by already experienced studio pupils of the "actors' class," for example, Blok's wife, who appeared as the society lady in the first play. Still, Gripich testifies that the entire studio worked on the production, from the dyeing of material to the sewing of costumes, besides playing all the parts. He adds: "The Blok show proved to be a very special test of new methods of direction devised in connection with Studio experiments since the summer

*Figures 3.3–3.6. Drawings by Vladimir Liutse of actors carrying each other. Though the drawings date from the period of "biomechanics" (1922), they obviously reflect the exercises used also in Meyerhold's prerevolutionary studio.*

*Figures 3.7–3.8. Costumes designed by Iurii Bondi for the studio on Borodinsky Street, in drawings by Aleksei Gripich. The notation reads, "Studio on Borodinsky Street, Gripich."*

theater in Terioki (1912); it became the chance to put into practice the principles set forth in the article, 'Balagan' " (*Encounters,* p. 137).

Blok's *Unknown Lady* was indeed suited to represent that dualism of romantic irony which Meyerhold advocated in his article, as *Farce* was suited to realize the "cabotinage" of folk theater. The theme of *The Unknown Lady* is the antithesis between the real world and the transcendental world of a poet's dream, personified when the unknown lady briefly appears on earth. The real personages of Meyerhold's production were all made to wear some mark of the clown: false noses or red wigs for the men, round rouge spots on the cheeks and mascara lashes for the women. Only the dream figures, the unknown lady, the man in blue, the poet, and the astronomer, wore none. True, the astronomer put on evening dress when he joined the real world of the society lady's reception. To emphasize the narrowness of the society world, Meyerhold confined it on the small conventional platform stage behind the footlights, whereas the play as a whole was acted also in the semi-circular space without ramp or curtain in front of the stage. Working in half darkness, stage assistants rolled back the floor covering of this forestage area and set the scene there while the actors took their places. Such open treatment of the theater illusion, which has be-

come routine today in many theaters, seemed shockingly radical then. However, another device of exposing the illusion which Meyerhold used in *The Unknown Lady* has not achieved wide acceptance in Western theater. This was the continued presence of stage assistants in half mask and tights during the performance, as in Kabuki theater: the stage assistants represented the falling of a star by extinguishing a long, lighted bamboo pole like a torch in water or showed falling snow by covering a character with a veil.

*Farce* was produced with much more clowning and cabotinage than in Meyerhold's earlier staging of 1906. An interlude prepared for the new emphasis in the second play: actors performed acrobatics and juggled oranges with which they then bombarded the audience; this was perhaps an advertisement for the magazine *Love for Three Oranges,* which was on sale in the lobby, or it might have been intended as the immediate direct contact through movement between actor and audience which Meyerhold had postulated as the essence of theater. Surely both aims were achieved in an aggressive act of essential theater to which modern sensibility easily responds.

Though the studio experiments found no direct outlet in performances at the Imperial Theaters, studio pupils did attend rehearsals at the Aleksandrinskii. And they actually played in at least one production, Lermontov's *Mas-querade.* There they not only performed all the pantomime at the masquerade ball, including the important moment when Nina loses her bracelet, but two studio actresses also took the two leads of Nina and Baroness Shtral. One of these performers, Elizaveta Timé, who played the baroness in 1917, recalled Meyerhold's return in 1938 to re-direct this most durable of all his pro-ductions. During the many years this last great production of the Imperial Theaters had continued in the Soviet repertory of the Pushkin Theater, Len-ingrad, she had, she admitted,

*thought up various realistic details, seemingly veracious and somehow help-ful to me in my role. . . . But at the first rehearsal of the revival Meyerhold at once called to me from the auditorium: 'What nonsense! Where did you get that from?' And Meyerhold strictly recalled me to the original form. He brought me out on the stage apron where I was altogether alone, isolated from furniture and properties, made me wring my hands 'so that the audi-ence could hear the fingers crack.' That is a stage direction in the text: 'I don't know why, but I love him. (Wrings her hands) [figs. 3.9–3.10].' " (Encounters, pp. 149–50.)*

Even after the war when Golovin's splendid sets and costumes had been lost in the siege of Leningrad, Iurev and Timé, the original Arbenin and baroness, continued to play their parts effectively on the bare stage. Meyerhold had taught them: "Strip the theater . . . leaving only the actor and the move-ments in which he has been trained, and you will still have theater."

The very splendor of Meyerhold's productions of *Don Juan* and *Mas-querade,* however, proved his com-mand also of the material elements of theater; and indeed the subjects of set, costumes, and lighting stood second only to movement among the topics for Meyerhold's course listed in the last number of his magazine. Properties, too, entered into the second year of studio work, when the actor was trained also in play with objects. On the bare constructivistic stage of the Soviet period Meyerhold later even derived thematic significance from the manipu-lation of things, for example, from Stella's play with a single paper flower, which communicated the unique con-trasting notes of purity and lyricism in Fernand Crommelynck's *Magnanimous Cuckold* (1922).

Noteworthy among Meyerhold's fur-ther topics for course study listed in the magazine was theater history, not only because it was then a new subject, but also because in Meyerhold's treatment it included contemporary directors (Craig, Evreinov, Komissarzhevsky, and Dalcroze), great actors, the circus, and folk theater. Finally Meyerhold re-

*Figures 3.9–3.10.   Figure 3.9.   Both Iurev as Arbenin and Timé as Baroness Shtral, photographed obviously in their own and* Masquerade's *greater age, are seen to gesture in all too great involvement with the furniture.   Figure 3.10.   Similarly melodramatic gestures, though tempered by the irony of worship before a loudspeaker, would recur in Nikolai Erdman's satiric comedy* Mandate *(1925), with* left, *Elena Tiapkina as Nastia and* right, *Natalia Serebrianikova as Mrs. Guliachkin.*

quired that the studio pupil "find himself as actor and artist" (no. 2 [1916], p. 144). The final examination included: musicianship (an instrument or voice), physical agility (physical training, acrobatics, improvised pantomime), clarity of enunciation (reading of a passage from a book), knowledge of verse metrics, accomplishments in the other arts (painting, sculpture, literature, dance, if those had been cultivated) and examples (if any) of the pupil's work in those areas, and reading in dramatic literature equivalent to secondary school requirements (as determined by answers to questions). By his final concern with the individual Meyerhold made way for that imponderable, the gift or talent of actor and director.

He depended finally on that imponderable in his own method of directing, as was made clear by his only article on one of his own productions—Aleksandr Ostrovsky's *Storm* (1916)—which he published in the magazine. He had insisted earlier that, despite years of historical research for *Masquerade,* Golovin and he never sought historical accuracy in their mounting of Lermontov's play. Maintaining rather that the director must find for each production its own "key," he rejected in *The Storm* the realism and folksiness that had crept into the acting tradition of this play and found his key idea rather in the restoration of its "mystery," its true folk feeling and poetry. With Golovin's set for the third act—and here he quoted Apollon Grigorev—he tried to capture the audience's imagination for "the rendezvous at night in the ravine with a sense of the nearby Volga and its fragrant grassy meadows," and, above all, "the whole fascination of deep, tragic, fateful passion" (*Articles,* 1:291).

## After the Revolution: The Meyerhold Workshop (1921–38)

If in the studio attention was paid to discovering individual talent, in Meyerhold's postrevolutionary instruction, especially at the start in 1921, the emphasis was rather on training large numbers of youth. In the autumn of 1921 a Meyerhold drama school was instituted, the first in Russia designed explicitly to teach directing, though the same courses were required of first-year students in both directing and acting. This institution, called here simply the Meyerhold Workshop, went through several stages of nomenclature; the designation GEKTEMAS (Gosudarstvennye eksperimental'nye teatral'nye masterskie), under which it first received government accreditation in 1923, remained longest in use. The workshop as such continued until the closing of the Meyerhold Theater in 1938. Perhaps the workshop's new emphasis on training and scientific technique, rather than genius and individual talent, made theater work in the new era seem suddenly accessible to eager students of average gifts.

Certainly young people came to the workshop by the hundreds, attracted not only by the physical culture program but also by the common cause of the Revolution which Meyerhold represented. For on the first anniversary of the Revolution it was Meyerhold who staged the first revolutionary play, Vladimir Mayakovsky's *Mystery-Bouffe* (1918), after it had been rejected by established Petrograd theaters. Further, it was Meyerhold who, at least for a short time, headed the Theater Division of Narkompros (People's Commissariat of Enlightenment), and it was he who announced the slogan "Put the October Revolution into the theater." Of course, the impulse to enlarge the field of art, and with it the theater, until it encompassed the world was widespread at the time. Apollinaire proclaimed in a lecture of 1917 *l'esprit nouveau* of a universal art,[6] just as Brecht in 1925 set himself the task of representing the world upon a stage, including the fluctuation of wheat prices on the stock market. The new spirit reflected the theater's sense of competition with a reality in which history was being made. Aleksandr Fevralskii, who joined the Meyerhold Workshop in

1922, describes political meetings in which pupils of the Meyerhold Workshop participated *en bloc* together with art students dedicated to Mayakovsky's art *engagé* and young actors working in the Proletkult, or propaganda theater—indeed, in this last one of the workshop's own students, Sergei Eisenstein, served as director.

Mass action and participation also characterized workshop living at Novinskii Boulevard (now Tschaikovsky Street), Moscow, where "the old man," as students called Meyerhold, lived in an unpretentious apartment upstairs, so that day or night he looked in on their work and they in turn went up to see him for advice. In the theater, too, there was now a broader public and a greater effort to reach an audience. Free tickets were issued for Meyerhold's earliest production there, a version of Emile Verhaeren's *Dawns* (1920) which Meyerhold tailored to revolutionary needs. Leaflets were tossed from the stage on opening night challenging the audience as workers of the world to repel the tyrannical pressure of capitalist countries on the borders, to form Soviets, and to hail the world commune of labor; political posters and slogans were displayed on the walls of the auditorium.

The effort to include the audience and the reality of the Revolution in the theater went even further at *Dawns* on the occasion of the capture of

Perekop. Long before Perekop, in fact since his first article, Meyerhold had in theory made clear his inclusion of the audience as the fourth element of theter; and in practice, since Blok's *Farce,* he had at least aesthetically broken through the fourth wall of the peepbox stage. But real success in moving the audience to active participation in both ceremonial communion and political debate came only after the Revolution. Even then Meyerhold never carried activation of the audience further than on the occasion of the announcement of victory at Perekop during *Dawns.* As Khrisanf Khersonskii describes it, at one moment in the play the general asks the messenger to report on the mood of the troops. Khersonskii, who played the messenger, also worked part-time at the news agency ROSTA. Every evening when he cycled to the theater he brought along the most interesting dispatches of the day, which he posted on the bulletin board backstage. An actor suggested also putting up news bulletins for the audience in the lobby. But Meyerhold, who was always searching for ways of incorporating reality into his plays and achieving audience participation, had a better idea. Upon the request for news in the play Meyerhold had the messenger read actual dispatches about the progress of the civil war against the Whites. There came an evening when the news was read from the stage of the capture of Perekop in the Crimea, which meant Soviet victory and the end of the war. Upon hearing this the audience rose to its feet and began to sing the International.

True, such audience participation was not wholly impromptu, for Meyerhold had provided a band which struck up the anthem from the back of the balcony. Still, two days later truly unprompted participation apparently occurred after the news reading, for a sailor in full battle dress rushed from the audience to the stage and made a speech in praise of the Red Army, concluding again with the singing of the International. The actors, who had suffered a moment's uncertainty about how to resume the play, relievedly carried on. However, Meyerhold's delight at the apparent improvisation proved unfounded: the sailor had been in the audience when the news from Perekop was read and had prepared to return and make his speech at the same moment in the play. The Meyerhold Theater never came closer than this to audience participation.

Meyerhold continued to flirt with the notion, but his other projects for various forms of mass participation remained unrealized. A "mass spectacle" planned for the Khodynskoe Field, Moscow (1921), and a political revue planned for the Manège Hall, Moscow (1922), never came off, though the last was designed by Eisenstein "with numerous interludes on contemporary themes" and adapted from Tieck's *Puss-in-Boots,* an exemplary play from *Love for Three Oranges* (fig. 3.11). Neither did anything come of Meyerhold's part in a conference on universal military training and art (1920), nor of his chairmanship of a Theater Division subcommittee for "the theatricalization of physical culture" (1921). Perhaps he was protected by some guardian angel from these last miscegenations of art and reality.

However, collaboration with amateur groups was successfully undertaken by the workshop. For this purpose a "Methods Laboratory" for clubs was organized in connection with the Meyerhold Workshop on 2 January 1924, which was to put the technical capacity of the Meyerhold Theater at the disposal of Red Army, peasant, and university clubs for staging propaganda theater (*agitteatr*). Corresponding membership was even provided for clubs in the provinces. Besides mass spectacles (for example, in 1924 a revival of *Earth Rampant* [fig. 3.12], a Meyerhold Theater production), a number of celebratory pageants (such as several productions in 1925 of the play *1917–1925*) and "living newspapers" (*Lenin Lives Among the Masses, The Ten Days, A Debate on Religion,* etc.) were produced during the first two years of existence of the Club Methods Lab.[7] But Meyerhold later protested against unprofessional

dilettantism in the theater and disavowed the Proletkult for its all too crudely realistic propaganda.

Consistently demanding art in the theater, he set out to train professional directors and actors for the much expanded work with amateurs, and many of his workshop pupils later served as directors for amateur groups. So in the drama club of the Kremlin police, Tamara Kashirina-Ivanova staged Vsevolod Ivanov's novel *Armored Train 14–69* (1924) three years before the author himself made of it one of the best known Soviet plays. And in answer to a request for help, Nikolai Ekk, later known as the director of the first Soviet sound film, *The Road to Life* (1931), was dispatched to work with a university drama group. Fevralskii recalls: "Meyerhold's people who worked in the clubs exchanged experiences, worked out common methods to overcome hit-or-miss dilettantism and to inculcate the politically worthwhile use of leisure. Meyerhold took an active part in criticizing his pupils' work and helping them to find the right direction" (*Encounters,* p. 196). The theater historian Boris Alpers sums up: "For a time the amateur stage of the clubs was almost wholly under the auspices of the Meyerhold Theater." [8]

Of course, the theater art which Meyerhold thus brought to the masses was intended to activate the audience ideologically quite as much as the

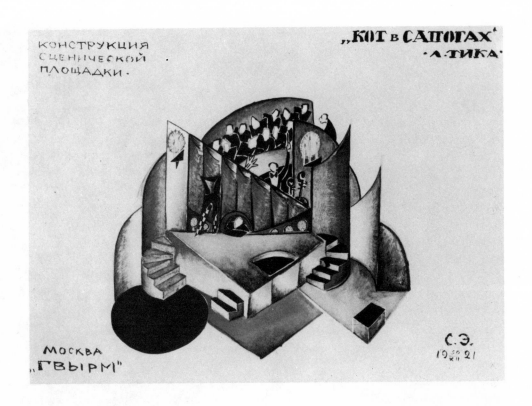

*Figure 3.11. Eisenstein's set design for* Puss-in-Boots, *labeled "construction of the stage space" and signed 30 December 1921, under Meyerhold Workshop auspices, shows footlights, prompter's box, and an imaginary audience behind the stage, while the real audience in front of the stage views the action as if from backstage.*

*Figure 3.12. Activation of the audience by means of artillery trained upon it in the second episode of* Earth Rampant *(1923)*

Proletkult. And though Meyerhold never ceased to reject crassly realistic means of projecting ideology, nevertheless a "key idea" of political or social message was communicated by all his Soviet productions. His first all-workshop show, Crommelynck's *Magnanimous Cuckold,* was meant as an example of the "flying theater." Osip Brik and Mayakovsky had demanded such a company in 1918 to take Soviet drama, like *Mystery-Bouffe,* to the people. So *The Magnanimous Cuckold* was staged with utmost economy, not just because Meyerhold at the moment lacked a budget and a theater, but also because he wanted to represent a model people's theater: "We wanted with this show to lay the foundation for a new kind of theater requiring neither an illusionistic set nor complicated properties, theater which could get along with the simplest objects at hand and progress from the spectacle acted by professionals to the free play of workers during their free time" (*Articles,* 2:47). The actors wore, instead of costumes, *prozodezhda* (work clothes [fig. 3.13]) and had, instead of a set, "constructions," or apparatus for acting, which consisted of a large revolving wheel (an allusion to Bruno's mill), a revolving door suitable for "antics proper to the theater," and finally stairs and a slide connecting platforms on various levels.

So the first studio maxim, "Strip the

*Figure 3.13. A "work clothes" costume sketched by Liubov Popova for* The Magnanimous Cuckold *(1922)*

theater," was realized, while the "key idea" (a concept which, as the last proposition of his method, Meyerhold insisted upon formulating for every show) was conveyed by the actors' movements. He took the key idea of this play to be the miller Bruno's unfounded jealousy of his wife, Stella; as Fevralskii formulates it: "The director underlined in the play those elements which show up the property instincts of the male animal, 'the head of the family' " (*Desiat let*, p. 30). Igor Ilinskii, perhaps the most gifted actor-alumnus of the workshop, played Bruno as a normal healthy fellow whose delusion about his wife nevertheless was shown up as obstinacy brooking no objection. Erast Garin, another distinguished actor-alumnus of the workshop, describes how Ilinskii provided satiric comment on the character through the dumb show of movement: Bruno, who has been sitting pensive, is observed by Estrugo, the town clerk (played by Vasilii Zaichikov):

BRUNO (*slapping the bench on which he sits as an invitation*): *Estrugo, come here!*
ESTRUGO (*hesitantly throws his leg astride and sits down barely on the end of the bench*).
BRUNO: *Closer. (He moves over).*
ESTRUGO (*comes a little nearer*).
(*The same play is repeated three times*).

BRUNO (*jumps up and threatens Estrugo with his fists*).
ESTRUGO (*frightened, lies down prone on the bench hiding his face and then after a pause looks up at Bruno*).
BRUNO: *Will you be quiet?*
ESTRUGO (*hides his face again*).
BRUNO (*seizes Estrugo by the face, raises it and shouts): Say, do you think Stella is faithful or not?*
ESTRUGO (*wants to answer, but Bruno pushes him back into his previous position*).
BRUNO (*writing with his fingers a question mark on Estrugo's back): The question arises. (Thinks for a moment). She's faithful! (Strikes Estrugo on the back with the flat of his hand). Like the sky is blue today. (Repeats the blow). Like the earth that turns. (Strikes). Yes! (Strikes again).*
ESTRUGO (*wants to say something, but Bruno holds his mouth with his hand. He raises his arms in sign of protest*).
BRUNO (*twisting his wrists): You agree—and even if you don't agree, you at least admit that a man may have his doubts* [fig. 3.14]. (Encounters, *pp. 316–17.*)

Garin comments: "This moment is satiated to the limit with movement and pantomime, but the pantomime here has nothing of aesthetic ballet

*Figure 3.14.* The Magnanimous Cuckold: *Bruno and Estrugo on opposite ends of the bench; between them the butcher (Aleksei Kelberer)*

prettiness but rather the purposefulness of action suited to concrete realistic content. In Estrugo's role there are elements of the Harlequin which bring out an ironic relationship to the subject, but the Harlequin element is not in the least coquettish or mannered. In the *Magnanimous Cuckold* principles of acting are crystallized which one may call 'biomechanics' " (ibid., p. 317).

Perhaps the basic principle of biomechanics thus "crystallized" in Bruno's scene was the conscious dualism between the actor's idea of the role and his performance of it. According to Alpers, the art of "presenting" the character rather than reliving it distinguished the Meyerhold-trained actor from those of all other backgrounds. It was this that made of the Meyerhold actor, "this half-athlete, half-mime, full of the joy of life," as Alpers describes him, also "a propagandist" and "a tribune":[9] that is, a critic of political values, such as Brecht too would later require his actors to be.

To return from such final results to a first definition: biomechanics was Meyerhold's method of actor training based on body movements, which he announced in 1922 and which represented a systematization and completion of studio methods in a new guise. The newness consisted chiefly in a theory and terminology borrowed from science and industry. The "constructivist" set for *The Magnanimous Cuckold,* designed by Liubov Popova, a leader of the new movement, alluded to industry, and Fevralskii has somewhat exaggeratedly called it "the industrialization of the theater" (*Desiat let,* p. 29). Meyerhold connected his newly revised method with science as well. Ivan Petrovich Pavlov, whose summary of research in reflexology, *Twenty Years of Experimentation,* had just appeared that year, provided the new scientific vocabulary. "Reflex sensitivity" was Meyerhold's new designation for the actor's gift, meaning a quickness at reaction which could be trained to the point of a "conditioned reflex." William James was the authority for an empirical psychology of reflexes, and another American, Frederick Winslow Taylor, the source of an efficiency system for rationalizing movements. But those modern saints of science and industry who were used to justify biomechanics merely corroborated the principles of theater art which Meyerhold had already enunciated.

Then in some five documents on the subject, one dated 1921, the rest 1922, he restated his basic theory, clothing it

anew in the trappings of exact science for the new Soviet age. He concluded the 1922 curriculum for his workshop with a signed definition which might as well have figured in a studio announcement but for its new pseudo-scientific vocabulary: "The biomechanics of Vs. Meyerhold attempts to establish laws of movement for actors in stage space; by experimentation it devises set exercises for training and works out methods of the actor's art based on exact calculation and regulation of the actor's conduct on stage." [10] And the conclusion of the 1922 pamphlet *Amplua aktera* (The Set Roles of the Actor's Art), by Meyerhold, Valerii Bebutov, and Ivan Aksenov, sounded like the Taylorization of the theater industry to avoid waste motion: "Once one knows with geometric clarity all the positions of biomechanics . . . then these motions are applied to certain types of roles by assimilating the roles characterized by these motions. . . . Usually this takes place by trial and error and is three-fourths unconscious. . . . The task of theater education is the systematization of such labor." [11]

"The Actor of the Future," Meyerhold's lecture of 12 June 1922, as reported in *Ermitazh,* a theater bulletin of which he was an editor, connected biomechanical training with constructivism, the industry-oriented movement in contemporary art: "Constructivism challenged the artist to become an engineer. Art must have a basis in scientific knowledge, for all artistic creativity should be conscious. The art of the actor consists in organizing his material, that is properly utilizing his body with all its means of expression" (*Articles,* 2:487). Clearly, then, Meyerhold taught both before and after the Revolution a theater art centered in "the actor and the movements in which he has been trained"; but after 1921 this characteristic method became "biomechanics" and a "science" of movements.[12]

Meyerhold's first-year Soviet curriculum, which like the studio's was identical for both actors and directors, formulated the aim of biomechanics for both alike: to inculcate conscious art, "a director's consciousness, an outside perspective on the material in its coordination with the stage space, partner, costume, and properties" (see Appendix 3). The actor himself was adjured to cultivate consciousness of his silhouette in the audience's eyes, variously called *risunok* (outline), *zerkalenie* (mirroring) or even *samozerkalenie* (self-mirroring), and *rakursi* (*raccourci,* or pose from a side view). Having given the audience more than just a frontal view of the actor through the use of the thrust or apron stage, Meyerhold later planned to place him in all-round perspective on the arena stage of his new theater building.

The ballet term *raccourci* seems to imply a ballet pose, and ballet was still included in the workshop curriculum for 1920. But in the fourth of the documents announcing biomechanics, a 1922 review of Tairov's book *Theater Unchained,* Meyerhold emphasized how much his method had evolved since the early pictorialism which Tairov learned from acting in the 1906 *Farce* under Meyerhold. How prettified were the ballet attitudes taught at Tairov's Kamerny Theater appears from Mayakovsky's barb of 1920: "the sweetish, ladylike futurism of Tairov." [13] Meyerhold also rejected this approach—"Leave elegance to tailors and shoemakers" (*Articles,* 2:38),—and pleaded rather that neither the comic nor even the grotesque should be neglected; besides the ballerina's tiny steps, he insisted on using the huge strides of the sailor over a rolling deck. In thus drawing the line between ballet and biomechanical movement, and between Tairov and himself, Meyerhold also differentiated between his own earlier and later selves, between the 1906 and 1914 productions of *Farce,* or between the pantomime for *Masquerade* and the bold movement of Bruno's scene in *The Magnificent Cuckold.*

The actor's consciousness of outline

and of self, the very essence of Meyerhold's teaching, was expressed by a mathematical formula in the workshop curriculum of 1922: $N = A_1 + A_2$. Here N means the actor, whose function is twofold. As $A_1$ he is a conscious, organizing intelligence, assigning the task to be performed. As $A_2$ he is also the body or instrument performing the task assigned. Thus, far from incarnating the role, as Stanislavsky taught, the Meyerholdian actor remained outside it with one part of himself, maintaining perspective on it, as Brecht would require. Again like Brecht and unlike Tairov, who ignored the public, Meyerhold specifically insisted that the audience too must remain conscious of the illusion: "The new spectator (I mean the proletariat) is in my opinion quite capable of being freed from the hypnosis of the illusion" (*Articles,* 2:43).

How such bold theories were put into practice in the biomechanical exercises is not quite clear from the workshop curricula. The 1922 curriculum prescribed "biomechanical gymnastics," legato and staccato movements with the greatest possible distinction between the two tempi. The gymnastics aimed at "placing the body and its extremities," that is, simply acquiring physical control of the body. Even the hands and fingers were drilled by juggling with wands, while the legs were exercised in Charleston and tap dancing. The "biomechanical exercises" purported to teach the actor to recognize his own center of gravity, to relate that recognition to his surroundings, and finally to coordinate with his partners on stage. Accordingly they were performed mostly in twos or threes.

Twenty-two biomechanical exercises were listed in the 1922 curriculum, some of which can be envisaged from the name: "the slap," "the blow with a dagger," "leapfrog," and "the quadrille." [14] All are said to have been recorded in a motion picture by Aleksei Temerin, an actor of the theater and also its photographer.[15] One exercise, "the bowshot," is known to have been adopted by Stanislavsky in his studio instruction; another, the "Di Grasso" or "leap to the chest," which Meyerhold named for a Sicilian actor whom he had seen performing it in 1907, occurred in various modifications in his productions, for example, in *Mystery-Bouffe.* Apparently, then, the exercises derived less from scientific experimentation than from the tradition of the theater, knowledge of which Meyerhold warmly recommended to his pupils even after the Revolution, when "the past" and "the tradition" became suspect.

As Meyerhold pointed out, the exercises were not intended for performance, but rather as material from which to shape a performance. Nor did they occupy more than a small place in the much larger whole of the curriculum. They were taught in the course on movement, under which they shared a subsection with physical training and succcessive trimester subcourses in science, dance, and "word-movement," this last a seminar announced under the joint auspices of Meyerhold and Sergei Tretiakov.

Many famous Russian theater people studied in the Meyerhold Workshop, though actors like Nikolai Bogoliubov or Lev Sverdlin are less well known in the West than directors like Nikolai Okhlopkov of the Realistic Theater or Valentin Pluchek of the Theater of Satire, and theater directors in turn are less well known than movie directors. Of those in the last category, Sergei Iutkevich has described his early experience under Meyerhold in an essay on Sergei Eisenstein, his fellow pupil in the workshop (Iutkevich, pp. 220–65). The two later famous film directors first met in 1921 while waiting to take the entrance examination to GVYRM (Gosudarstvennye vysshie rezhisserskie masterskie—State Graduate School for Theater Directors, as the Meyerhold Workshop was then called): Iutkevich points out that the idea of a training course for directors was Meyerhold's. In the auditorium of the three-story former high school on Novinskii Boulevard, the same street where the workshop and Meyerhold's upstairs apartment were located, the two candidates came before an admissions committee made up of Ivan Aksenov, poet, translator, and author of the only Russian monograph on Picasso; Valerii Bebutov, Meyerhold's directorial assistant and an authority on Elizabethan theater; and Valerii Inkizhinov, a specialist in body movement, who later played the lead in Vsevolod Pudovkin's film *Storm over Asia*. At the head of the committee, Meyerhold himself managed to look impressive despite a costume designed for warmth: red fez, wool scarf, faded sweater, trousers stuffed into soldier's leggings, and thick-soled shoes.

The entrance examination had three parts, first an oral exchange to determine the candidate's cultural background, second a directorial assignment, and third a test of expression in acting. Iutkevich, whose name came at the end of the alphabet along with Eisenstein's, reports that both were given the same test of expression, to shoot an imaginary bow and arrow, and the same directorial assignment, to stage "Six in pursuit of one." In answer to the directorial assignment Eisenstein drew on the board a stage set with six doors, a solution Iutkevich recalled five years later when he saw Meyerhold's production of *The Inspector General* with its décor of eleven doors for the bribe scene.

Naturally both candidates achieved admission to the workshop and were soon sitting eagerly close to the teacher's desk. Meyerhold announced at the first lesson two subjects for study, stage direction and biomechanics. He wanted to make directing, like biomechanics, an exact science, insisting that it must be possible to formulate the whole process of creative direction. "He proposed," according to Iutkevich, "that we should draw graphs and work out a scientific system of all stages in creating a production. . . . It was interesting to watch how this born artist of improvisation tried to teach us a method in which, as he declared, nothing should be left to chance" (Iutkevich, p. 224). Eisenstein, however, growing tired of circles and squares, after several lessons decided to make Meyerhold disclose the secret of directing. Indeed the two friends found Meyerhold easy to detain after class with questions about his staging of Blok's *Farce* or his Paris production for Ida Rubinstein of D'Annunzio's *Pisanella*. Soon the pupils had converted the master to seasoning his classes with concrete discussions of plays he had produced in the past or hoped to produce in the future, like *Hamlet*. As Iutkevich reports, Eisenstein first learned what directing was from these accounts of Meyerhold's.

Meyerhold asked his class in biomechanics for help in laying the groundwork for this experimental subject. After introducing Zinaida Raikh as his assistant in the course, he himself demonstrated the first exercise; the pupils, each with a partner, were to aim for utmost expression and economy of motion. As Iutkevich describes it, the exercise "combined acrobatic play with a clown's entrance. One partner provoked the other, who, taking aim, traversed the whole room at a run, ending by feigning to kick his opponent in the nose with his pointed toe. The partner then felled the aggressor with an imaginary slap; whereupon the partners changed places" (Iutkevich, p. 227).

Meyerhold refused to recognize Delsarte and, as Iutkevich twice insists, was altogether opposed to "Duncanism." Indeed, biomechanics avoided "stylization" and the demonstrative emotional pantomime taught in ballet. Instead, acrobatic training accompanied the work in biomechanics. As the requirements of athletic prowess increased with successive lessons, Eisenstein, the heavy for Iutkevich, one day almost failed to catch his partner on the salto mortale. "From then on," Iutkevich admits, "we tried to cut acrobatics, saying we already had sufficient preparation in it" (ibid.). Finally projects were given out. Iutkevich recalls that for the independent project assigned to Eisenstein, the staging of the literary classic *Puss-in-Boots* by Ludwig Tieck, Eisenstein planned to put a stage upon the stage and to place his actors between two audiences with the imaginary one behind the scenes.

Movement was but one of six principal courses taught in the Meyerhold Workshop, of which the others were the word, dramatic literature, stage set and properties (including lighting), music, and the technical course. The importance given to literature was commendable; in 1927–28, for example, the noted writer Andrei Belyi taught poetry in the workshop. A similarly prominent place was given to music in the workshop, taught in 1927–28 once more by Gnesin. Such emphasis had been characteristic of Meyerhold's method since the studio; of course, music has today become so much a part of theater art that we are no longer surprised to find composers listed for Meyerhold's productions from 1905 on, among them such noteworthy names as Glazunov, Shostakovich, and Vissarion Shebalin.

However, music was then an innovation, even in the primitive function of melodramatic moodmaker, as Meyerhold had early used it in *The Death of Tintagiles*. Fevralskii terms Meyerhold's later use of music, in the Soviet period, "by no means a 'musical accompaniment' but an inalienable component of the production" (*Desiat let,* pp. 21–22). Was it Meyerhold's own training in music, his early reading of Appia, or his experience as opera direc-

tor, which made him seek in this art an added dimension of theater? As late as 1910 he had himself acted the non-dancing part of Pierrot in Fokine's ballet *Carnival* by Schumann; of this occasion Fokine wrote: "I think this was his first contact with the art of rhythmic motion to music. At the first two rehearsals he showed that he belonged to another world. He lagged behind the music in his gestures. Frequently he did not come in on time and did not exit with the music. But at the third rehearsal our new 'mime' had altogether come of age, and at the performance he gave a wonderful interpretation of the melancholy dreamer Pierrot." [16]

With this experience of the musical cue in ballet Meyerhold came to make music part of the metaphysics of time and space in the theater: "Great events are concentrated within so small a space as the stage and in such a short space of time as from eight to ten or half-past ten o'clock," he said in a seminar for directors in 1933. "And as soon as we have admitted that a law of time or space is here at work, we have come upon the inevitability of being musical. As it is essential that we be able to verify the time and to dispose ourselves in space . . . we must be able to count the time without taking out our watch. . . . There must be rhythmicality" (*Articles,* 2:272–73). Accordingly, Meyerhold sometimes rehearsed his actors to music, only to omit it from the final performance. And with or without music he held the time dimension of a production to be of greatest importance. He checked "chronometrage," trying to combat what he called the "wearing out" of his productions, that is the gradual slowing down during a long run.

For the director, then, the rhythm or tempo of a production becomes an essential part of its overall composition, similar to the timing of a role for the actor. As Meyerhold put it in his Intourist seminar of 1934: "All the art of producing a play consists in the art of successive variation of tempo" (*Articles,* 2:296). He himself used musical terms to denote the timing of a scene and considered the director's notebook deficient if it lacked the dimension of timing. He exploited tempo to convey ideology in the revue *D.E.* (1924), in which Soviet sailors, representing the hope of the future, did brisk gymnastics, while the bourgeois representatives of a decadent past danced languidly in a nightclub. (The American jazz ensemble which Meyerhold engaged to accompany the dances in *D.E.* is said to have inaugurated the still current vogue of jazz in the USSR.) However, in order not to obscure ideology by so "culinary" an enjoyment, as Brecht would have called it, Meyerhold also indoctrinated the audience by projecting scene titles and facts about the personages on a central

screen, as well as critical commentary and quotations from revolutionary leaders on side screens.

The silent motion picture, which had just become enormously influential, doubtless inspired such use of "titles" in Meyerhold's work, as in that of Erwin Piscator in the early twenties. Not only contemporary works like *D.E.* but also the classics received cinematic treatment: Ostrovsky's five-act play *The Forest* (1924) was divided into seventeen brief cinematic episodes, and Angelo Ripellino calls the effect of the quick succession of incidents in Aleksandr Sukhovo-Kobylin's *Death of Tarelkin,* as produced by Meyerhold in 1922, a "ritmica percussione sui nervi." [17] This *Tarelkin,* Meyerhold's third, evidently made radical use of circus and cinematic tricks: a chase took place as in the old Keystone comedies, and a character swung his way to safety over the heads of his pursuers on the end of a rope, the trademark trick of the silent-film star Douglas Fairbanks.

If such double speed and cinematic acrobatism showed biomechanics at an accelerated tempo, Meyerhold's pivotal production, Aleksei Faiko's *Bubus the Teacher* (1924), exemplified its application in slow motion. For in *Bubus* Meyerhold demonstrated the three elements comprising each movement according to biomechanical analysis: first, pre-action, or preparation, as in the backward sweep of the arm before the forward thrust; then action, or the movement itself; and finally, reaction, or recovery. Meyerhold extended pre-action to mean also the psychological preparation of the audience, which he found exemplified in a great performance by Aleksandr Lenskii as Benedick in Shakespeare's *Much Ado About Nothing:* alone on stage after overhearing Beatrice's pretended profession of love for him, Benedick allowed a triumphant smile to creep over his face, which set the audience off in laughter even before he pronounced a word of his monologue. By using such pre-action, actually a pause, before each action, Meyerhold evidently drew *Bubus* out to excessive length. In this way he demonstrated by nonobservance the validity of his principle that the director must compose his production with varying tempi in successive scenes.

The last principle of Meyerhold's method, the imponderable of creativity, may seem to have been jeopardized in the Soviet period by increased systematization. Though the actor must possess the gift of "reflex sensitivity," according to Meyerhold's theory at that time, apparently any normal young person so endowed needed only undergo the necessary physical training to become an actor. Especially *Amplua aktera,* the pamphlet classifying the set roles of the actor's art, seemed to sug-gest that, given the necessary physique, any trained person might master any of the great roles of dramatic literature. Further, as Garin showed on a gala evening honoring Meyerhold in 1924, workshop training resulted in virtuoso command of the art of "transformation," that is, the performance of numerous quite different roles in quick succession. Finally, the erudition on which Meyerhold continued to insist for actors quite as much as for directors inculcated in both the reasoned, conscious exercise of theater art.

Yet, despite the emphasis on training, skill, and erudition, the actor's creativity remained in practice the last essential. For at the very moment when Meyerhold seemed to dictate the outline of the role by demonstrating it, he required the actor to re-create it according to his own individuality. Iurii German, author of *Prelude* (1933), described Meyerhold's demonstrations during rehearsals of his play: "But if they copied him blindly he flew into a rage. He required that the artistic individuality to whom he had shown the rudiment of the part should create some new compound—of his own self and that distinct shape (*risunok*) which Meyerhold taught him" (*Encounters,* p. 451). Unfortunately, the demonstrations to actors, like the key ideas and plans for Meyerhold's productions, are often irrecoverable. And Meyerhold's later notebooks are said to be either almost indecipherable, with but a few hieroglyphs, or altogether clean and empty. Like the orchestra leader who conducts a score from memory, Meyerhold ever more frequently toward the end carried the whole composition in his head. Thus Meyerhold's method, especially with the actor, can be finally studied only through recollections of its realizations in the theater.

The director's creativity, then, was given, if anything, increased scope in the Soviet period. Meyerhold saw the theater as an art in its own right, not merely illustrative of literature or imitative of reality; therefore, he more and more created plays wholly in the theater. So Meyerhold collaborated extensively with the Soviet writers Mayakovsky, Iurii Olesha, Vsevolod Vishnevskii, and Iurii German. With Vishnevskii, for example, who brought with him only a scenario, the play *The Last Decisive Battle* (1931) was wrought in the theater. And Meyerhold continued to rework or "contemporize" the classics for the modern stage, though he did not wholly rewrite them as Brecht rewrote Shakespeare's *Coriolanus,* for example. Meyerhold was able thus to sign his perhaps most important work of the Soviet period, Gogol's *Inspector General* (1926), as "author of the production." Nevertheless, adaptation and collaboration on stage never reached with Meyerhold the point of collective creativity in the theater, as

was recently the case with Peter Brook's *US* at the Royal Shakespeare Society. Rather, Meyerhold insisted only on the right and duty of the theater director to read a play in his own way, just as the orchestra director or musical performer must read a piece of music.

In a 1938–39 course for directors at the VTO (All-Russian Theater Society), Moscow, Meyerhold again recommended extensive reading and "cultural experience" through travel and museum visits as a source of background essential to the director's interpretation. And he continued to send directors and actors, as he said, "scurrying" to libraries (*Articles,* 2:444). When in the twenties with the new socialist state the folk theater began to die out, Meyerhold drew instead on the tradition of circus and music hall and the new popular art of the cinema. On the basis of such background then, the director must develop the key idea of his production, and Meyerhold recommended "hitting the actors on the head" with it at the first meeting. More than one such meeting of explication and discussion around a table, however, he considered not desirable. Rather, he prescribed a rehearsal immediately thereafter, using as much material setting for the production as can be made available from the start.

In sum, though no handbook of Meyerhold's teaching remains, his method is clear in large outline. Indeed, his fundamental assumption that the art of the theater depends on interaction between the actor and the audience has become a familiar basic premise of the major preceptors, like Antonin Artaud, Brecht, or Brook, and a foundation of the best work in theater today. Likewise, his conception of acting as a conscious art is the only possible exact and comprehensive hypothesis on which to base the training of actors and directors. Several possible styles of acting which Meyerhold sponsored in succession, the choral recitation of Greek tragedy under Gnesin's tutelage, the *commedia* pantomime with Solovev's assistance, and the acrobatism influenced by the cinema of the early twenties, were superseded one after another in his own practice. Indeed, the zigzag of trends in the rich variety of his own productions might almost suffice as twentieth-century history to be studied in its own right.

Meyerhold's own teaching derived from the long tradition of the theater and cannot be subsumed under the pseudoscience of biomechanics. His work contained much that is attacked today under such slogans as "the non-literary theater," "the theater of noise" or of "gimmickry," the "high-production director's theater." However, not only some abuses but also some fine recent achievements derive from the Meyerholdian tenet that director and actor alike have the duty and right as artists to reinterpret the classics and to create contemporary drama as viable art in the theater. Music can hardly be considered a part of Meyerhold's general method, since his use of it depended very much on his own individual genius, but his insistence on timing was basic. The "key idea," too, defied systematization because it involved inspiration as much as erudition. With these exceptions, though, Meyerhold more than any other single master provided the principles and practice of a method peculiarly suited to the theater in our time.

# Chapter 4: Soviet Productions (1918-39)

In the interim between the February and October Revolutions of 1917 Meyerhold appeared to retain his position as director of the former Imperial Theaters, now the "academic" theaters of Petrograd. However, Iurii Elagin, author of the only complete biography of Meyerhold, has called this period in his life one of unobtrusive withdrawal.[1] He is contradicted by the artist Iurii Annenkov, who was present at *Masquerade,* Meyerhold's final imperial production and somehow the epitome of an era. Annenkov describes emerging from the première into a February night, made strange by the inexplicable silence of the streets, which was then followed by the sound of machine gun fire—that is, Annenkov found himself confronted with a revolution. Meyerhold, whom he met a few days later, seemed far from "withdrawn," as Elagin calls him; instead he was almost gleeful: with an imitation of the shots, " 'Trakh-tararakh,' " he cried, " 'Now we'll pull the theater out of its rut ourselves.' "[2]

In August Annenkov found him still bent on change; this time Meyerhold asked how to get an interview with the Provisional Government in order to obtain needed funds. " 'I want to save the theater, rejuvenate it,' " he told Annenkov.[3] Meyerhold's effort at rejuvenation was evidently part of what Aleksei Gripich describes as a general burst of activity set off by the Revolution: the opening of an experimental theater in the Hermitage, the launching of a journal edited by Meyerhold, and the founding of institutes, one for theater history and one for "The Living Word." The first courses ever organized specifically for theater directors were doubtless Meyerhold's most important achievement of the interim period, for they became the precedent for similar training which he then offered in his Moscow workshop. Gripich finds a new sense of purpose in the courses: artistic experimentation was replaced by instruction in theater craft and the preparation of professionals to guide an expanding theater in a new age.

At this time a new spirit was being felt in the West as well, even without a revolution. In France just before the war, Guillaume Apollinaire, the John the Baptist of surrealism, had preached his destructive "futurist antitraditionalism," and then after the war the more constructive "esprit nouveau": "Let no one be surprised if with the sole means now at their disposal they [the poets] try to make ready for this new art (more vast than the simple art of words), in which, conducting an orchestra of unheard-of extent, they will have at their beck: the entire world, its sounds and sights, thought and human language, song, dance, all the arts and artifices, more mirages than Morgana could call up" (fig. 4.1).[4] Again in the prologue to *The Breasts of*

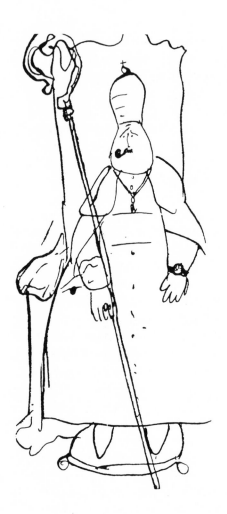

*Figure 4.1. "L'esprit nouveau":
caricature of Guillaume Apollinaire
by Pablo Picasso*

*Tiresias* (1917), Apollinaire presaged the total theater which Meyerhold's new building was to make possible in the mid-thirties. True, in an interview for the surrealist journal *Sic* in 1917, Apollinaire found the cinema better suited than the theater to rendering "an art of total playwriting," as he called it.[5] Yet it was a theater director, Brecht, who as playwright in 1925 set himself the task of rendering the world upon the stage.

Russia, meanwhile, had its own futurist prophet and playwright, Mayakovsky, who wrote "the first revolutionary play," as Lunacharsky termed *Mystery-Bouffe*. This play, produced by Meyerhold in honor of the first anniversary of the Revolution (1918), is a "mystery" in the sense of the medieval mystery and miracle plays—it shows Heaven, Earth, and Hell. It is a "bouffe" or "bouffonade" in the sense that it makes fun of miracles by turning one upside down; as Lunacharsky summarized it: "This is the merry symbolic journey of the working class which after the flood of the Revolution gradually rids itself of parasites on its way through hell and heaven to the Promised Land —which last turns out to be our sinful earth." [6]

This so eminently communist notion of paradise is not the only parodistic reversal of orthodoxy in Mayakovsky's play. The Sermon on the Mount is preached for believers in communism, not Christianity, and the Christian dialectic of the blessed and the damned is punningly reversed to express the class struggle. The traditional *lubok* (folk woodcut) showing the *blagochestivye* (the blessed) dining amid the joys of heaven, while the *nechestivye* (the damned) banquet below with devils, is transformed by Mayakovsky to show a class struggle between the *chistye* (the clean or white-collar bourgeois), who are doomed, and the *nechistye* (the unclean or working class), who shall inherit the earth (figs. 4.2–4.3). Both classes set sail together on an ark as the earth is inundated by revolution. The set, representing the top of the world as part of a sphere, was designed by the suprematist Kazimir Malevich. Hell was shown as a Gothic hall in red and green, though the Promised Land was abstract, suggesting a suprematist machine.

Not only the hierarchies of heaven and hell recalled the medieval mystery; so did the manner of casting the play. Rejected by established theaters, *Mystery-Bouffe* was cast by a town cry for actors: volunteers, many of them students, came to a trial reading of the play by Mayakovsky on 13 October 1918 in the auditorium of the Tenishevskoe high school, where Meyerhold and his former studio colleague Vladimir Solovev took down the names. One of them, Nikolai Golubentsev, describes Meyerhold's work with this diverse cast, consisting partly of experienced actors, mostly contemptuous of the play's vernacular verse and its farcical style (*balagan*), and partly of youthful amateurs, enthusiastic but inexperienced. Golubentsev tells how Meyerhold reproved one of the devils in hell for setting too slow a pace: " 'Don't you know what devils are?' . . . And executing an incredible dance step on the apron stage, Meyerhold is suddenly beside the second devil, jumps upon his back and, riding crouched at first, then rising to full height, piercingly cries out the text: 'Life is cheap,/ They're climbing onto the very devil's horns' " (*Encounters,* pp. 170–71). Such drastic movement was far removed from psychological finesse, and indeed the whole dramatic conflict between revolution and reaction was brought out with the farcical naïveté of folk theater.

Many of the play's propaganda slogans, promulgated at its two performances of 7 and 8 November 1918 in the Petrograd Theater of Musical Drama, were aimed at the realistic conventions of established theaters, not at political targets. Malevich's nonrepresentational sets (lost in 1932), like the drawings Meyerhold had produced as models for them, struck a blow for avant-garde art. But if Malevich conceived the stage as a cubistic picture, as he told Fevralskii, then surely Meyerhold and his codirector

  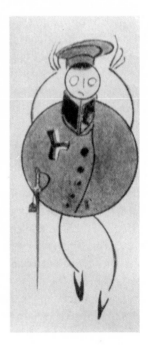

*Figures 4.2–4.8. Mayakovsky's sketches for* Mystery-Bouffe *(1918).    Figure 4.2.*
*"Clean" or white-collar people:* left, *the Australian,* middle, *the American,* right, *the*
*student.*

*Figure 4.3. Two devils*

Mayakovsky broke the frame with clowning and with at least one unconventional entrance: "The American rode down the aisle on a motorcycle." [7]

The second production of *Mystery-Bouffe* in its revised version (1921) was abstract too (as the drawing of the set in *Encounters*, p. 179, shows). Together with *Dawns* by Emile Verhaeren (1920), also in the Theater RSFSR I, Moscow, it constituted a political and artistic assault on "the United Front of the hypnotic theater," as Alpers calls the academic theaters, the Art Theater, and the Kamerny.[8] Yet for all their artistic interest, Alpers considers these two shows nevertheless primarily of political importance. "There was more polemical impudence in them and less genuine theatrical mastery." [9] Still, with the constructivist-oriented set for its second production, *Mystery-Bouffe* marked an artistic milestone in the theater.

Later Meyerhold twice defined constructivism: in 1927 he called it a vertical arrangement of scene (*Articles*, 2:492), and in 1930 he called it acting on a vertical axis (ibid., 2:497). In this sense constructivism began only later with Meyerhold's production of *The Magnanimous Cuckold*. Nevertheless, the instructions received apparently from Meyerhold himself by the set designers of the second production of *Mystery-Bouffe*, Viktor Kiselev, Anton Lavinskii, and Vladimir Khrakovskii,

were constructivist, though the acting on such a set could hardly have been so. The actress Mariia Sukhanova, who played three parts in *Mystery-Bouffe*, describes its vertical set:

*The peepbox stage had been scrapped. The action was transported into the auditorium, from which several rows of orchestra seats had been removed. In front in the foreground the globe of the earth, or rather part of the globe, had been built. Paradise was piled up on constructions under the ceiling at the very back of the stage. We in Paradise (I was an angel) stood with arms raised; at our backs little white wings trembled with every movement. . . . The devils had their place at the foot of the globe. The things [also characters in the play] and machines were placed in the box seats. The Man of the Future appeared near the ceiling on a platform especially built for the purpose.[10]*

In this second variant *Mystery-Bouffe* was more specific and political. The set, a partial globe marked "Earth" in printed letters, could be turned to the other side to show "Hell." Unfortunately, the costumes for the hero figures, the workers especially, made them monotonously alike, whereas the villainous characters remained memorable: the caricatured bourgeois, the devils, and especially the Menshevik—this last played unforgettably as the typical opportunist by Igor Ilinskii with umbrella and the clown's red beard and wig (figs. 4.4–4.11). Fevralskii characterizes the whole production as based on movement: "In accordance with the spirit of the play, the directors inventively used methods of the popular folk theater [*balagan*]; acrobatic and circus elements were brought in" (*Desiat let*, p. 28). And Boleslav Rostotskii singles out Ilinskii: "Perhaps most brilliant and persuasive of all, the political poster was combined with circus and clown devices in the role of the fellow-travelling Menshevik, with which Igor Ilinskii gave a wonderful example of sharpest political satire." [11] Fevralskii testifies to the success of such methods in truly activating the audience: "The struggle between two forces —revolution and reaction—unfolded not only on the stage but also in the auditorium" (*Encounters*, p. 184).

If the second *Mystery-Bouffe* marked the revolutionary May 1 holiday, *Dawns* of the same theater season marked the third anniversary of the Revolution. Indeed, Fevralskii calls *Dawns* the first truly revolutionary play; its theme is the fall of capitalism and the rise of social revolution, both of which were given the color of Soviet reality in Meyerhold's adaptation.

*The main aim in direction was to end the division between auditorium and stage. . . . The show took place with the house lights on full. In the orchestra pit in front of the stage a chorus was placed which cried out phrases of comment on one or another moment of the action. . . . The actors hurled out the words, . . . there was little motion on stage, only the characters' long speeches. . . . A stage set, soon to be abandoned, was still used in* Dawns *but differed radically from the usual. It consisted of non-objective geometrical forms (disks, triangles, cubes, etc.); the stage was cross-hatched with cords. These elements of the set were made of genuine materials —iron, wood. The designer, V[ladimir] V[ladimirovich] Dmitriev tried not to represent a city, but to give a general, abstract impression of one. Make-up and wigs were not worn.* Dawns *was Meyerhold's last production to use a curtain. However, the curtain too was nonobjective, brightly lighted. (Desiat let, pp. 26–28.)*

Like the cubist set, Dmitriev's curtain too used abstract forms: on a black background a huge, somewhat distorted red circle, dissected from the right by a large yellow wedge and labeled in the center with the letters RSFSR (*Encounters*, p. 181). Since the Russian Revolution was not the content of *Dawns*, as it was of *Mystery-Bouffe*, Meyerhold strove by other means to bring October into the theater for this production. For this reason Meyerhold abandoned the pleasing pictorial box set and strove in the spirit of Tatlin to build

*Figures 4.4–4.5.  Two of the "unclean" (workers): a washerwoman (fig. 4.4) and a lamplighter (fig. 4.5).   Figure 4.6.  Methusaleh (played by Mayakovsky).*

*Figure 4.7.  Heaven (act 3, scene 2)*

*Figure 4.8. The Promised Land (act 3, scene 3)*

*Figures 4.9–4.11. Sketches by Viktor Kiselev for the second version of* Mystery-Bouffe
*(1921). Figure 4.9. Set design of the Land of Things for act 5.*

*Figure 4.10. An angel*

*Figure 4.11. The Menshevik, played by Ilinskii*

*Figure 4.12. Maquette of cubist set designed by Vladimir Dmitriev for* Dawns *(1920)*

on the open stage, though Dmitriev's designs remained cubist in inspiration (fig. 4.12). Also for this reason Meyerhold created the atmosphere of a political meeting in the play and announced news of the civil war from the stage. Fevralskii distinguishes sharply: "The problem of the revolutionary play was solved differently in these two productions: there [*Dawns*] an elevated solemnity, here [*Mystery-Bouffe*] the merriment of the liberated people" (*Desiat let*, p. 29). Though both shows were intended to affirm the revolutionary cause, both were denied the approval of the highest authority. Lenin himself expressed his complete distrust of Mayakovsky's "futurism" (referring, it is true, not to *Mystery-Bouffe*, which he never saw, but doubtless to the 1916 play *Vladimir Mayakovsky*, and Lenin's wife, Nadezhda Krupskaia, published an unfavorable review of *Dawns* in *Pravda*. Soon thereafter the Theater RSFSR I, which had housed both Meyerhold shows, was closed.

So it was at the Zon Theater, Sadovaia Street, that Meyerhold produced Crommelynck's *Magnanimous Cuckold* (1922) with his own workshop players, the first group trained together in his methods. If the production was the first to realize the biomechanics of acting, it was also, thanks to its constructivist set designer, Liubov S. Popova, the first wholly to realize constructivism (fig. 4.13). As a drawing of

the set has shown, the stage was bared to the back brick wall to make way for "apparatus for acting" with working parts.[12] One such construction, reminiscent of a windmill, had blades and two wheels which moved with increased speed at moments of tension. Further, two raised platforms, connected with each other by a ramp and connected with the stage level by stairs and a slide, made possible the near acrobatics of the actors. Of these the trio of principals, Ilinskii (Bruno), Mariia Babanova (Stella), and Vasilii Zaichikov (Estrugo), were called "the three-bodied actor" because they played together with such absolute harmony (fig. 4.14). We have already seen proof, in the excerpt from the play described by Garin (chapter 3), of how Estrugo "in physical movement gave an exact pantomimic accompaniment to the mad actions of the jealous Bruno, thus commenting like the chorus of Greek tragedy on the whole experience of the 'magnanimous cuckold.'" Of the third in the trio Aleksei Gvozdev wrote: "Babanova (Stella) revealed astonishing gifts of musicality which made possible the rightness of her fast tempi and her development of her character; thus she showed the whole range of the woman persecuted by jealousy from idyllic cloudless happiness to complete psychological torture" (fig. 4.15). Gvozdev concluded: "The mass scenes, disclosing with stormy joy of life the

*Figure 4.13. Liubov Popova's construction for* The Magnanimous Cuckold *(1922)*

*Figure 4.14.  Actors at work on Popova's working construction for* The Magnanimous Cuckold

gymnastic skill of the young actors, filled the platforms and stairs of the 'construction' with a whirlwind of acrobatic movements." [13]

Meyerhold's ironic antiproduction of *The Magnanimous Cuckold* departed far from a boulevard comedy of adultery. To be sure, Meyerhold could take as authority for such treatment of a quite conventional play the suggestions of the Italian futurist Filippo Marinetti, whom he had quoted in a polemical statement only the year before:

*Did not Marinetti recommend the following remedies to theaters sunk in sweet dozing and weary psychologism: "To substitute mass scenes for adultery on stage, to show plays in the reverse order of their action, to utilize for the theater the heroism of the circus and techniques of the machine age, to pour glue on the seats of the auditorium, to sell the same tickets to different people, to distribute sneezing powder, to stage fires and murders in the area of the orchestra seats, to use the intermission for contests—running around the theater, discus-throwing: all this in honor of speed and dynamism." (Articles, 2:29.)*

The Crommelynck play might thus be viewed as heralding the artistic revolution that followed soon after the political revolution represented in *Dawns.*

Quite as ironic and drastic as his revision of the original *Magnanimous Cuckold* was Meyerhold's alteration of a play from the Russion ninteenth-century repertory, *The Death of Tarelkin,* by Aleksandr Sukhovo-Kobylin (1922). Garin calls Meyerhold's *Tarelkin* a confirmation of the methods of acting developed in *Cuckold* and names a number of acting successes, such as Dmitrii Orlov as Raspliuev (fig. 4.16) and Nikolai Okhlopkov as Kachala. However, though work clothing had been used in *Cuckold,* he criticizes its use in *Tarelkin.* Garin calls *prozodezhda* unconvincing here because it is irrelevant to a classic play of the previous century; others objected to the single blob into which the undifferentiated costumes faded (figs. 4.17–4.20). Yet Garin finds that *Tarelkin* initiated the line Meyerhold was to take in his further adaptations of the classics, a line which Garin considers by no means drastic compared with the "annihilation" treatment such works were receiving just then from others, notably Eisenstein with his *Even A Wise Man Stumbles,* after Ostrovsky. Certainly Meyerhold's treatment of *Tarelkin* as a folk-theater and circus farce exposing the czarist police state seems disrespectful enough of a conventional realistic play.

The designer for *Tarelkin,* again a leading constructivist, Varvara Stepanova, made everything on stage func-

*Figure 4.15. Babanova as Stella in* The Magnanimous Cuckold

*Figure 4.16.  Dmitrii Orlov as Raspliuev in* The Death of Tarelkin *(1922)*

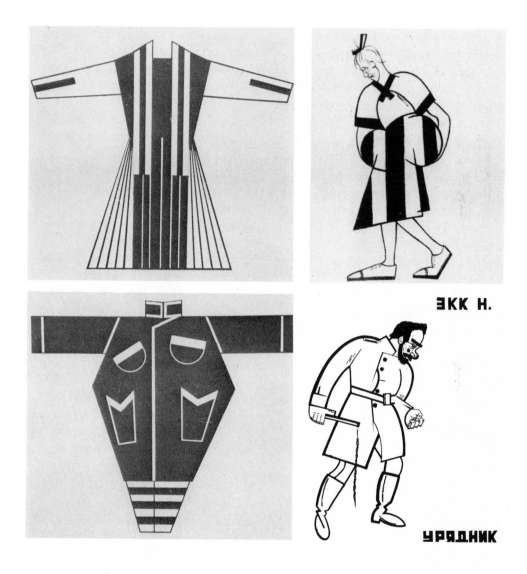

ЭКК Н.

УРЯДНИК

*Figures 4.17.–4.18. Two costume designs by Stepanova for* The Death of Tarelkin.
*Figures 4.19–4.20. Two of Stepanova's costume designs for* Tarelkin *in drawings by Ilia Shlepianov; figure 4.20, the policeman, is marked for Nikolai Ekk, later known as director of* The Road to Life, *the first Soviet sound film.*

tional from a kind of squirrel cage with a revolving wheel for the transport of prisoners, to chairs with false spring seats, to a wooden chest in which an actor could hide and then reappear like a jack-in-the-box (figs. 4.21–4.22). The actors fired shots from pistols and indulged in farcical fisticuffs. The role of the huge washerwoman Brandakhly-stova was played by a male actor, just as Mama in Brecht's *Seven Deadly Sins* was sung by a bass (fig. 4.23). And Zaichikov, as the victimized hero *Ta-relkin,* used clowning gestures as when, panting for thirst, he pathetically held out to the audience an earthen bowl for water, but then in quick reversal iron-ically rejected it by taking a pull from his pocket flask of wine. Rostotskii criticizes this gesture as the actor's, not the character's, "wink of understanding with the audience" by which he "breaks out of the role" and "destroys its unity and wholeness." [14] Western critics would doubtless approve it as an ex-ample of "alienation." Other devices used in *Tarelkin* to achieve tempo and cinematic effect have been hailed as the "cinematification" of the theater.

Unlike the radically produced *Tarel-kin,* another classic, Aleksandr Ostrov-sky's *A Profitable Post* (1923), was staged in a rather conservative manner at the Theater of the Revolution, though it, too, clearly aimed to expose the old regime. Dark wooden panelling, simple wooden furniture, a stairway at

each side, and a small chamber visible on the upper level—Viktor Shestakov's set interpreted a traditional play con-structivistically (fig. 4.24). Alpers crit-icizes the production as neither fish nor fowl, that is, neither a radical re-vision nor the reverent realization of a classic.[15] Others praised it for its subtle synthesis, a fine interpretation pushed only imperceptibly toward satire. To be sure, the folksiness often found in Ostrovsky was gone, for Meyerhold, consistently opposed to naturalism, "exclude[d] the genre-picture," [16] and relied instead on type characters. The most memorable of these were Baba-nova as Polina and Orlov as Iusov. Orlov was not above clowning; he used the comedian's trick of descending ever deeper into a knee bend before entering the master's door, thus caricaturing the pose of servility. Babanova went to no such extremes, yet admirably rendered the character of a foolish girl altogether the product of her petit bourgeois en-vironment. The constructivist spiral staircase served further to demonstrate servility: climbing it to the master's door, Belogubov (played by Vladimir Belokurov) bowed at each turn like a machine, not a man (figs. 4.25–4.27). Thus by ironic emphases Meyerhold reaffirmed Ostrovsky as a satirist in the great tradition of Gogol and Sukhovo-Kobylin.

*A Profitable Post* was one of the two productions which Meyerhold staged

*Figure 4.21. Stepanova building her construction for* Tarelkin

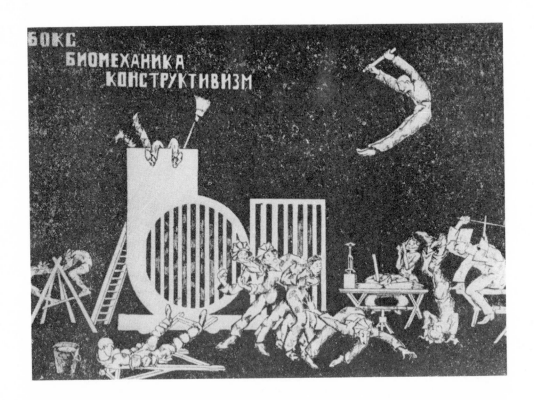

*Figure 4.22. I. Makhlis's drawing of the* Tarelkin *set (labeled "Boxing. Biomechanics. Constructivism.")*

*Figure 4.23. Mikhail Zharov as Brandakhlystova in* Tarelkin

*Figure 4.24. Viktor Shestakov's set for* A Profitable Post *(1923)*

*Figures 4.25–4.27. Woodcuts of three actors in leading roles of* A Profitable Post. *Figure 4.25. Babanova as Polly.   Figure 4.26. Vladimir Belokurov as Belogubov.*

*Figure 4.27. Orlov as Iusov*

for the Theater of the Revolution during the brief period of his artistic directorship there (1922–24). For all its brevity his leadership evidently set a definitive course for the company, later renamed the Mayakovsky Theater. None other than Olga Kameneva (Trotsky's sister, director of the Theater Division in 1920 at the same time Meyerhold was acting director) has written the early history of this theater in an illustrated volume issued in honor of its tenth anniversary. Originating as TEREVSAT (Theater of Revolutionary Satire), 1920 to 1922, the Theater of the Revolution had at first consisted of travelling propaganda units, singing popular songs near railway stations from which soldiers departed for the Civil War, or doing a few vaudeville acts as the "artistic program" at political meetings. When this troupe, accustomed to performing on street corners and in small clubs, moved into its own building, the former Potopchina Operetta Theater on Nikitskaia Street, "it looked pitiful and ridiculous on the big, brightly lighted stage, surrounded by the accumulated stage sets and properties for musicals." [17] So Meyerhold was invited to reorganize the group, and he "determined for some years the theater's artistic character"; he "brought to the Theater of the Revolution an enormous heritage of theater culture, which he was easily able to inject into the young organism because he spoke the same political language. . . . Even in the most radical productions at the Theater of the Revolution Meyerhold could teach the actor the best from the acting heritage of the Art Theater, the school which this gifted master had himself gone through at the start of his stage career." [18] Osaf Litovskii in an anniversary article on the theater cites A Profitable Post as combining both a new radical interpretation of the play and a classic delineation of character.

Meyerhold's other production at the Theater of the Revolution, Aleksei Faiko's Lake Liul (1923), has a plot as complicated as a James Bond movie, in which it is hard to know which agent is working for whom. Of course, in the end the communist idealists successfully launch the Revolution, and Maisie, the chambermaid heroine, unflinchingly shoots down her beloved Toni for having yielded to capitalist blandishments. No wonder that the chief interest of the production seemed to lie in Meyerhold's devices for scene change, which later, revised and simplified, served also for the production of D.E.

The French play Night by Marcel Martinet, completely rewritten as a propaganda play by Sergei Tretiakov, was the production with which Meyerhold opened his own theater (1923). Renamed Zemlia dybom (Earth Rampant), the new version made the original five acts into eight tableaux: Down with war, Attention!, Truth in the

*Figure 4.28. Earth Rampant (1923): a scene from the third episode*

trenches, The black International, All power to the Soviets, The Revolution betrayed, Sheep shearing, and Night. The play depicted events at the end of World War I, especially the contrast between the generals and the simple peasants. Produced in something like arena style, it was given several times outdoors, once, for example, in June 1924, in the Lenin Hills for delegates to the Fifth Congress of the Comintern as a "mass spectacle" or pageant (fig. 4.28). Slogans, announcements, and the portraits of revolutionary leaders projected on a screen underlined its relevancy to current events, and actual machines of everyday life—an automobile, a field kitchen, a harvester, a machine gun, and motorcycles—were brought on stage in an effort to inject reality into the theater (fig. 4.29). Actors planted in the audience shouted "Hail the Red Army!" or "Onward to the dictatorship of the proletariat!" One of the rare vulgarisms to be found in Meyerhold's work occurred in an interlude of this production and proved most effective: the German kaiser used a chamber pot on stage. As Meyerhold saw the aim of this most successful show: "Thus the play develops in close connection with contemporary life and is staged as a heroic propaganda poster with the interpolation of the grotesque interlude, General Bourbouze and the Emperor [figs. 4.30–4.31]" (*Articles*, 2:52).

Meyerhold's next show, his version of the classic play *The Forest* (1924), by Ostrovsky, managed to leave the text intact while altogether changing the feel of the original. Alpers's account, though written from the prejudiced perspective of 1937, perhaps best explains how this was done.[19] Ostrovsky's original exposes the narrow milieu of the estate owner Gurmyzhskaia, in which everyone is dependent on the power she derives from her great wealth. Nevertheless, in the confrontation between rich and poor, which means also between wickedness and purity of heart, Gurmyzhskaia's machinations are frustrated by her vagrant actor nephew, Neschastlivtsev. Meyerhold changed the whole sense of the play by breaking up the classic structure of five acts into the quick movement of thirty-three episodes and by removing events from their bourgeois milieu through use of scenically neutral ramps and a circular swing as an apparatus for acting (figs. 4.32–4.34).

The text, which was spoken unchanged, was accompanied by what Alpers calls pantomime études in movement, which achieved a new emphasis. For example, in the first encounter between Gurmyzhskaia and her nephew, the man got the better of the rich old woman by going on with his shaving throughout the dialogue, while she retreated to one side of the stage. When he finally waved a stick at her, she ran

*Figure 4.29.  Meyerhold in the mid-1920s: the leather coat he is wearing might well be the one in which he made his promised appearance in* Earth Rampant, *riding down the aisle on a motorcycle.*

*Figures 4.30–4.31. Drawings by Ilia Shlepianov show the "propaganda poster" treatment used in* Earth Rampant. *Figure 4.30. A caricatured priest (played by Stepan Kozikov). Figure 4.31. The heroic role of Favrol (Ivan Savelev).*

*Figure 4.32. Vasilii Fedorov's construction for* The Forest *(1924): semicircular bridge mounting left, used as exit ramp; maypole, in the center, used as circular swing; entrance to Gurmyzhskaia's property, so labeled, under right-hand theater box*

*Figures 4.33–4.34. Shlepianov's costume sketches for Ilinskii as Schastlivtsev (fig. 4.33) and for Boris Zakhava as Vosmibratov (fig. 4.34)* in The Forest

away. He ended by inverting the shaving bowl on his head, thus giving his words a last touch of defiance. In the original, Alpers feels, the nephew lacked independence, but in the swift movement of the Meyerhold production he and the other dependent characters were liberated: Aksiusha, the orphaned poor relative of the house, punctuated her talk with Gurmyzhskaia by flattening the washing with blows of a wooden roller so that she too frightened her guardian. Aksiusha's beloved, Petr, who in the original must bend to his father's will, became in Meyerhold's production a lover-liberator, thanks to the accompaniment not only of lively physical action but also of lively music played on the accordion. Alpers admits that liberating the underdog personages in this way enlivened the play and pleased the public with an optimistic tone, but he accuses Meyerhold of oversimplifying reality.

As part of the action, while Aksiusha and Petr talked of setting off into the great world, they propelled themselves with each new destination named to ever higher leaps on a merry-go-round rope swing (*gigantskie shagi*) (fig. 4.35). Meyerhold considered the dynamism by which he transformed Petr so essential that he replaced in the role that excellent actor Orlov, who was afraid to use the "giant-leaps" swing, and thus lost him from the Meyerhold Theater for good. The two players

chosen (Raikh as Aksiusha and Ivan Koval-Samborskii as Petr) displayed their skill on this gymnastic apparatus to an accordion tune called "Kirpichiki" (Little Bricks), to which accompaniment the young people also departed in the end. The piece was composed by Valentin Kruchinin to the melody of an almost forgotten popular waltz, "Dve sobachki" (Two Little Dogs), with new naive words by Pavel German; through Meyerhold's show it became popular as the theme song of the two young lovers. Pantomime was deftly used in the play as the older pair of wandering actors (fig. 4.36), who helped the young couple to victory, enacted their life of the open road; a high point was reached when Ilinskii, as the comedian Schastlivtsev, gave by a flutter of the hand the illusion of catching a fish when none was there. In this way, by the physical action of biomechanics, Meyerhold transformed *The Forest*'s theme of bourgeois repression and conveyed a new sense of freedom and optimism without altering the text.

*D.E.*, adapted from two novels, *Trust D.E.*, by Ilia Ehrenburg, and *The Tunnel,* by Bernhard Kellermann, concerns an American effort to destroy Europe (Trust for the Destruction of Europe) and a Soviet countereffort to save it. The play is interesting for the collective origin of its text, which was compiled from suggestions made by students of the Higher Military Pedagogical Insti-

*Figure 4.35.  Petr (Ivan Koval-Samborskii) and Aksiusha (Raikh) in* The Forest

*Figure 4.36.  Neschastlivtsev (Mikhail Mukhin) and Schastlivtsev (Ilinskii) in* The Forest

tute, and for the musical accompaniments which characterized the opposing sides: the briskly acrobatic Soviets as against the languidly tangoing Western decadent bourgeois. The final memorable effect of *D.E.* resulted from the use of movable wooden screens for the sets. These were arranged in different combinations for different scenes or, changing while the characters ran between them and projectors flashed, were incorporated into the action, thus giving *D.E.* its sense of dynamism. Costumes were used once more and so were projected "titles"—facts and revolutionary comment shown on three screens. Mikhail Zharov enjoyed in his role as master of ceremonies the chance to improvise his text with fresh topicality every day. The large number of characters required the doubling of roles, at which Garin especially excelled with his seven "transformations," clearly underlined as such, in the space of one brief episode. (Meyerhold even caused a peephole to be made and had old-time vaudeville music played during the changes so that the audience might admire the actor's art and also view the characters ironically, not seriously.) As a political review, *D.E.* was rewritten in 1930 and brought up to date with new references to current events and a "political interlude" honoring the thirteenth anniversary of the October Revolution.

After staging an optimistic, joyous show in *The Forest* and a dynamic and breezily "urbanistic" one in *D.E.*,[20] Meyerhold deliberately reversed all these trends. In his next show, Faiko's *Bubus the Teacher* (1925), instead of a bare stage and work clothes he used an elegant set, screening off the acting area by a semicircle of bamboo hangings, and employed ornate costumes and makeup. Finally, as Alpers emphasizes from the hindsight of the campaign against the Meyerhold Theater in the thirties, Meyerhold pointedly retarded tempi by interpolating marked pauses. Unlike Stanislavsky's pauses for "experiencing" the action, Meyerhold's were introduced for the sake of *predygra* ("pre-acting"), a moment of pantomimic communication between actor and spectator, a kind of winking at the audience.

However, Faiko's text could not well sustain such emphasis. It was admittedly a weak play about a weakling, a compromising liberal, a role later acted by Ilinskii, who had so successfully played the compromising Menshevik in *Mystery-Bouffe*. So Meyerhold worked, not on the text, but on an elaborate system of movement for each character. Pre-acting and acting were performed against an elegant musical background of Liszt and Chopin, to which the words were spoken as well. The music was intended not as background but as a "co-construction," in Meyerhold's word for it, an added dimension of psychological characterization. Meyerhold discussed it thus in a talk to his troupe: "Wagner introduced two new elements—the leit-motiv and the unending melody. . . . In the orchestra he notes those psycho-logical impulses which must be com-municated to the audience, and he ex-presses them not only in words—for words are spoken in those dialogues of Wagner's own making—but also so as to save time: that is, while the character is speaking the orchestra plays such melodies, and so constructs harmony, that various thoughts must come to mind for the audience and it must ex-perience associations" (*Articles*, 2:66). Clearly, then, Meyerhold hoped to acquire for stage plays the added di-mension of the musical leitmotiv.

Unfortunately, unlike the orchestral score of a Wagnerian opera, the Liszt and Chopin accompaniment never be-came an integral part of *Bubus,* and so the association between leitmotiv and character did not necessarily take place in the audience's mind. Nor were there any titles and texts, like those projected in *D.E.,* to help the mystified spectator. Perhaps the *Bubus* experiment could succeed only in such a work as *The Threepenny Opera,* in which music and ironic counterpoint are truly integrated from the start. Surely the Germans Brecht and his composer Kurt Weill needed no such theater experiment by Meyerhold in order to exploit Wag-nerian techniques in their opera.

Apparently the price paid for the almost intolerable retardation caused by Meyerhold's pre-acting was mis-understanding and boredom on the audience's part. Nor did the intended "alienation" strike home, despite the instructions to the audience in the pamphlet-program:

*With the words he speaks on stage and the situations he plays, the actor-tribune wants to let the audience know his atti-tude to all this, tries to compel the audi-ence to understand in one certain way the action developing before his eyes. . . . Before the audience's very eyes the actor-tribune reveals the true nature of the personage he has created, as if peer-ing from under the costume cape of the personage; he pronounces not only the words prescribed by the dramatist but also something like the very word roots. He must re-assess the elements of his art and restore to the theater what the theater lost in the period of political reaction when it fell into the rut of apo-litical conversationism.* (Articles, *2:94.*)

But if the experiment of pre-acting did not succeed in *Bubus,* the device of accompanying physical motion did serve as a rich commentary on the ac-tion a year later in *The Inspector Gen-eral.* And if *Bubus* was too slight to sus-tain the greater weight Meyerhold wanted to give it, still it did mark in his career a turning point toward increased seriousness.

Meyerhold pushed the comic toward the tragicomic in *Bubus* and again in his next production, Nikolai Erdman's *Mandate* (1925). The play shows a petit bourgeois milieu on the outskirts of Moscow where eight years after the Revolution a trunk containing clothes from the court of the last empress is stored for safekeeping. The cook Nastia, who dons the clothes, is actually named Anastasiia Nikolaevna, so that she is taken for the Grand Duchess of that name. Thus the clothes act as a catalyst for the wish dream of all the die-hard characters who have secretly hoped the Soviet era might soon be ended and the czarist past return (figs. 4.37–4.38). The ghost of such wishful thinking rises in the demand of the daughter's suitor, Smetanich, that a powerful relative be found as a "dowry" for Varvara Guliachkin (fig. 4.39). Interestingly, her brother realizes that the small store, the family's former source of income, is irrecoverable and that only a party document can guarantee prosperity in the new age. (The document, supposedly a membership card in the party, is later revealed to be only an identity card from the *uprav-dom* [house warden].) To his own horrified surprise the brother finds himself pretending to have such a document, or "mandate," and tyrannizing over his neighbors with it (fig. 4.40). In the end

his forgery of the identity card is exposed, yet is not even taken seriously enough to warrant his arrest, so that the play's last lines, "What have we to live for?" sound like the epitaph of an entire outlived class.

This first full-length play by Erdman, witty as it is, does not yet have the sureness of means and economy of language usual with an experienced writer of comedy. So Meyerhold heightened certain effects by theatrical means. He rolled out pantomime scenes on two concentric revolves, which at times moved in opposite directions (fig. 4.41), and he again used music as ironic commentary. He thus put the play in the direct line of the classic social satires of Gogol and Sukhovo-Kobylin; indeed, Stanislavsky too expressed admiration for "the Gogolian power of the best scenes." And it was Gogol to whom Meyerhold turned with his next great production of a classic, *The Inspector General* (1926).

The following play at the Meyerhold Theater, Tretiakov's *Roar China* (1926), was not staged by Meyerhold alone but in collaboration between Meyerhold and his pupil Vasilii Fedorov. In a newspaper interview Meyerhold described the actual incident of 1924 on which the play was based: In reprisal for the death of an American, killed in a quarrel with a Chinese boatman, the captain of the British gunboat *Cockchafer* threatened to bomb a

Figure 4.37.  *Mama Guliachkin (Serebrianikova) receives from Tamara Leopoldovna Vishnevetskaia (T. Inger) the overwhelming charge to preserve "all that remains of old Russia in the new"* (The Mandate, *act 1*).

*Figure 4.38. Mama prays before the phonograph* (Mandate, *act 1*).

*Figure 4.39.* The Mandate: *the Guliachkin family:* left to right: *Mama (Serebrianikova),*
*Pavel (Garin), and Varvara (Raikh)*

nearby Chinese village unless two Chinese were delivered to him for execution. Since the guilty man had fled, two innocent Chinese, selected by lot, were executed, and the execution was actually approved by a resolution of the House of Commons (fig. 4.42). Meyerhold went on to explain the idea of Fedorov's production: "The director decided to treat the European scenes in the manner of the theater of masks; the Europeans in their relationship to the event talk and act automatically accordingly to schematic patterns worked out for them, clichés and stereotyped commands. The real human feeling they lack is the exclusive property of the Chinese and therefore the Chinese scenes are developed as a realistic depiction of life" (*Articles,* 2:99). Here the several devices which Meyerhold called the "mask" and which he used to such good effect in the 1914 studio production of Blok's *Unknown Lady* were reapplied to show a negative attitude toward the bourgeois figures who had also been the villains of that earlier play.

*Roar China* ends with an assembly of the aroused populace. To heighten the realistic depiction of everyday Chinese life, Meyerhold added nonspeaking "figures," as he called them: the knife-sharpener, the barber, the rickshaw boy, each with his own distinguishing cry or musical trademark. For the Chinese crowd in general, in Gvozdev's description, "the voice was used against a soft-pedaled background of musical accompaniment, and pitiful moans and gestures reached a tormenting tragic crescendo of a mass movement growing from nothing." [21] Besides the musical leitmotivs for the nonspeaking roles, Fedorov repeated the *Bubus* device of showing the psychology of the oppressed by means of pauses, again, however, too long drawn out. Fevralskii cites various effective elements of this production: the spectacle of the crowd scenes with the gunboat in the background, the melodrama of a musical accompaniment aimed at touching the emotions, and finally the sheer machinery by which the *Cockchafer* was made to move forward in the end, guns trained on the audience. For all their effectiveness, Fevralskii admits that the devices were used without "due economy," so that "the production was over-heavy" (*Desiat let,* p. 53). Nevertheless, other productions of *Roar China* were staged all over the world, including a Theater Guild production in New York (1930).

Meyerhold's series of social satires from *The Death of Tarelkin* through *The Mandate* culminated in the masterpiece *The Inspector General,* by Gogol (1926), in which his experiments of the first five years with the Meyerhold Theater and Workshop now bore fruit.[22] Considerable erudition, too, was drawn upon for *The Inspector*

*Figure 4.40. Scene from act 3 of* The Mandate. *Note the "working-class relatives," paid to be such as guests at the wedding; by their position in the pit they linked stage and audience.*

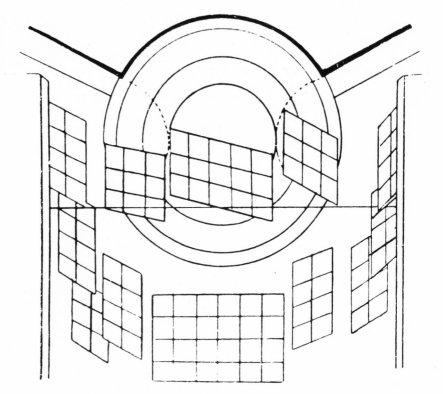

*Figure 4.41. Diagram of concentric revolves and movable background pieces used in* The Mandate

*Figure 4.42. The white men react to the death of one of their kind in* Roar China *(1926).*

*General,* as it had been for *Masquerade.* Meyerhold and his collaborator Mikhail Korenev restored to Gogol's text some of the passages which had been cut by imperial censors, and they added personages and portions of scenes from other works by Gogol, *The Gamblers,* for example. Further, Meyerhold moved the play from its limited small-town setting to a more important provincial city. He intended thus not only to renew Gogol for our time but also to make him for the first time altogether himself. For despite Gogol's objections, his comedy had been reduced in his own time to farce. By what means, Meyerhold asked in a report on his production in Leningrad (1927), was the play to be restored to Gogol's larger conception of truth?

*We have tried in this production to approach realism by new means: by biomechanics . . . and through the element of music. We saw that we had to compose the show according to all the rules of orchestral composition, that the 'score' of each role would have to have resonance by itself, that we had to fit it into the mass of instrument-roles, weave the instruments into a very complicated orchestration, mark in this complicated structure the path of leitmotivs, and make it all resound together like an orchestra: the actor and the light and the movement and even*

*the properties that are shown on stage. (Articles, 2:140.)*

Of course, it was not an innovation in Meyerhold's theory to postulate music as the organizing principle of a production, but to realize the theory with such eminent success as in *The Inspector General* was a great achievement. And moreover, to apply biomechanics in minimal space, as Meyerhold did in this production, was quite new. Instead of his well-known expansive motion and pantomime over an area extended in all three dimensions, Meyerhold used the opposite solution of concentrating on intensive economical motion in small space, or what he called "close-ups." "Remember Chaplin," Meyerhold reminded his actors on 20 October 1925, in his explication of Gogol's play,

*what complicated scenes he does, or Keaton—and he acts in a space of a couple of yards, sometimes half that, sometimes simply sitting on a chair. . . . By the way, we shall thus increase our range: we have learned to act in a wide area, now we shall play in a small one, sitting in an armchair or on a table, or lying on a bed or sitting on a sofa. What is mimicry? Is it facial expression alone? No, it is also acting with both hands and pose, not only the turn of the head and shoulders, but also the* *"composition" of the whole figure in the chair or armchair, etc. (*Articles, *2:110.)*

In order to achieve a faster pace and to expand the scope of meaning, as well as to make possible the close-ups he intended, Meyerhold broke up the play's classic five acts and almost complete unity of place into fifteen episodes set in various places. In rapid succession all but four of these short scenes took place on small platforms twelve by sixteen feet, which, with the actors already prepared in their positions, were shot far forward at the audience on rails. Even when the full stage was used in the other four episodes, it was partially masked off by a broad oval of eleven doors set in highly polished mahogany panelling (figs. 4.43–4.47). Indeed, the elegance of earlier Meyerhold productions, like *Don Juan* and *Masquerade,* returned to supersede the bare stage and work clothes of the first Soviet years. For Meyerhold wanted to contrast the outward splendor of the reign of Nicholas I with its inward corruption and meanness of soul, the elegance of the painter Karl Briullov's portraits of the period with the "pig snouts" of the officials Gogol portrayed in his play. The large stage space was used when the bribes, not offered singly and successively as in the original, were held out simultaneously by disembodied hands from each of nine doors.

But if Meyerhold used the device of "multiple uniformity," familiar since his early days, to heighten the satiric effect, he nevertheless abjured on the whole the cheap effects of farce and "the antics appropriate to the theater" which had characterized his studio work. He even repudiated the romanticism and exaggeration Briusov found typical of Gogol. Still he sought romantic irony, the sudden strangeness which unexpectedly infuses the most ordinary moment in broad daylight at the start of a tale by Hoffmann: "We found in Gogol," wrote Meyerhold, "the fantastic element so characteristic of that other remarkable creative spirit, E. T. A. Hoffmann, who so artfully makes one believe that the old woman selling apples from her applecart has a little tail under her skirts. That doesn't mean we have to put the Devil in a skirt. It only means that Gogol skilfully shows the world as real but with a shade of the fantastic—not the mystical, but the fantastic" (*Articles,* 2:142–43). In this way Meyerhold remained true to his early impressions. For he had read early an essay familiar to the circle he frequented since his first visit to Petersburg in 1905, Dmitrii Merezhkovskii's *Gogol and the Devil* (1906). And his enthusiasm for Hoffmann had been evident ever since he devoted a

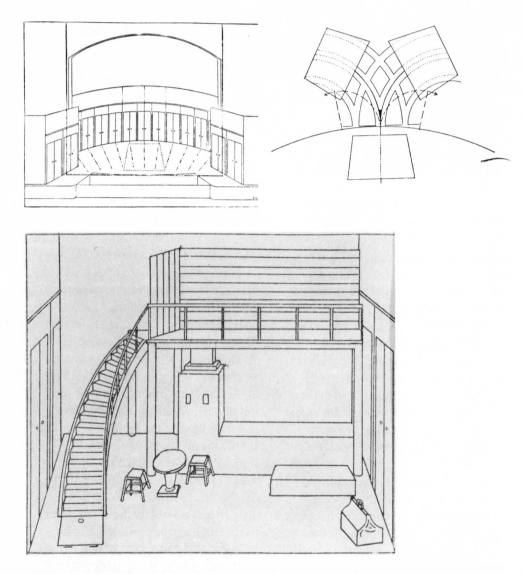

*Figures 4.43–4.47. Diagrams of full stage and the placement of trolley platforms for*
The Inspector General *(1926).    Figure 4.43.  The large stage lined with a half-circular
segment of doors (trapezoidal floor diagram indicates the position of trolley on the full
stage).    Figure 4.44.  Small stage on trolley and the rails on which ready-built scenes, with
the exception of the inn scene, were rolled in.    Figure 4.45.  The inn scene, moved forward
through the central opening above the doors (see fig. 4.43).*

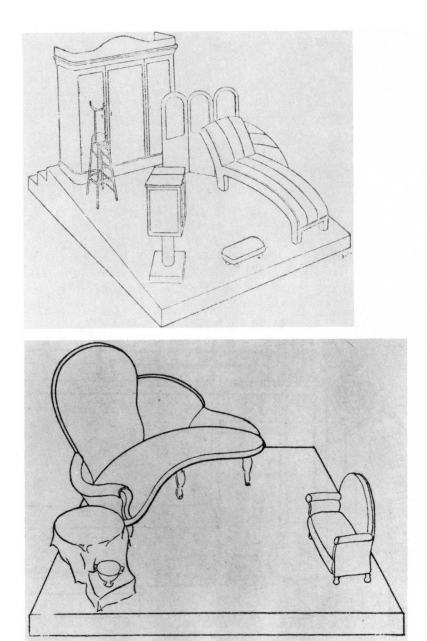

*Figure 4.46.   Anna Andreevna's closet.   Figure 4.47.   sofa.*

*Figure 4.48. Khlestakov (Garin) descends the stairs as if from another world in act 2 of*
The Inspector General.

regular section of the magazine *Love for Three Oranges* to Hoffmanniana (fig. 4.48).

The Khlestakov of his production was not the devil, however, nor was he the everchanging universal character which some critics averred that the actor Garin, with his skill in the art of transformation, was really playing. Nor was Khlestakov the lightweight dandy, one tradition of the role which Meyerhold explicitly repudiated as inadequate and boring. Meyerhold underlined rather two traits in Khlestakov, his frankly physical greed and his rascally opportunism, the motif represented in the inn scene when he and his companion, the transient officer, work with a false deck of cards. Meyerhold symbolized his insatiable hunger by a bagel, which Khlestakov wore like a medal in his buttonhole. He showed him deriving advantage from his concupiscence by the courtship of both mother and daughter after the maxim of "Pluck ye roses while ye may." Other themes, not particularly significant in themselves, Meyerhold enlarged to encompass a whole era. Thus Khlestakov's square-rimmed glasses were suggestive of the intellectual in Nicholas's time, who, like the hero of *Woe from Wit,* could perhaps seem a threat to bourgeois complacency (fig. 4.49). And Meyerhold added the nonspeaking roles of Khlestakov's companions, one of them a transient officer reminiscent of Lermontov's outsider, the "hero of our time."

If the character of Khlestakov was thus given depth, so too was that of Anna Andreevna, the mayor's wife. More than merely flirtatious, she was made wholly sensual and corrupt. Meyerhold constructed her role with notable economy of gesture around one characteristic, the smile (fig. 4.50). He represented her endless affairs with men through a pantomime which he devised from a mere stage direction in the original: the direction that the mayor's wife change costume four times. This instruction was imaginatively extended to show her wish dream for thousands of suitors. For in her voluminous clothes cabinet were concealed, along with numerous dresses, Dobchinskii, whom mother and daughter discovered acting the voyeur while they changed, and numerous other young officers who burst out of hiding to kneel at Anna Andreevna's feet and serenade her, one even shooting himself for love of her (fig. 4.51). Thus the role of Anna Andreevna was epitomized in smiling lasciviousness. Meyerhold commented on "the fat-bellied clothes closet": "So a certain erotic atmosphere is created. . . . After all, we want the audience to feel, when Khlestakov appears, that in this comedy people not only take bribes, eat and drink, but also make love, perhaps

*Figure 4.49.* Inspector General: *Khlestakov (Garin).*   *Figure 4.50.* Inspector General: *Anna Andreevna (Raikh).*

in a peculiar manner, but still make love" (*Articles,* 2:114).

Just as Meyerhold considerably invigorated the character of Petr in *The Forest,* so in Gogol's play he made Osip no longer the faithful old retainer but rather a bold young fellow, a close relative to the rebellious Figaro. The mayor too, younger than usual, was shown as the leader of a chorus. And his chorus of officials functioned as a group, offering their bribes simultaneously and echoing Khlestakov's remarks in unison. The frequent mention of the "musical composition" of the show does not refer to an actual continuum of musical background, as in *Bubus,* though music by contemporary composers, including Mikhail Glinka, was used; it rather denotes the strict observance of a carefully calculated variety of tempi, culminating in a finale of ever greater crowds on stage and a crescendo of sound. Throughout, numbers of officers and officials crowded in a small space were the leitmotiv of the bureaucrats' scenes, and for such scenes of officialdom a "benighted" half darkness of candlelight was used as well. The scenes with the ladies (the roses of enjoyment) were typified, on the other hand, by light and movement.

To contrast the two milieus, Meyerhold also varied tempi, changing the whole mode suddenly by a device he called *perekliuchenie* (sudden change-

over). At the announcement party for the mayor's daughter, for example, the bright light and movement of the ball suddenly yielded to crowding and the flickering of candles as the guests put their heads together to read Khlestakov's letter mocking them all. While the mayor spoke his monologue, the doctor managed to confine him in a strait jacket. The sound of bells preceded the gendarme's arrival amid the flashing of spotlights. Then a curtain rose from below, bearing in black letters the gendarme's announcement that a true inspector had arrived. As the curtain moved on upwards, all those on stage were transformed to life-size mannequins, frozen in horrified poses. For the first time Gogol's "silent scene" could be held for minutes as he had directed (fig. 4.52). Evidently the audience too was held in shattered silence for a time before the applause began.

Meyerhold next produced—after long preparation—the Russian classic *Woe from Wit,* by Griboedov (1928).[23] In the overall view of the two postrevolutionary decades Meyerhold staged Russian classics in almost equal alternation with new Soviet plays. He included quite regularly from the beginning most of the great Russian dramatists; only the great foreign playwrights, so frequently represented among his pre-1917 productions, disappeared almost wholly from his Soviet repertory (except for Dumas's *Camille*

Figure 4.51. *Anna Andreevna and the officers in her wish dream, interpolated by* Meyerhold into The Inspector General. *(The youngest officer, holding aloft a bouquet*

*of flowers, was played by Valentin Pluchek, later director of the Moscow Theater of Satire.)*

*Figure 4.52. Meyerhold and Garin modeling poses for the mannequins which in the "silent scene" at the end of* The Inspector General *replaced the crowd of officials and socialites, as all stood horrorstruck to learn the Inspector General was yet to come*

[1934]). The remaining three or four plays by Western writers done in this period he made his own, through complete revision, for example, *Earth Rampant,* after Martinet. Among the classic writers whom Meyerhold staged after 1917—Lermontov, Sukhovo-Kobylin, Ostrovsky, Gogol, Chekhov—his production of Griboedov's play may well be ranked for its importance in the canon of his work with *The Inspector General.* Indeed, Lunacharsky did so pair the two in his speech (1929) honoring the one hundredth anniversary of Griboedov's death.[24] In intent, at least, the production of *Woe from Wit* aimed at even higher significance than did *The Inspector General.*

Griboedov's play not only represents a negative satiric assault upon nineteenth-century society, as does Gogol's, but also puts before us a positive hero, such as Gogol's comedy lacks. Indeed, the depth and human portent of Griboedov's protagonist Chatsky push the play beyond comedy toward tragicomedy. The hero, a gifted young intellectual modelled on prototypes of the time, possibly Wilhelm Kiukhelbeker or even Griboedov himself, returns from travel and study abroad to marry, as he hopes, his childhood playmate Sophie Famusov and to realize his liberal ideals in the Moscow of the early 1820s. He fails to grasp the all too obvious, that Sophie is in love with her father's secretary, Molchalin, a shameless careerist, and that she will be forced in the end to marry the suitor her father has picked out, the desk officer Skalozub, already preferred to high rank. Nor will Chatsky compromise his ideals to achieve status himself in either military or government service. Mercilessly bombarding Moscow society with his witticisms, he finds himself the victim of a rumor that he is insane. No other than Sophie has thoughtlessly launched the rumor, which she then allows to reach harmful proportions out of pique against Chatsky's scorn of Molchalin. In the end both Sophie and Chatsky are forced to confront the void of lovelessness in those they love.

A great distinction of the play is that it is written in a free-rhythmed rhymed verse of often epigrammatic wit, more of which has become proverbial in Russian than have lines from any other play. If Lermontov's hero in *Masquerade* is the Russian Othello, then Griboedov's Chatsky comes closest to Hamlet. Yet this is nevertheless a comedy, at darkest a tragicomedy, and surely the time which Chatsky was born to set right does not feel itself out of joint. Moscow society at the moment when Chatsky returns from some unnamed Wittenberg is characterized by brazen self-satisfaction. That is, Meyerhold in his explication to the cast singled out the trait of self-satisfied contemptibility (*khamstvo*) as the key to the exploitation practiced notably by Famusov and Molchalin in the play. Meyerhold compared the unabashed meanness of this nineteenth-century world to his own time as caricatured by George Gross. This was his key idea and therefore the tragic possibility of the play in his production. Still, despite the serious emphasis, he kept within the limit of comedy, he insisted, comparing Sophie's infatuation with Molchalin, not only to Desdemona's with the Moor, but also to Titania's with donkey-headed Bottom.

Besides the serious tendency, Meyerhold wanted to add a political accent to deepen the meaning of the play. The aristocratic society gathered for an evening at Famusov's provided a historically authentic background against which Chatsky was to declaim his brilliant verse tirades. Meyerhold broadened that background into the aura of an age, the ideological precondition of existence for such a "hero of our time" as Chatsky—and Meyerhold suggested rereading Lermontov's biography in order to understand the ironic acerbity of Chatsky's speeches.

The name Chatsky suggests as a possible prototype a freethinker of the 1820s, Petr Chaadaev, much admired by Pushkin and the whole younger generation of avant-garde intellectuals, all of whom, like Griboedov himself, were close to the radical movement of the abortive December revolt (1825).

Chaadaev was later officially declared insane, a political measure by no means unique to that time and place. However, this declaration occurred after Griboedov's death in 1829 and after the publication of the first of Chaadaev's *Philosophical Letters* (1836), so that Griboedov's play, if prophetic of the event, cannot actually allude to it. Meyerhold not only amplified the text by collating several versions of the play, which had been censored in its time, but also added parts for Chatsky's Decembrist friends. These were not silent roles like those of the added figures in *The Inspector General;* rather, they were to recite verse by Pushkin and Kondratii Ryleev (who was hanged for his part in the uprising of the fourteenth of December).

Meyerhold intended these weighty verses to contrast with the light bright lines of Griboedov's play. As authority for his interpolations, Meyerhold cited the historian Vasilii Kliuchevskii, who in his famous course on Russian history said, "A Decembrist served as the ideal from which Chatsky was copied" (*Articles,* 2:170). By establishing this connection with history Meyerhold generalized the meaning of the play as effectively as the arrival in the end of an actual inspector general deepens the significance of Gogol's play: Griboedov's hero thus became the poet-thinker, prophet of truth, who, misunderstood and victimized by society, suffered a fate common to those ahead of their time in all ages. The best recent productions of *Woe from Wit* have included this further dimension of Griboedov's classic, first added by Meyerhold.[25]

Though Meyerhold particularly urged his actors to work on the verse with its peculiarly Griboedian lightness, he nevertheless added another dimension of sound: music was superimposed. Griboedov was himself a musician and collected folk melodies; indeed, he passed one on to Glinka, for which Pushkin then wrote words, now well known as the "romance" (Russian art song) "Do not sing for me those sad songs of Georgia." Shortly before opening night Meyerhold explained his reason for the music; in a newspaper interview in *Pravda* on 12 March 1928 he said, according to Fevralskii, "The show is saturated with music. The approach to Chatsky's character through music will make it possible to overcome its apparent intellectuality. The emotional charge in Chatsky will be revealed in his musical improvisation, taken from the enormous musical culture of the age (Beethoven, Mozart, Bach)" (*Articles,* 2:171). So Meyerhold's Chatsky was made to represent not only "wit," or intellect, in his critical attack upon an indifferent age, but also romantic depth of feeling in his friends' readings from poetry and his piano improvisations (fig. 4.53). Unfortu-

nately criticism was directed against the production for its use of so much music, which evidently at times made the lines inaudible.

Did Meyerhold sense a growing antiintellectuality in his own time and intend to be topical when he changed the accepted title of the play, making it *Woe to Wit?* Or was he pretending scholarliness by using Griboedov's earlier variant of the title? Or did he seek through the title change to call attention to his renewal of an otherwise all too familiar classic? At any rate the changed title emphasized the persecution of wit, or intelligence, though the audience, of course, was meant to side with the defense and not the prosecution. Historically the perhaps most important group of Decembrists had also espoused the cause of intelligence by its very designation: *Obshchestvo umnykh* (Association of Intelligent Men); this is, of course, the stand of the hero, Chatsky, an intellectual pitted against an antiintellectual society.

Meyerhold further changed the play by removing it, after the fashion of the twenties, from its almost single setting and by breaking up the four acts of the original into seventeen episodes—four of which were apocryphal.[26] Yet the play owed nothing of the larger reference it gained in Meyerhold's adaptation to these changes. For the time of action still remained within the classic limit of twenty-four hours, and all but

*Figure 4.53.* Woe to Wit *(1928): Meyerhold's Chatsky (Garin) at the piano*

one scene in a tavern, Meyerhold's addition, still took place at Famusov's. Superficially the list of episodes seems to give ground for Rudnitskii's criticism that apparently "Meyerhold wanted to show the audience all the rooms of the Famusov house" (Rudnitskii, p.381). Of course, as Rudnitskii is well aware, the various locations were not realized naturalistically. In order to allow Meyerhold the benefit of his own recognition of faults, however, let the revival of 1935 serve as the subject of description, for in it he made certain corrections; he also proved by reviving *Woe to Wit* how important he felt it to be.[27] In 1935 the scenes, reduced to thirteen, no longer carried a place designation; they were numbered only, each with an epigraph of significant lines, all taken from the play except four quoted from Pushkin, Corneille (*Le Cid*), Sophocles (*Oedipus Rex*), and another work by Griboedov. The second production was dedicated to Mei-lan-fang, the Chinese actor whose Moscow appearance (14 April 1935) had been introduced by Meyerhold and attended by Brecht, among others.

The single set for *Woe to Wit* was a construction, used for all scenes. It consisted of a high platform upstage center with connecting bridges at each side leading into a stair, which descended right and left forward onto the apron. The construction was not meant to reproduce or even suggest the interior of a nineteenth-century noble house; rather, it made an impression of constructivist modernity. It was built of gleaming metal and the space beneath the platforms closed off with screens of Chinese orange red. Though bright metal and bright color together gave a sense of geometric abstraction, the screens were concretely practical, that is, movable, so as to mark off now this, now the other, locale. A transparent curtain delimited the area beneath the central platform upstage, which, when back-lighted, allowed a view of such silent scenes posed behind it as Decembrists reading verses while downstage Famusov and Skalozub met. In the first production the platforms were not used for acting, according to Rudnitskii, but in the revival Chatsky spoke his impassioned monologues from on high, as if to raise them

above the real world of the society he confronted, thus clearly separating his thought from the action about him (fig. 4.54).

The real world, as Meyerhold conceived it, was not to be caricatured and dark like that of the bureaucracy in *The Inspector General*. Rather, he intended the world of Famusov's Moscow to be bright, fresh, and healthy. Indeed, the kaleidoscope of colorful uniforms and evening dresses, servants in white wigs and knee breeches, gave an impression of movement and gaiety (figs. 4.55–4.58). Only at the climax of Meyerhold's production did the life of the show freeze in still confrontation. The ball scene at which the rumor of Chatsky's madness circulates was transposed from the dance floor to the banquet table. Behind a single long table across the entire stage and as far forward as possible, as if for a close-up, the whole company faced the audience. Like the four mystics lined up behind a table in Meyerhold's seminal production of Blok's *Farce* in 1906, the many times more numerous personages of *Woe to Wit* sat, also stiff, as in a roll call, staring into space. In his handbook on directing, written in the mid-thirties, Sergei Eisenstein called such a novel staging effect the "opposite" (*naoborot*) solution, contrary to nature or to tradition of a classic scene. "In *Woe to Wit*," Eisenstein pointed out, "the lines about

*Figure 4.54. The evening reception in the 1935 production of* Woe to Wit: *both levels of the set were used, whereas the upper was evidently not in the first production in 1928.*

*Figures 4.55–4.58. Makeup sketches by Aleksandr Kostomolotskii for* Woe to Wit *(1928).*
*Figure 4.55. Famusov (Ilinskii): the inscription, signed by Meyerhold, reads, "I very*
*much like the wig, the face too."    Figure 4.56. Repetilov (Nikolai Sibiriak).    Figure 4.57.*
*Khlestova (Serebrianikova).    Figure 4.58. A hussar.*

Chatsky's madness are always delivered in the full heat of the ball—so deliver them motionless, seated at table." [28] If this were not in itself a sufficiently dehumanizing effect, when Chatsky appeared on the opposite side of the table from them, all the society people began to chew with brutal appetite, as if grinding his fate between unfeeling jaws (fig. 4.59).

The hero of Griboedov's play lends himself to an almost Hamletian variety of interpretations, and even the two conceptions of the role in Meyerhold's two productions of 1928 and 1935 were quite different. In a review of a traditional mounting of the play in 1930 at the Malyi Theater, Moscow, Lunacharsky cited the innovative traits already introduced for Chatsky by Meyerhold two years before:

*It has been customary almost everywhere to see Chatsky as leading man and lover, attractive as usual; only the caprice of an eccentric author had endowed him with a strong admixture of boring preachment. The dullness of his moralizing had to be overcome by an unusually agreeable actor's baritone and a pathetic manner of declaiming, accentuated by clutching the breast. Meyerhold has already changed all that in his remarkable, though somehow insufficiently finished presentation of* Woe to Wit. *His Chatsky, as you recall, was an ineffectual rich man's son,* not of this world, a pale dreamer, a musician and gentle soul like Lensky [Onegin's friend in Pushkin's greatest work].[29]

Indeed, Chatsky was played in 1928 by Garin, a slight slender youth whose highly mobile features and near dancer's skill of movement, so satirically used for Khlestakov in Meyerhold's *Inspector General,* were contrasted with Molchalin's self-satisfied good looks. The scene of their dialogue, each placed with architectural symmetry facing the audience beside a column at dead center, was generally admitted to be another high point of the first production (fig. 4.60).

In Meyerhold's second production of *Woe to Wit* the role of Chatsky was played by Mikhail Tsarev, who had shortly before joined the Meyerhold Theater to play Armand Duval, Marguerite's lover in *Camille.* His manly beauty lent persuasiveness and weight to the political revolutionary emphasis Meyerhold had intended for the part. Sophie in the revival was played by A. Kheraskova, not, as in the first production, by Meyerhold's wife, Zinaida Raikh, who had been criticized as too mature and sexually appealing for the part of a young girl. Ilinskii as the first Famusov was replaced by Petr Starkovskii. Doubtless Rudnitskii is right that at least these last two replacements weakened the show.

However, Rudnitskii concedes that the second Molchalin, played by Gennadii Michurin, gained by a more active interpretation. True, only if Molchalin has some stature—and in the handbook *Amplua aktera* Meyerhold ascribed to the role the importance of "second lover"—does the fascination Sophie feels for her father's secretary become comprehensible. Rudnitskii quotes in support of his praise the criticism D. S. Mirsky gave Meyerhold's second production in *Literaturnaia gazeta* (24 September 1935), for Mirsky there perceived the new meaning gained by the role: "Molchalin becomes the synthetic embodiment of the whole Russian bureaucracy" (Rudnitskii, p. 392). This is the breadth of meaning which Meyerhold extended to the whole society of which the careerist Molchalin is a part, and he achieved it without the obvious signal of benighted candlelight used in Gogol's play.

In the elegant bright light of Griboedov's aristocracy Meyerhold again satirized the ruling class. However, as Rudnitskii makes clear, satire was no longer sufferable in the realistic thirties. This climate of opinion largely explains the negative criticism which one of Meyerhold's most important productions received in the Soviet press of the Stalinist decade. Though *Woe to Wit* as revived in 1935 partook of the mastery typical of Meyerhold's late work,

rather than the experimentation of his early and middle periods, this made it only the more admirable. Even Lunacharsky used Meyerhold's show as the yardstick by which to measure the traditional production of *Woe from Wit* at the Malyi in 1930, which he praised by calling it "worthy to be placed alongside Meyerhold's." [30] So the memorable productions of Griboedov's classic today inevitably hark back to the precedent of Meyerhold's great *Woe to Wit*. Both recent reinterpretations of *Woe from Wit,* one at the Malyi (1963), the other at the Leningrad Gorky Theater (1962), while faithful to the classic text, show complete awareness of Meyerhold's inventive reading of it.

After exposing old-regime corruption in two productions of the classics, Meyerhold staged *The Bedbug* (1929), which the author, Mayakovsky, had intended as an "exposure of petit-bourgeois vulgarity today" (fig. 4.61). A decade after *Mystery-Bouffe,* "the first revolutionary play," Mayakovsky and Meyerhold again joined forces to produce *The Bedbug,* the first Soviet classic. Mayakovsky delightedly reported how the hero of *The Bedbug* soon became folk legend: on a trolley he overheard one comrade annihilate another with the invective, "You scum, you bedbug out of Mayakovsky!' " [31] To be sure, Prisypkin's name has not become folk legend to the same extent as that of Osip Bender, Ilf and Petrov's

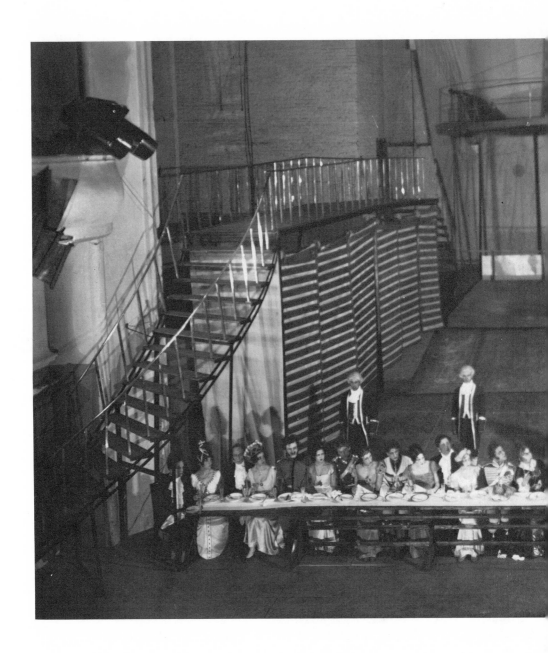

*Figure 4.59.* Woe to Wit: *Chatsky stands alone.*

*Figure 4.60.*  Woe to Wit: left, *Chatsky, and* right, *Molchalin (Mikhail Mukhin), in symmetrical juxtaposition, rivals before Sophie's door*

*Figure 4.61.  Mayakovsky's poster for* The Bedbug *(1929). The text reads, "Hurry to see*
The Bedbug. *There's a line at the box office and a crowd inside. Only don't get mad*
*at the bug's antics; they touch* NOT YOU *but your neighbor."*

*Figure 4.62.* The Bedbug:
*Prisypkin (Ilinskii)*

*Figure 4.63.* The Bedbug:
*Rosalie Renaissance (Serebrianikova),
doing comparative shopping
for herring*

epitome of the opportunist, perhaps because early in the get-rich-quick process Prisypkin changes his name to the more elegant "Pierre Scripkin," with a sound like violin music (fig. 4.62).

Prisypkin abandons not only his real name but also his working-class origins, thanks to the bourgeois machinations of Rosalie Renaissance, owner of a beauty parlor (fig. 4.63), who persuades him to marry her daughter Elzevira for the Party card he will bring into the business. However, the wedding feast, held in the beauty parlor, ends in a drunken brawl in which fire breaks out and destroys the premises. All are lost save Prisypkin, who is fortuitously preserved in the deepfreeze resulting from the firemen's hoses. In the second half of the play, which takes place fifty years later, Prisypkin is defrosted, but due to his deplorable bourgeois tastes of 1929, finds himself wholly isolated and misunderstood in the purified, perfect communism of 1979. Unfortunately, Prisypkin's addiction to alcohol and tobacco and his love of jazz and the romantic are infectious even in the brave new world, and he is finally confined in a cage at the zoo where, a unique exemplar of an extinct species, "petit bourgeois vulgaris," he serves as habitat for another unique surviving specimen of the bourgeois past, the common bedbug.

Undoubtedly Mayakovsky was the greatest Russian writer whose entire canon Meyerhold might claim to have created in the theater. Actually Meyerhold did more, for not only did he stage all three plays of enduring interest by Mayakovsky, it was he who cajoled this first revolutionary dramatist into writing *The Bedbug,* possibly the greatest of his plays. The juxtaposition of the bourgeois and communist worlds, which remains abstract in *Mystery-Bouffe,* is made concrete in *The Bedbug*. Sets for the first part of the play, which caricatures the unregenerate bourgeois of 1929, were designed by a team of newspaper cartoonists, the Kukryniksy (figs. 4.64–4.70), while the second part, with its picture of the communist world of 1979 as it appeared to the popular imagination, was designed by the constructivist Aleksandr Rodchenko (figs. 4.71–4.73). Of course, the second part allows a rich ambiguity of interpretation. To Western eyes it seems as much a satire of an unendurably rationalized future as Aldous Huxley's *Brave New World;* but it was intended, according to Fevralskii, as "a parody of petit bourgeois notions about the future" (*Desiat let,* p. 68). In the Western view Prisypkin's all-too-human tastes make him the only likable being in a drearily sanitized world, and as the house lights go on just before the end, revealing the audience to him, he appeals to the audience from the confinement of his cage as to his brothers. Yet Meyerhold was preparing a revision of

*Figure 4.64. The Kukryniksy, designers of the first half of* The Bedbug, *which takes place in the caricatured bourgeois world:* left to right: *Mikhail Kupriianov, Porfirii Krylov, and Nikolai Sokolov*

part 2 in 1936 which was to make the bourgeoisie unambiguously the target of attack. From the Western point of view one must be grateful that the revision was not completed and the intended revival went no further than the rehearsal of two scenes from part 2, the dormitory and wedding scenes.

Meyerhold mounted Mayakovsky's play, as usual, under interesting musical auspices. Having turned first in vain to

Prokofiev, who was much occupied at this time—his ballet *Le Pas d'Acier* having just been staged by Diaghilev (1927)—Meyerhold commissioned the music for *The Bedbug* from Dmitrii Shostakovich, then at the start of his career and serving as pianist in the Meyerhold Theater. Shostakovich's music, of which there were several numbers as well as an orchestral interlude used between the two parts of the

*Figures 4.65–4.68.  Costume sketches by the Kukryniksy for* The Bedbug.    *Figure 4.65.*
*Vendor of cheap books (scene 1).*

*Figure 4.66. Vendor of fur bras (scene 1)*

*Figure 4.67. Baian, instructor in etiquette and ballroom dancing (played by Aleksei Temerin)*

*Figure 4.68.  Elzevira Renaissance*

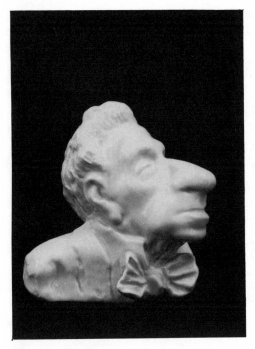 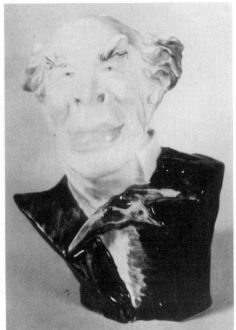

*Figures 4.69–4.70. Caricature busts by the Kukryniksy.    Figure 4.69. Meyerhold.*
*Figure 4.70. Stanislavsky.*

*Figure 4.71. Prisypkin displayed in a cage at the zoo as a "contagious contaminator* [porazitelnyi parazit]" *in scene 9 of* The Bedbug.   *Figure 4.72. Shostakovich and Meyerhold in 1928.*

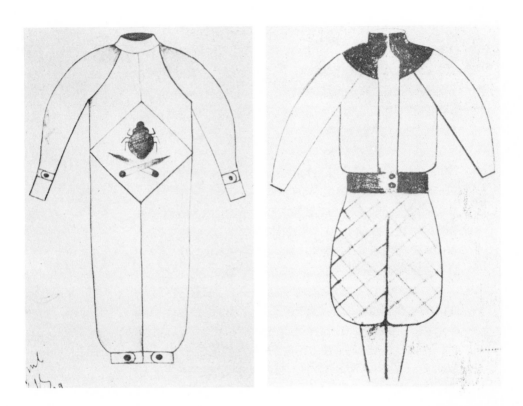

*Figure 4.73–4.74. Costume designs by Aleksandr Rodchenko for the world of the future in* The Bedbug

*Figure 4.75. Preserved of Dmitrii Shostakovich's music for* The Bedbug *was the "Pioneer [Boy Scout] March" for the world of the future.*

play, is said to have been lost, though this seems either inexcusable or implausible (figs. 4.74–4.75.) The verse passages of Mayakovsky's text, such as the vendors' cries in the first scene, were set to music: the peddlers of automatic snap-on snaps, unbreakable glue, and fur bras went down the aisles, crying their wares amidst the audience to musical accompaniment. Such merging with the audience from the start created potential sympathy with Prisypkin's final appeal for human imperfection and therefore antipathy toward the decontaminated future of glass and metal —involuntarily one recalls Dostoevsky's similar rejection of the nineteenth-century glass palace.

Mayakovsky's *Bathhouse* (1930), the only new play produced at the Meyerhold Theater the following year, unambiguously satirizes communism, at least the communist bureaucracy's suppression of inventiveness and initiative (figs. 4.76–4.79). Again the world of the future serves as the yardstick by which to measure the imperfections of today. An inventor has devised a machine for launching the present generation ahead in time as a rocket is launched into space. Meyerhold sketched projects for the constructivist stage picture of the launching, with platforms at several levels and connecting stairs, and designs for the costume of the Phosphorescent Lady of the future. These were realized by the

designers, Sergei Vakhtangov, son of the theater director and architect of the new Meyerhold Theater building, and Aleksandr Deineka, an artist well known in the Soviet Union. The music, though composed by Vissarion Shebalin, who collaborated perhaps better and certainly more often with Meyerhold than did any other composer, is said to have made the text inaudible. Of course, inaudibility of the lines is particularly regrettable when the poet's words are thought to be especially fine. At least once, in the scene of Pobedonosikov's self-scrutiny, Mayakovsky's wit was used only topically in a polemic against enemy literary and theatrical trends of the time. His parody of a propaganda pageant is only remotely funny today, like the parody of a Restoration fop or a Wildean dandy, which may only slightly amuse a modern audience. The post-Stalinist production of *The Bathhouse* (1953) by Valentin Pluchek, director of the Theater of Satire (who had played Momentalnikov in Meyerhold's original production), simply omitted these scenes.

Still, however topical certain allusions were, Mayakovsky's stand opposing the aesthetics of realism continues valid. Meyerhold too remained true to constructivism both in his suggestions for the set and his representation of the Phosphorescent Lady in a space-age constructivist costume, which was criticized for its nonrealism (fig. 4.80).

*Figure 4.76. The Kukryniksy's poster for* The Bathhouse *(1930) shows the bureaucrat Pobedonosikov (played by Mikhail Shtraukh) in the pose of a leader with the forbidding slogan on upraised hands, "I can't see you without an appointment." Three weapons appended to him defend his authority: telephones or dictaphones (three in number), his briefcase of documents, and an enormous fountain pen.*

*Figure 4.77. The constructivist set for* The Bathhouse *also shows slogans, movable like the slats of a Venetian blind.*

*Figure 4.78.*  The Bathhouse: left, *real people—the inventor and his assistant—are refused help by the bureaucrat, Mr. Optimist (Zaichikov), from the world of unreal paper work. Note the petitioners,* right, *wooden mannequins.*

*Figure 4.79.*  The Bathhouse: *the bureaucrat, Mr. Optimist, prizing paper documents*

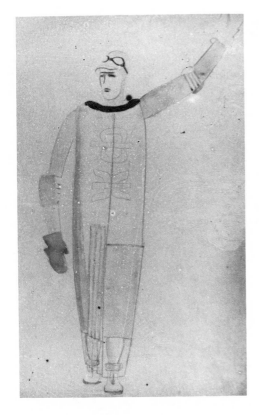

Pluchek rectified this interpretation in his recent production by making an un-exceptionally realistic figure of today out of this ideal of future Soviet woman-hood. Doubtless the first lukewarm re-ception of *The Bathhouse* was due not so much to faults of Meyerhold's produc-tion as to increasing Stalinist insistence in 1930 on a realism contrary to Maya-kovsky's and Meyerhold's incorruptible aesthetics. The changed climate of opinion is one reason often adduced for Mayakovsky's suicide (1930), which deprived the Meyerhold Theater of its major Soviet playwright.

The undoubted dwindling in both the number and the success of Meyerhold's productions at this time must be ascribed less to the failure of his powers than to the increasingly difficult plight of the arts under Stalinism. The number of his productions forbidden presents sad testimony to the growing repression. In particular, problem plays produced at the Meyerhold Theater either never opened or did not remain long on the boards; examples are Tretiakov's *I Want a Child* (1927–30), Erdman's *Suicide* (1932), and Iurii Olesha's *List of Assets* (1931). Even produc-tions of the classics, to which Meyer-hold resorted almost entirely in his last five years, proved not wholly a safe way out. Apparently even the straight re-cre-ation of a classic work did not always receive official support, for Meyerhold had to announce to Golovin the impos-

*Figure 4.80. One of Aleksandr Deineka's costume sketches for* The Bathhouse; *the initials on the front identify the Phosphorescent Lady (played by Raikh).*

sibility of their project to collaborate on Aleksandr Dargomyzhskii's opera *The Stone Guest,* based on Pushkin's play.[32]

Nor did heroic plays, three of which entered the repertory of the Meyerhold Theater in as many years, escape criticism; they were blamed for overemphasizing the tragic or underlining individual conflict. Thus Ilia Selvinskii's heroic verse play *Commander of the Second Army* (1929), which returned for its subject to the Civil War of the early twenties, is criticized by Rostotskii for its depressing tragic end and for the overly complicated introspection of its un-Bolshevist intellectual hero, Okonnyi. In his portrayal of a leader who, despite his success in battle, is executed for unauthorized seizure of power, the author meant to show, as Fevralskii quotes him, "the problem of the leader and the masses, of self-designated ideological authority, of technology versus the poetic impulse, the clash of bourgeois revolutionary ideals with proletarian goals, the confrontation of the erring genius with a mediocre but competent functionary, the development of socialism as revolutionary feasibility, and so on" (*Desiat let,* p. 69).

If Meyerhold simplified and sharpened the issues and appreciably reduced the many long monologues, he did so in order to get this first play by a promising young author onto the boards. Meyerhold's defense of the play before the Artistic Political Council of the

Theater gives some idea of the nature of the council's opposition: "I have become involved with this play because it will bring fresh air to our stage. We will get at last a text in a perfectly astonishing language. We have no tragedy in our repertory—this is an attempt to create a tragedy, a real tragedy . . ." (*Articles,* 2:180). And, Meyerhold continued at a later meeting of the council, "We must not lose Selvinskii as a playwright. . . . Are we so rich in playwrights then? We must save Selvinskii for the theater. Where will he learn? Do you think a dramatist learns when you send his play back to him, especially if you tell him his play is badly written? [Dramatists] learn by experiencing the reactions of an audience, reading the criticism of the press, hearing different points of view at discussions of the play" (ibid., 2:181).

After the production Meyerhold congratulated the theater on bringing to the stage still another of those strong young poets who considered the proletariat capable of understanding the great problems of their time and who did not feel obliged to talk down to the "people" and "enlighten" them. Of course, Meyerhold's furtherance of young playwrights was not only advantageous to the "people" and to the writers themselves but also essential in supplying the very life blood of the theater, new plays.

The stage set for *Commander of the Second Army* was a construction de-

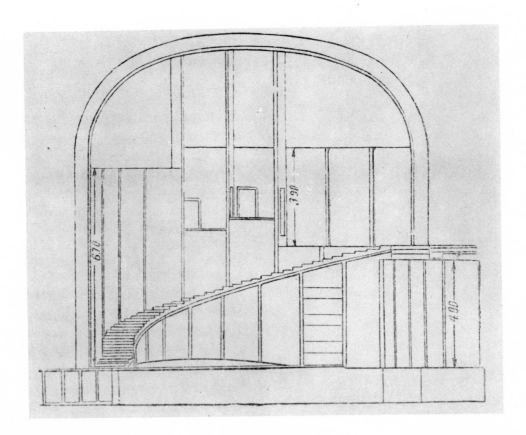

*Figure 4.81. The set for* Commander of the Second Army *(1929)*

*Figure 4.82.* Commander of the Second Army: *the discussion meeting scene, showing the full sweep of the set with two landings*

signed by Sergei Vakhtangov (fig. 4.81). A high semicircular wall formed the background, along with a wall mounted from left to right along a curving stair with two small platforms or landings (fig. 4.82). This gave the production a broad sweep, against which the crowd scenes were most impressive, among them the meeting in the steppe, the interlude "War," which Meyerhold devised without immediate plot connection but in the sense of the play's large theme, and the final scene in which the sentry sings a sad little song. Fevralskii's description concludes: "The powerful reading in chorus on the one hand, and lyric speech and singing on the other, the wide and rhythmic scope of motion all found support in the lively and emphatic music of V. Shebalin and the typically Meyerholdian musical structure of the whole production" (*Desiat let,* p. 72).

In his production of Selvinskii's play Meyerhold insisted on showing the hero's execution on stage: "In this we must learn from the Japanese Kabuki theater and not think the audience so sentimental that it must tremble at a shot" (*Articles,* 2:182). So Meyerhold pushed in the direction of restoring seventeenth-century horror effects to the stage, a trend which has gone still further today under Artaud's misunderstood slogan "Theater of Cruelty."

The last play of 1929 produced at the Meyerhold Theater, Aleksandr Bezy-menskii's *Shot,* was staged not by Meyerhold himself but by four of his pupils under his supervision. One would therefore like to exculpate him from this potboiler, which reads like a parody of Soviet propaganda. Against opposition from at least four villains—a power-seeker, a bureaucrat, an infamous foreign engineer, and a band of hooligans—the play spares no hindrances on the way to achieving its uninspired goal, the construction of a trolley car. Just as catholic in its deployment of artistic as of propagandistic devices, it uses a revolving stage, a quick episodic scene, direct address of the audience, and audience involvement in celebrating the final triumph of good over evil; it resorts to movies, motion, and music for establishing leitmotivs, and the lines are even in doggerel verse. Fevralskii claims for the production a political effectiveness of which the Meyerhold Theater had great need now that it had come under attack: "The manner in which the play and the production were constructed gave the upswing, the electrical charge of class motivation and alertness so essential to us all in everyday work; it was a bold, courageous, sometimes even daring and brash production, a challenge to work indefatigably and to carry on the class struggle" (*Desiat let,* p. 77). If indeed the production achieved such brilliant results with such shabby material, then Meyerhold need never have apologized for

"Meyerholdianism," the abuse by others of his bag of tricks.

Like *Commander of the Second Army,* Vsevolod Vishnevskii's *Last Decisive Battle* (1931) was a heroic representation, this time not of the already legendary past, the Civil War, but of a possible imperialist attack in the future. As in *D.E.,* the contrast was underlined between Western decadence and Soviet discipline, only this time with a tragic ending: all twenty-seven men of a Navy unit die blocking the invasion. This early play of Vishnevskii's, which was largely filled in from a scenario during rehearsal, as Garin testifies in *Encounters,* points ahead to the same author's outstanding success with *An Optimistic Tragedy* (1932), staged a year later by Tairov. The film version (1963) of the later success even borrowed the effective ending used in Meyerhold's earlier piece: the device—unusual on the screen—of a direct address to the audience. Meyerhold is said to have outdone himself in the effectiveness of the ending of *The Last Decisive Battle:* before every member of the little unit had died in the vainly heroic holding action, the last man, dying, managed to chalk up on the blackboard the figure of the total Soviet population minus the twenty-seven of the unit's dead, thus showing how many millions would soon join those few in resisting invasion. Against a background of real blanks fired from machine guns at the audience the an-swering cannon blasts from the balcony had to be toned down. One shot was still used by the lone survivor to silence at the last moment a radio, on which in almost too pointed contrast a jazz song by Maurice Chevalier had been heard. In the sense, then, of "an optimistic tragedy" the dying man admonished the millions who would win victory in his stead: "Don't surrender. Arise, comrades . . ."

Iurii Olesha's *List of Assets* (1931), Meyerhold's other production of the same year by a Soviet author (fig. 4.83), was unfortunately not so straightforward in its final charge to the audience. The heroine Elena Goncharova, a successful Soviet actress, has the intellectual maturity to find faults as well as virtues in the Soviet system. Unfortunately, while playing in Paris, she is threatened with the publication of her notebook, in which she has all too naively kept a written list of the debits and credits of Soviet society. Once caught in the net of Western corruption she finds no difficulty in opting for communism: she joins a Marxist street demonstration, in which she is killed by a stray police bullet. But her tragic end seems only a dramatic solution rather than a true resolution of her doubts. Her final atonement seems a matter of chance and individual fate which does not particularly serve the cause of the proletarian revolution, whereas her hesitations, still unrefuted at the end,

*Figure 4.83. Eric Mordmillovich's caricature of Meyerhold and Iurii Olesha (1931)*

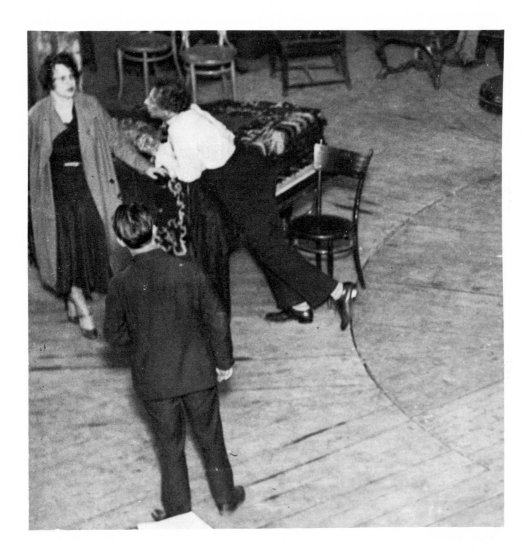

*Figure 4.84. Meyerhold rehearsing with Raikh in* A List of Assets *(1931), as if to draw from her one of the fine performances she is said to have given especially at the end of her career*

can be generalized for the intelligentsia as a whole.

*A List of Assets* was sharply criticized on ideological grounds and soon dropped from the repertory despite fine performances by such leading actors as Raikh, Mikhail Shtraukh, Bogoliubov, Zaichikov, and Sergei Martinson (fig. 4.84). The author Olesha in a preproduction article, "The Theme of the Intellectual" (1930), had announced his intention of exposing, above all, the impossibility of life in Europe: "The theme of the play is 'The European spirit,' if you can put it thus." [33] And Meyerhold in his preparatory discussion with the cast listed reasons—"unemployment, depression, competition for markets"—why the European powder barrel must soon explode and be destroyed (*Articles*, 2:253). Yet for many viewers the play was reminiscent of an actual instance of an intellectual's opting for the West: the actor Mikhail Chekhov was then spending his third year abroad with no return to the USSR.

Meyerhold evidently meant to present both sides of the case, not just to caricature negatively viewed European figures. He demanded that the role of the émigré journalist Tatarov, for example, be created as at the Art Theater with a past and an "address." Nevertheless, on the whole the play was apparently pushed toward the melodrama which it inherently is (figs. 4.85–4.86). The actress Sukhanova, who under-

studied Raikh for the lead, mentions the projectors turned on Tatarov when he villainously steals Goncharova's notebook. And Goncharova's audition before Marzheret, consisting of excerpts from *Hamlet* accompanied by what amounted to a ballet of movements for manipulating a cape, ends in an offer insulting to a lady and great artist (figs. 4.87–4.93). All in all, the Meyerhold Theater was taking on a more romantic tone. Far from abandoning a persistent theme, though, *A List of Assets* showed the same conflict between the capitalist West and Soviet communism as did most of Meyerhold's productions from *Mystery-Bouffe* and *D.E.* on. Only the tone changed in the thirties, from ironic-satiric to tragic-heroic.

In an explication Meyerhold underlined another feature of his production of *A List of Assets* which was to become characteristic of his sets in the early thirties, a means of escape from the confinement of the proscenium arch: "I don't like having to design all our shows frontally; that is, the stage is always squared off, facing squarely forward so that you feel: Everything is symmetrical and parallel" (*Articles*, 2:250–51). In *A List of Assets*, then, as in *Commander of the Second Army* and *Camille* (1934), Meyerhold used a diagonal set. This allowed the audience a sense of seeing the production as if from the wings and freed the actors

*Figures 4.85–4.86. Caricatures of exploitation under Western capitalism in* A List of Assets. *Figure 4.85. The little man in the guise of Chaplin (V. Maltsev). Figure 4.86. The predatory manager (Mikhail Shtraukh).*

*Figures 4.87–4.93. Drawings by Boris Kelberer of the cape exercises which Goncharova (Raikh) uses in her role as Hamlet in* A List of Assets

*Figures 4.88–4.91*

*Figures 4.92–4.93*

from "posing," since they were observed from the side. With this last innovation Meyerhold seemingly reversed his principle that the actor must remain always conscious of the pose.

Like *The Last Decisive Battle* and *A List of Assets,* Iurii German's *Prelude* (1933) also ends tragically. In this the play departs from the novel, the young author's first success, which Meyerhold commissioned him to adapt for the stage. German described more vividly than any other memoirist in *Encounters* the origin of a play under Meyerhold's guidance: after the failure of German's novice try at a stage version Meyerhold himself took over, helping him to write the play which would be the last work by a Soviet author produced at the Meyerhold Theater. Again, Meyerhold insisted on the castigation of the West as the key idea. The play has a double story line: the German engineer Kelberg after an assignment in China becomes so disillusioned with the exploitation of the masses under capitalism that he goes to the Soviet Union to work with the people for the people. Likewise, the German workman Hanzke, deprived of his job thanks to an invention of Kelberg's, emigrates to find work in the Soviet Union. The play omits the novel's third part, which shows the further life of the two men in the USSR, concentrating rather on two tragic scenes in Europe. At a reunion of engineers, Nunbach, Kelberg's un-

employed colleague, commits suicide: in the Meyerhold production, a final close-up in the spotlight showed Nunbach confronting a monumental bust of the great humanist, Goethe, with the question why an engineer must descend to selling pornographic postcards instead of fulfilling his true vocation as a builder of houses (fig. 4.94).

In the other climactic scene Hanzke was also shown at a turning point, the funeral of his son, whose death has been caused by the bad working conditions at the factory that employed him. The spotlight again seized a close-up of a face distorted by sorrow and protest. A victim of the middle class, Hanzke saw himself in a mirror ridiculously decked out in the bourgeois funeral uniform of tall hat and tail coat, whereupon he tore off the garb of the enemy class (fig. 4.95). Not only the director's ideas of bust and mirror, but also the music composed by Shebalin, again no mere accompaniment, added comment and emphasis.

After the four "heroic tragedies" of the years 1929 to 1933, *Commander of the Second Army, The Last Decisive Battle, A List of Assets,* and *Prelude,* Meyerhold turned to four productions of the classics in his remaining years of work (1933–37). In his comments on the first of these, Sukhovo-Kobylin's *Marriage of Krechinskii* (1933), he declared that his revision was much

*Figures 4.94–4.95.* Prelude.   *Figure 4.94.  The engineer Nunbach (Lev Sverdlin) confronts Goethe.*

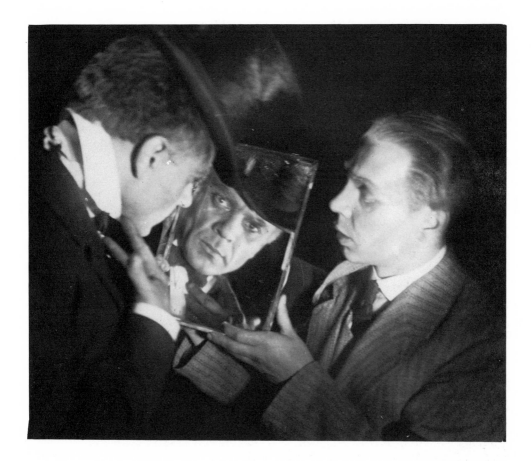

*Figure 4.95. The worker Hanzke (Nikolai Bogoliubov) confronts himself in the funeral masquerade of the enemy class.*

less drastic than those in the twenties of *The Inspector General* and *Woe from Wit.* The play was not divided into brief episodes, though the acts were subdivided into scenes for which titles and Meyerhold's "stage directions" were shown on a white curtain lowered at the start of each.

Further, Meyerhold took a fresh look at Krechinskii, viewing him as typical of the nineteenth-century upper classes, and so added nonspeaking characters of the same sort, his "fellow-conspirators." The wealth Krechinskii conspired to achieve by a rich marriage was to be spent solely in enjoyment, and Meyerhold found this attitude typical of his class as described in Marx's essay "Money": "The example of Krechinskii, as shaped by Sukhovo-Kobylin and pointed up in our thoroughly revised dramatic material, will show the difference between the importance assigned to money in the capitalist and the socialist system. *The Marriage of Krechinskii* reveals not just the conflict of persons in society, but the tragedy of people concerned with money, connected with money for the sake of money, in the name of money" (*Articles,* 2:265). Krechinskii's helper, Raspliuev, a mere comic-relief figure in the original, was interpreted in Meyerhold's production to suggest the sinister police spy he becomes in the last play of the trilogy, *The Death of Tarelkin.* To mention *Tarelkin* is to recall Meyer-

hold's impudent 1922 production and to measure the distance traversed by the Meyerhold Theater in the decade between the two productions from the trilogy. But then the changes in twentieth-century history were equally great: Meyerhold mentioned, in connection with Raspliuev, the rise of fascism, which came to power that year in Germany.

Obviously Meyerhold still sought authority for his interpretation of a play, though in political ideas rather than in the artistic sources he had drawn on before the Revolution. If Marx supplied justification for the key idea of Krechinskii, it was Lenin whom Meyerhold invoked in support of his conception of *Camille,* by Alexandre Dumas fils (1934): "Liadov tells in his recollections of Lenin how Lenin and [his wife] Krupskaia both saw a performance of *Camille* in Geneva. And when during the play Liadov turned toward Lenin, who was sitting in the depths of the box, he saw that Ilich was embarrassedly wiping away a tear. It isn't hard to guess the cause of Lenin's tears at this play. He saw in it artistic confirmation of the enslavement of women under capitalism" (*Articles,* 2:285).

From this somewhat contorted justification by authority for choosing *Camille,* Meyerhold went on to formulate the purpose of his production and the "charge" it was intended to carry for the audience: "In producing Dumas fils's *Camille* we raise the question of the attitude toward women in our country, and the attitude toward them in capitalist countries. Audiences which have seen our play will fight with greater obstinacy to maintain the new way of life, to strengthen the new morality, that very communist morality of which Lenin often spoke" (*Articles,* 2:286). Yet Meyerhold only stressed in his production the author's meaning; as Dumas wrote in his preface of 1867, "En refusant à la vertu le droit d'être un capital, vous avez donné au vice le droit d'en être un" ("By denying virtue the right to have value as capital, you have given value as capital to vice").[34]

Meyerhold changed the period of the play from the mid-century of Dumas's original to the seventies. This change of emphasis could hardly have been made for purposes of ideology but was due instead to Meyerhold's preference for the rich artistic background of the later time. He mounted his production with the help of paintings by Manet and Renoir and descriptions by Flaubert, insisting the while that this "helped us strengthen the play's social significance" (*Articles,* 2:286). He revised the text, he said, with the same aim, inserting a Flaubertian personage and restoring to the play Marguerite's monologue "Confessions of a Courtesan" taken from the novel *Camille,* from which Dumas himself had derived his stage adaptation. The revision was not evident as such,

however, and Meyerhold was charged with inconsistency for drastically revising some plays while leaving others like *Camille* untouched. He denied the charge: "I re-worked *Camille* very considerably, only I succeeded in doing it so artfully that the basting stitches of the revision are not easy to find" (ibid., 2:351). Nor did the setting attract attention as anything but beautiful; with it Meyerhold reverted to his prerevolutionary practice of using materials of elegance and expensive authenticity (figs. 4.96–4.100). But despite the success Meyerhold achieved with audiences, thanks to the rich background of *Camille,* he was criticized for investing too much luxury in a superficial play.

Meyerhold was further accused of choosing this classic "vehicle" for the sake of the rewarding role it afforded Zinaida Raikh, his wife, who played Marguerite. The vast amount of work done on the role by director and actress led to doubtless the best performance of Raikh's career (fig. 4.101). Leonid Varpakhovskii, then secretary of the Meyerhold Theater, who took notes on Meyerhold's last productions in complicated transcription, also remarks the research Meyerhold did, not only in art and literature, but also in the theater history of Marguerite's role as played by Eleanora Duse and Sarah Bernhardt. Varpakhovskii attributes to Duse a moment at the beginning of the last act which Meyerhold reused.

*Figures 4.96–4.100. Ivan Leistikov's sketches for* Camille *(1934).* *Figure 4.96. Act 2.*
*Figure 4.97. Act 4.*

*Figure 4.98. St.-Gaudens (Vasilii Zaichikov) and Olympia (S.I. Subbotina).   Figure 4.99.*
*Marguerite (Raikh).   Figure 4.100. Gaston (Mikhail Sadovskii).*

Shortly before her death Marguerite reads aloud the letter in which Armand's father has promised to send Armand back to her: in the Meyerhold version she gradually put down the letter while continuing to recite the words, thus showing that she had reread it so often as to know it by heart. Other gestures of the role were cool and subtle in the same manner, not melodramatic and sentimental.

In the music, which Meyerhold commissioned from Shebalin, he also sought contrast, not emphasis. At the evening supper, for example, when Armand joins Marguerite's gay circle for the first time, some slightly off-color verses by Pierre-Jean de Béranger set to Shebalin's music gave ironic counterpoint to Armand's fresh, pure love for Marguerite. Again, for the end of the same scene, Meyerhold gave Shebalin most detailed specifications for music in contrast to the action. Here the whole worldly company, donning bits of Spanish costume, joined in a mock masquerade, against which the music of a genuine Breton folk song was heard. The set for this scene was designed on the diagonal, giving Marguerite a greater distance to traverse when she made her first appearance, whip in hand, driving her harnessed suitors across the stage. In return for the great amount of thought and rehearsal expended, *Camille* ran for 725 performances. Indeed it was on the bill for the last evening performance before the enforced closure of the Meyerhold Theater on 8 January 1938.

Not merely the chance of history, however, lends *Camille* a certain finality; its merits as well rightly place it at the end of Meyerhold's career. Certain details of inventiveness from *Camille* are memorable. For example, Meyerhold foreshadowed in act 3 the moment in act 4 when Armand Duval publicly slanders Marguerite by showering her with bank notes: "You have sold your heart like a piece of merchandise. . . ." Meyerhold prepared for this an earlier contrasting moment when, during their brief idyllic respite in the country, Armand showered her with rose petals. Just such rhythm of parallels and contrasts "in strict subordination to theme" caused Eisenstein in his *Rezhissura* (A Director's Handbook, 1934) to use *Camille* as a model of "how with absolute strictness to coordinate space and meaning in the composition of separate scenes in a production." [35]

Meyerhold made a virtue of necessity when, to gain space, he composed most of the scenes in *Camille* on the diagonal, a solution, Eisenstein felt, which came from "longing for the large dimension of a theater with a wide proscenium. Let us not forget the proscenium of the Zon Theater," Eisenstein reminded readers, "where Meyerhold realized his whole epos of the Revolution years. Let us not forget either that under these

*Figure 4.101. Armand (Tsarev) and Marguerite (Raikh) in act 4, scene 3, of* Camille

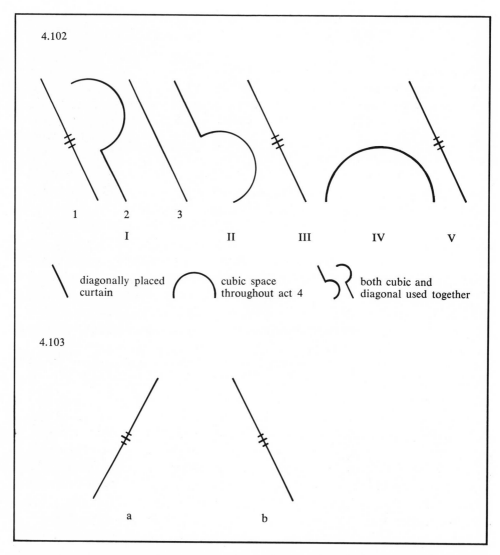

*Figure 4.102. Eisenstein's scheme of the sets for* Camille. *Figure 4.103. Eisenstein's alternative diagram for act 3 of* Camille. *He suggested substituting* a *for* b *to avoid confusing the onlooker, who would not at first realize, when confronted by a diagonal wall with a window in act 3, that he was outdoors (the scene in the country), not, as in acts 1 and 5, indoors, where a similar wall with a window indicated Marguerite's Paris apartment.*

conditions he used almost without exception a frontal stage picture (*Dawns, Cuckold,* the ball in *Woe from Wit* with its long dinner table parallel to the footlights, the shots fired straight into the audience in *The Last Decisive Battle*)." The diagonal rather than frontal presentation of scenes in *Camille* resulted in sets for which Eisenstein made diagrams (fig. 4.102). "From the simple combination of these figures a superb classic rhythm in alternation of space resulted: the diagonal was used in odd-numbered acts, cubic in the even-numbered ones." [36] Eisenstein further pointed to repetition in up- and down-stage blocking to emphasize parallelism in lyric moments, and to the use of height in crises: just as Armand declaimed his love poem from a height in the second scene, so in act 4 he hurled the money at Marguerite from the height of stairs.

Though Eisenstein was doubtless right in criticizing the set Meyerhold used for act 3, the idyll in the country, it does not follow that Eisenstein's own plan for a substitute background (fig. 4.103) is the right solution. Quite rightly Eisenstein objected that if a curtain with a wide central window denoted an interior in acts 1 and 5, then a similar curtain with a similar window in act 3 could hardly be taken to denote an exterior wall and an outdoor scene. Almost schematically, it seems, Eisenstein suggested that at this turning

point of the play the opposite diagonal in the first half of the act might indeed give a different impression of outdoors and might yield in the middle of the act to a change of scene indoors with the coming of the father, indicated by the same constant diagonal used before. Despite his preference for a different setting for act 3 Eisenstein lauded Meyerhold for masterfully underlining the theme in a wholly formal rhythm of scene changes.

Like *Camille,* Meyerhold's next production—three one-act plays by Chekhov (1935)—brought up the question whether such light pieces were worth the effort (fig. 4.104). Meyerhold answered in a *Pravda* article with the claim that the three, *Jubilee, The Bear,* and *The Proposal,* had social significance, while he rejected the major plays of Chekhov as no longer relevant. To emphasize ideology in the first of the three, Meyerhold rearranged the text so as to bring the bank director Shipuchin to the fore and connect him with implications of fraud. In fact, Chekhov had published an article and had written *Jubilee* to point out an actual case of fraud at the Skopinsky bank (fig. 4.105). Further, Meyerhold made the number of comic collapses, which occur frequently in all three plays, their common denominator, calling the production *33 Fainting Fits;* he meant thus to make such collapse symptomatic of the state of the bourgeoisie of the time

*Figure 4.104. Certainly Viktor Shestakov's set for 33* Fainting Fits *(1935), with the usual circular staircase but now writhing nightmarishly in multiple curves, seems somewhat overweighted.*

*Figure 4.105.* The Jubilee: left to right: *Merchutkina (Serebrianikova), Shipuchin (M. Chikul), Chirin (Aleksei Kelberer)*

*Figure 4.106.* The Bear: *Popova (Raikh), Smirnov (Bogoliubov)*

(fig. 4.106). Nevertheless, arguments of social significance, while still admissible for *Camille,* seem farfetched indeed as applied to Chekhov's delightful little comedies. Social satire by means of Gogolian exaggeration and witty use of language, yes, but hardly a pretext for more than a sense of the ridiculous and of universal human comedy.

Of course, as artist and director, Meyerhold was undoubtedly interested also in the devices which he had called in the studio "antics appropriate to the theater." The most prominent of these, the fainting fits, were particularly

emphasized by Shostakovich's music. Viktor Gromov, who played the father in *The Proposal* (fig. 4.107), describes in *Encounters* a brass band at the left of the stage which fanfared the fainting of the men, while stringed instruments at the right intoned for the women; Meyerhold even set up a scoreboard to show the total number of fainting fits.

Gromov also describes the manner of Meyerhold's direction, which had by then become typical of his work with actors, even with such an experienced master as Ilinskii, who rehearsed the suitor's role in *The Proposal*. The director stopped the actor literally at every word and gesture, even when the acting was good, to add suggestions which the actor was to synthesize with his own interpretation of the part. If Meyerhold approved the synthesis, as subsequently verified in a run-through, the painstaking analysis was not repeated. The stenographic records and eyewitness accounts of rehearsals, more plentiful for Meyerhold's last years than for the first, reflect such microscopic treatment of classic roles. The iconoclasm of early shows like *Tarelkin* and *The Forest* was replaced by "the opposite solution," i.e., a detailed reversal of the tradition for every single speech. For example, the proposal of marriage was traditionally recited in a rapid patter to show it had been learned by heart, but Meyerhold changed this treatment: he had Lomov (Ilinskii)

*Figure 4.107.* The Proposal: left to right: *Mashka (Fefer), Chubukov (Viktor Gromov), Lomov (Ilinskii)*

first put on frock coat, gloves, and tall hat, and then, gasping from stage fright, enunciate each word with a swallow of water between. Meyerhold cited Stanislavsky's example and Stanislavsky's term *subtext* during such careful work on the role. Altogether, Meyerhold at this point seemed to hark back to his beginnings in dedicating this production to the seventy-fifth anniversary of Chekhov's birth.

After *33 Fainting Fits,* the Meyerhold Theater's last completed production, several plays were rehearsed which never opened. Two of them were partyline propaganda plays, Lidia Seifulina's *Natasha* and a dramatic version of a heroic biography, that of the Soviet hero Nikolai Ostrovskii, which could only have detracted from Meyerhold's reputation if they had been finished. The other two projected plays showed Meyerhold as single-mindedly devoted to theater art as ever. Both were classics by Pushkin. One, the verse play *Boris Godunov* (1936), would eminently have repaid the minute study it was receiving if only it had been completed. The other, Tschaikovsky's opera after the Pushkin story *Queen of Spades* (1935), was completed at the Malyi Opera Theater, Leningrad.

*The Queen of Spades* provides yet another example of Meyerhold's careful study and rearrangement of a text, aimed this time at reducing the distortions of Modest Tschaikovsky's libretto and bringing the opera closer to the original Pushkin story. Meyerhold, of course, was no novice at producing opera, thanks to a decade of work at the Mariinskii Theater before the Revolution. But, unfortunately, most postrevolutionary work for him in opera had been frustrated. An invitation to serve in 1929 as artistic consultant at the Bolshoi, Moscow, for Shostakovich's opera *The Nose* and Prokofiev's ballet *Le Pas d'Acier* never materialized, and his final directorship at the Stanislavsky Opera Studio (1938–39) ended prematurely with his arrest. However, *The Queen of Spades,* Meyerhold's unique Soviet opera production, deserves to be rescued from the oblivion which has long surrounded it.

As usual, Meyerhold had an important innovation in mind for his production of *The Queen of Spades:* "To satiate the atmosphere of P. I. Tschaikovsky's marvelous music with the ozone of Pushkin's still more wonderful story" (*Articles,* 2:299). Though Tschaikovsky certainly derived his inspiration from Pushkin's classic story of the 1830s, he and his brother, the librettist Modest Tschaikovsky, working at the behest of Ivan Vsevolozhskii, director of the Imperial Theaters, nevertheless created an opera in the lush style of the late nineteenth century. Meyerhold found the key idea of his return to Pushkin in the epigraph to chapter 5 of the original story, a quotation from Swedenborg: "That night the deceased Baroness von B . . . appeared to me. She was all in white and she said to me: 'Good evening, M. Privy Councillor.' " Meyerhold saw in this apparition the synthesis of dream and waking so essential to the story, and he meant to substitute it for the opera's melodramatic exploitation of the supernatural. "What a blunder opera directors of the *Queen of Spades* make when they try to mobilize all possible theater machinery to frighten the audience with the Countess's ghost when she comes to Hermann in his barracks room" (ibid., 2:301). The usual staging reveals the countess in a flash of lightning high on a platform, dressed in her shroud. "So they disturb the whole texture of Pushkin's story," Meyerhold continued, "which so artfully interweaves reality with fantasy" (ibid.). In Meyerhold's version of the fateful card game the countess was merely present instantaneously in the crowded gaming room, as if alive.

Meyerhold changed Modest's libretto, he insisted, only where Petr Ilich gave him the right to do so. Accordingly, the new production did not begin in the park of the Summer Garden with a chorus of nursemaids walking crowds of children in the park amid flirtatious guardsmen. For Petr Ilich had expressed dissatisfaction with this scene in a letter to the grand duke Constantine: "I'm afraid it has turned out a little like cheap musical comedy." The

new production opened in Pushkin's original setting, the gaming room at the cavalry officer Narumov's. Meyerhold reverted to the original in another respect by eliminating Eletskii, Hermann's rival for Liza's love, and her romantic suicide in the end, both inventions of Modest. When the dead countess suddenly appeared, not on high in a clap of thunder, but still more alarmingly at Hermann's elbow at the gaming table, she then could speak the fateful words, "Your queen of spades has lost!" Hermann did not die in romantic contortions in the gaming room but rather, as with Pushkin, in a hospital gown at the asylum. Without the interpolated love plot, Hermann's thirst for gambling became once more the motive force. The element of class, too, could be brought out: Hermann, a member of the Third Estate with the ambitious profile of a Napoleon, was pitted like Stendhal's Julien Sorel against titled aristocracy in the person of the aged countess.

Still, Meyerhold did not insist on the element of class conflict but justified his production with artistic arguments, including the musical purpose of bringing out in the score certain little-noticed passages. To this end he employed not only cuts and simplifications but also an acting technique requiring movement not in unison with the score but in counterpoint to it: "Down with music à la Dalcroze, in unison: in the music a

triplet and so in the movements a triplet; in the music a pause and so in the
movements a pause. . . . The idea of the
role created by the actor must follow
the idea of the score" (*Articles,*
2:308–9). Indeed, the depth of Tschaikovsky's music in this particular opera
caused Meyerhold to claim the composer as an ally in his cause against the
superficial librettist. Modest considered
Pushkin's story charming but mere fluff,
whereas Petr Ilich was haunted by its
images.

In the set design, too, Meyerhold fo-
cused not on Modest's interpolated love
story but rather on Hermann's confrontation with the countess and on the
passion for gambling which makes him
guilty of her death. Though Hermann
pretended love for Liza in order to get
into the house, once inside he rushed
past her room and on to the countess's.
Meyerhold built the countess's room in
the center of the stage at the top of a
horseshoe staircase—true, a horseshoe
distorted on the diagonal, a curved
mounting ramp like the one he had used
for productions from *The Forest* on
through *Commander of the Second
Army.* Meyerhold had Hermann slowly
mount the long side of the staircase,
pausing before the ancestral portrait
above each step, and then threaten the
countess with a revolver in order to
learn her secret of the winning cards.
Upon her collapse, dead from fright, he
ran down the short side of the stairs and,

after only a brief exchange with Liza,
escaped. Meyerhold's "new word" on
opera staging was, in sum, that the score
rather than the libretto conveyed the
emotion and the rhythm of the work.

There was little time left. In Meyerhold's brief period as director at Stanislavsky's Opera Studio he completed
Stanislavsky's production of *Rigoletto*
(1939), posthumously dedicated to
Stanislavsky, and drew up plans for his
own production of Prokofiev's *Semen
Kotko* (1940), which was then completed by Serafima Birman after Meyerhold's arrest and, of course, necessarily
presented without credit to Meyerhold.

Though opera was important
throughout Meyerhold's career from
*Tristan and Isolde,* his first impressive
production at the Imperial Theaters, on
to his last days as opera director for
Stanislavsky, his auspicious beginnings
in opera before 1917 were not followed
by any significant operatic production
in the Soviet period except *The Queen
of Spades.* Nor did he create the Soviet
"polit-musical," despite suggestions for
"contemporizing" operettas with satire
of social significance when he became
Theater Commissar in Moscow: in his
second official letter he wrote: "In order
to embark upon cutting musical satire
in the tradition of Aristophanes so as to
strike at those phenomena which hinder
the progress of the Communist cause,
so as to ridicule the vain efforts of our
enemies and harass the world Socialist

movement—to this end we should re-examine the texts of operettas with good music (Offenbach, Lecocq), discard texts outmoded for our time and revise those which offer possibilities for revision." [37] Here he retracted his prerevolutionary deemphasis of the word for the sake of music and movement and returned in the new political age of the Soviet state to prime concern with meaning. So music, which he had insisted was central to opera, became only an adjunct, however important, to the dramas he staged after 1917.

As a whole, Meyerhold's postrevolutionary period offered a wealth of ideas which have since borne fruit. In the first half of the twenties, in particular, Meyerhold conceived of many possibilities that were then, as Vakhtangov noted, not fully exploited. The next half decade was Meyerhold's great period of fulfillment in the vein of satire, especially with *The Mandate* and *The Bedbug*. Thereafter his shows were distinguished by the pathetic heroism typical of *The Last Decisive Battle*. His career ended not only with the realization of careful detail in such stage classics as *Camille* but also with detailed work on Pushkin and with plans for *Hamlet*, though unfortunately Meyerhold's mature potential for the great classics, as for opera, was never wholly realized.

# Chapter 5: Meyerhold and Other Arts and Artists

## Other Arts

### The Visual Arts

Meyerhold's actual accomplishment in the theater, like that of any director, died with him, since a performance in community with an audience is perforce unique. Yet, paradoxically, his ties with other arts, groups, and artists and even his unrealized plans have been perhaps quite as influential in the long run as his real achievement on stage. The numerous activities into which he plunged immediately after February and before October 1917 show how much he hoped to change the theater through the Revolution. Indeed the slogan "Put October into the theater," which he propagated, surely meant not just politicizing the theater but also revolutionizing theater art. In this he himself set an example by employing artists representative of avant-garde trends, especially constructivism, from Malevich (*Mystery-Bouffe*), Popova (*The Magnanimous Cuckold* and *Earth Rampant*), Stepanova (*The Death of Tarelkin*), Viktor Shestakov (*Lake Liul*), Rodchenko (*The Bedbug*), even to El Lissitzky (the unrealized *I Want a Child*). Camilla Gray in her pioneer book on the subject, *The Great Experiment: Russian Art (1863–1922)*, even regards Meyerhold's own system as part of constructivism, calling his biomechanics "the application of constructivist ideas in the theatre." She

adds, "Constructivism achieved its mos, complete realization in these [Meyerhold's] theater productions and in Sergei Eisenstein's early films." [1]

With this view a contradiction between constructivist theory and practice is immediately felt. The constructivists strove in theory to translate art into life, to take it out of the dream world of the atelier and reshape the real environment by its means. Tatlin accordingly went to work in a metallurgical factory and Popova used her art in designing textiles. Another term for constructivism, *production art,* reflects the aim of a mass-produced art, just as the term for Popova's costumes for *Cuckold, prozodezhda,* means work or factory clothes. Stepanova's *Tarelkin* costumes closely resembled her drawings for sport uniforms,[2] another practical and popular use for good design. Indeed, the constructivists explicitly abrogated "easel art" and sought instead to apply their art to real materials and to the structuring of real space in functional buildings. What a contradiction, then, that in the early twenties their constructions achieved only ephemeral, not lasting, realization in an imaginary, not a real, world of wood upon a stage, as at Meyerhold's theater; or in layout on paper, as in Mayakovsky's magazine *Lef* and in the volumes of his work, such as *Pro eto,* designed by Rodchenko; or on the walls at avant-garde art exhibits like El Lissitzky's *Proun* room at the Russian Art Exhibit in Dresden

(1926). Gray blames the failure to coordinate design with production in Russia on the backwardness of industrialization and the crises consequent upon war and revolution there. But Mies van der Rohe's design for a glass skyscraper (1920) was left unexecuted in the West, just as was, in Russia, Tatlin's Tower of the same year, model of the Monument to the Third International. More likely the lag in taste behind advanced ideas in both East and West is to blame. Not until the present age of "neoconstructivism" has resistance to architecture and design in this style been overcome.

Almost from its start, as at the present time, the constructivist style has ambiguously embraced several trends. Among several constructivist-related statements, El Lissitzky's *Proun* manifesto may serve as an example, if only because it comes so close to formulating the aims of Meyerhold's postrevolutionary theater art. Actually, of course, Lissitzky conceptualized in it his own "new art," exemplified in paintings which, beginning in 1919, he numbered successively "Proun 1," "Proun 2," and so on, and about which he wrote: "At my early exhibitions in Russia visitors asked, what does it represent? . . . My aim—and this is not only my aim, this is the meaning of the new art—is not to represent, but to form something independent of any conditioning factor. To this thing I give the independent name

*Proun* [*proekt utverzhdeniia novogo* (project for affirmation of the new); also, in 1920, called *unovis, utverzhdenie* or *ucherezhdenie novogo v iskusstve* (affirmation or establishment of the new in art)]." [3] In his manifesto Lissitzky set the goals of the new art: "a) Repudiation of art as a mere emotional, individual, romantically isolated matter; b) 'Material' creation, in the silent hope that later the resulting product will eventually be regarded as a work of art after all; c) Conscious fixity of purpose in creating an architecture based on previously worked-out, objective scientific principles which presents a coherent artistic impression. This architecture will actively raise the general standard of living." [4]

Like several constructivists, Lissitzky incorporated in one person the interdisciplinary, international nature of the new art. First trained as an architect, he became acquainted during his study in Darmstadt (1914) with the ideas of Walter Gropius, who founded in 1919 the German school of architecture and design, the Bauhaus (closed in 1933 by its last director, Mies van der Rohe, upon the advent of Hitler). After studying in Germany, Lissitzky returned to his native Russia, where he worked with Malevich in Vitebsk in 1920 and then with Tatlin in Moscow. Thus, the most advanced ideas of theater building took shape before Meyerhold's eyes when Lissitzky built the set model for *I Want a Child* in 1939, about which Lissitzky wrote, "If Meyerhold needs the stage set for a new play, then I design the layout, transforming the whole interior architecture of theatre with its traditional picture frames" (figs. 5.1–5.2).[5]

The architects of the plans for Meyerhold's new theater (1932), Mikhail Barkhin and Sergei Vakhtangov, also represented the new Soviet achievement in architecture (Barkhin's father, Grigorii, had been one of its leading representatives).[6] The two architects in an article of 1956 mention discussing at length with Meyerhold both his needs and such precedents, ancient and modern, as the theaters of the ancient Greeks, Shakespeare, and Max Reinhardt, as well as the ideas of Le Corbusier, Tatlin, and Mayakovsky.[7] The principles they finally selected seem, except for the last two, surprisingly modern:

1. *Stage and auditorium in one.*
2. *Action to be surrounded on three sides by the audience.*
3. *Action to be conceived in depth and assimilated by the audience axonometrically, from above and from the side.*
4. *No front curtain, footlights, or orchestra pit to separate actors and audience.*
5. *Auditorium to be lit by natural light.*
6. *Actors' dressing rooms to be linked directly with the acting area.*[8]

After three variants they arrived at final plans which, to reduce costs, incorporated the existing walls of Meyerhold's old building, the Zon Theater (fig. 5.3). Despite this predetermined outline, the resemblance of these plans to Gropius's plans for a total theater (1927) is noticeable. Indeed, the two architects included a sketch in Gropius's style for consideration (*Encounters,* p. 570). (Meyerhold showed an awareness of Gropius by mentioning him in *Reconstruction of the Theater* (1930): "Bravo Piscator, for finding in the architect, Walter Gropius, such a talented collaborator!" [9]) This is not to call derivative the building planned by Meyerhold and his Soviet architects but rather to place it in the great stream of avant-garde art, so much an international phenomenon in the twenties until reduced by the thirties to a trickle of conflicting nationalisms.

The international character of constructivist art went hand in hand with what might be called its "interdisciplinary" nature, or "mixed media" might be used to describe the combination of architecture, acrobatics, and music presented in Meyerhold's early Soviet productions. The art of the cinema as such, however, invaded the theater only in the work of other directors, such as the inclusion of Eisenstein's first film strip in his *Wise Man* (1923), or Erwin

*Figure 5.1. Inspecting the "transformation" of Meyerhold's theater from traditional picture frame, as Lissitzky designated it, to arena style.* Left, *Adolf Milman;* above, *Meyerhold;* center, *Pavel Tsetnerovich;* right, *I. E. Maltsin.*

*Figure 5.2. Lissitzky at work on his model for* I Want a Child *(1929)*

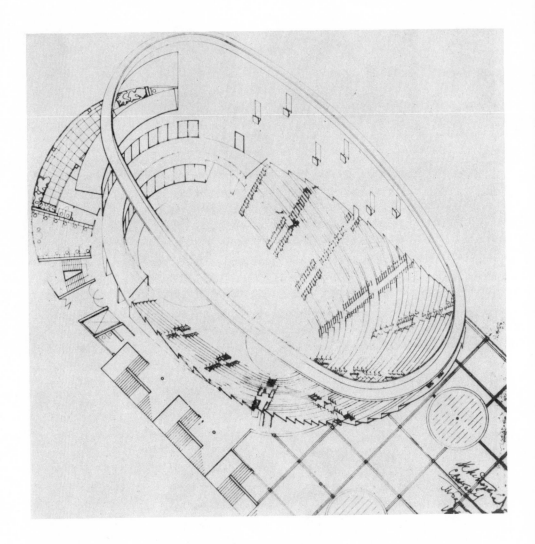

*Figure 5.3. Mikhail Barkhin's plan for the Meyerhold Theater (1932)*

Piscator's use of motion pictures in Alfons Paquet's *Flags* (1924). Meyerhold projected only stills and titles in *Earth Rampant* and *D. E.* The cinema in Meyerhold's work was rather an implicit influence, especially in his early Soviet work, to the point that Ripellino speaks of his "cinematification of the theater" in *The Death of Tarelkin,* codirected by Eisenstein. Though at the time the relationship of *Tarelkin* to circus and the devices of the traveling fair impressed some critics even more strongly, Meyerhold's productions in general had evident cinematic features: episodic structure (the five acts of the classics were broken up into numerous scenes, fifteen in *The Inspector General*); pantomimic characterization (a single trait would be brought out, as if to project it visually as in the old silent film: for example, Orlov as Raspliuev in *The Death of Tarelkin* carried a pistol and the "little man" in *A List of Assets* assumed the unmistakable guise of Charlie Chaplin); the rapid tempo of pre-*Bubus* productions (the dynamism of *Tarelkin* and *D. E.* is said to have reminded of an old Keystone comedy); the intensity of the close-up (the sit-down scenes, each on a small platform, of *The Inspector General* were composed in emulation of the close-up). Of course, Meyerhold expressly aspired in *Reconstruction of the Theater* to achieve a theater art which

might be as popular as sport or the cinema.

In two lectures concerning cinema, one sociological, *Reconstruction of the Theater,* the other aesthetic, "Chaplin and Chaplinism" (1936),[10] Meyerhold discussed cinematic art in the age of Hollywood. His criticism in the lectures and his own practice in making and acting in motion pictures belongs to this past age as his theater art does not. His two motion pictures directed during World War I are hard to judge, as both have been lost. Jay Leyda in his basic book on the Russian cinema, *Kino,* rates Meyerhold's achievement in *The Picture of Dorian Gray* very high: "The resultant film was acclaimed by critics of vision, and pretty generally disliked by the public at large. It was original and daring as few films before it or since have dared to be. Russian artists who saw it and then *The Cabinet of Dr. Caligari* a few years later in Europe, tell me that if it had been shown abroad it would have surpassed *Caligari's* reputation as a heightening of film art. It was undoubtedly the most important Russian film made previous to the February Revolution."[11] Leyda cites as distinctive Meyerhold's use of contrast, "bold black and white masses—with dramatically lit figures against dark backgrounds or striking silhouetted figures against bright backgrounds, as in Dorian's caped figure outlined against a huge high-keyed theatre poster lit by a single street light overhead." [12] Meyerhold sought, as always, the third dimension of contrapuntal comment, which he achieved by a mirror image: "One of the most vividly original episodes was a scene from 'Romeo and Juliet' shown as reflected in the large mirror of the loge behind the watching Dorian" (figs. 5.4–5.5).[13]

Meyerhold, who himself adapted the novel to the screen, used Wilde's epigrams for titles. In a lecture of 1918 assessing the film Meyerhold urged the importance of the poetic memorable word, surely a lost art since the disappearance of titles. However, he emphasized other elements of perennially great cinema: composing the frame as picture, rhythm or pace, and the art of montage in Eisenstein's sense of a meaningful succession of shots contrasted to convey an idea.

The motion picture *The White Eagle,* directed by Iakov Protazanov (1928), in which Meyerhold acted the role of the senator, has evidently been preserved in the Soviet Film Archive. In it Protazanov reinterpreted a typical prerevolutionary story of indifferent Fate, *The Governor,* by Leonid Andreev. In Protazanov's version the title figure, played by the Moscow Art Theater actor Vasilii Kachalov, was presented as experiencing guilt: having given the order to fire on petitioning strikers, thus killing also women and children, the governor then suffered from conscience despite the award to him of the Order of the White Eagle. In contrast to Kachalov's psychological acting, Meyerhold's portrayal of the senator was sharp in outline, even grotesque (fig. 5.6). Protazanov in the judgment of Soviet historians took ready-made from other films of the Revolution his most memorable images; Eisenstein's epoch-making *Ten Days That Shook the World* is said to have "left the imprint of its intellectual metaphors on the sequence in the Winter Palace, for example Meyerhold's long progress through the enfilade of Palace apartments as the senator bearing the Governor's official report on the massacre." [14]

*Music*

Meyerhold's achievement in opera in the Soviet period consisted unfortunately of but the one production, *The Queen of Spades,* which he interestingly brought closer to the Pushkin original of Tschaikovsky's libretto. In view of Meyerhold's innovative prerevolutionary contribution to opera and ballet, the failure of his several Soviet plans to materialize seems indeed an overwhelming loss. Perhaps one unrealized project, the plan to produce Aleksandr Dargomyzhskii's *Stone Guest* with Golovin at the Bolshoi, was all too

*Figure 5.4.* The Picture of Dorian Gray *(film), directed by Meyerhold in 1916:* left,
*V. Ianova as Dorian;* right, *Meyerhold as Lord Henry. Note that the play on stage,* Romeo
and Juliet, *is reflected in the mirror in the background of the box.*

*Figure 5.5. Meyerhold as Lord Henry in* The Picture of Dorian Gray

*Figure 5.6. Iakov Protazanov's film* The White Eagle *(1928):* left, *Meyerhold as the* senator; right, *Vasilii Kachalov as the governor*

classically routine and therefore not greatly regrettable. However, two works by Prokofiev which Meyerhold planned and failed to produce, as well as the music commissioned of Prokofiev for the unfinished production of Pushkin's play *Boris Godunov,* represent major omissions from the canon of Meyerhold's work.

On a trip to Russia in 1929 Prokofiev worked with Meyerhold on the production planned for the Bolshoi of Prokofiev's ballet *Le Pas d'Acier,* which had been premiered by Diaghilev in Paris. However, Prokofiev's and Meyerhold's explications of music and production plans failed to convince the musicians' union, which almost unanimously rejected the project.

In 1936 Prokofiev returned to Russia for good, and by November was able to play for the Meyerhold Theater company the eighteen fragments of music he had already completed for Meyerhold's long-intended production of the Pushkin play *Boris Godunov.* Fevralskii, an eyewitness, describes the occasion and the music in his article, "Prokofiev and Meyerhold." [15] Unfortunately, this Meyerhold project of some two decades' standing, rehearsals of which were begun in the spring of 1936, was not completed; along with this, Meyerhold's only dramatic production of a great tragedy, Prokofiev's music too failed to come to fruition.

Prokofiev's opera *Semen Kotko,*

promised to the Stanislavsky Opera Theater, of which Meyerhold became chief director, entered the planning stage in the spring of 1939. The composer met often with Meyerhold and Valentin Kataev, author of the story "I Am a Son of the Working-Class," who himself wrote the libretto; together they had already made considerable progress toward mutual understanding of book and music. Meyerhold had also begun work on his production plans when his career was abruptly ended.

These three projects were not the only ones on which Meyerhold and Prokofiev began collaboration. Fevralskii mentions others in his article, of which perhaps the most important was the "production" of the part to be played by physical training students from the Lesgaft Institute of Physical Training in an All-Soviet physical training show and parade (6 July 1939, Leningrad, and 18 July 1939, Moscow). Both composer and director began work on this commission; Fevralskii lists the music Prokofiev conceived for the project at Meyerhold's request.

## Other Artists

*Contemporary Russian Directors*

From Meyerhold's first director's plan (1902) for a production he never realized, Lev Mei's *Girl from Pskov,* Volkov concluded: "The completed plan for *The Girl from Pskov* gives a clear idea of Meyerhold's starting point, of its connection with Moscow Art Theater methods. Indeed Meyerhold's first season [as a director, 1902–3] in Kherson was based on the application of those methods" (Volkov, 1:160). Quite as noticeable as Meyerhold's dependence on the Moscow Art Theater in his first year at directing was his recognition during the second year at Kherson (1903–4) of the need to depart from the past. What were these early Moscow Art Theater methods which undeniably shaped Meyerhold's beginnings, first his dependence, then his reaction to them?

Meyerhold spoke of the "two faces" of the Moscow Art Theater, meaning the surprising duality characteristic of the theater when he made his acting debut there in 1898 as a member of the original company. Stanislavsky, its co-founder, at first directed his main effort toward bringing "external truth" to the theater. This was the theater's first face: the "naturalism borrowed from the Meiningen players" (*Articles,* 1:113), as Meyerhold explained it. The theater pioneered this use of historical accuracy in its first productions, Aleksei K. Tolstoi's *Czar Fedor Ioannovich* and *The Death of Ivan the Terrible,* both of which appeared also on Meyerhold's list of productions during his first season as a director of repertory theater.

The second face of the Moscow Art Theater related to Chekhov's true dramatic intent. It was the other founder of the theater, Nemirovich-Danchenko, Meyerhold's drama-school teacher, who had imbued his pupils with faith in the still untried dramatist. Yet the theater's first decisive success with Chekhov, whose play *The Sea Gull* supplied its emblem, was due to a paradoxical interpretation of him. For the theater's basic trend toward outward realism contradicted the very substance of Chekhov's psychological mood and symbolism. David Magarshack points out this antithesis, only in somewhat different terms, when he remarks that Stanislavsky's methods "bring out in Chekhov's plays of indirect action the latent action";[16] that is, Stanislavsky showed all that was hidden in Chekhov. Where Chekhov insisted that not a single property be brought on stage unless for a purpose, Stanislavsky filled the stage with objects to manipulate, as he put it, so as "to give the actors something to do in the long Chekhovian pauses." And mood, implicit in the Chekhovian "atmosphere," was created by realistic sound effects like the croaking of frogs and the chirping of locusts.

Meyerhold, emulating the master, planned a background of realistic sound for Mei's *Girl from Pskov* in his first director's notebook: the cooing of doves and the clop of horses' hooves, "if they can be successfully imitated"

(Volkov, 1:158). However, like Stanislavsky, Meyerhold aimed at more than sound imitation; he sought atmosphere as well. Thus for a love scene in act 2 of this early production he prescribed: "Frogs, night birds in indeterminate sounds. Something hidden, mystic" (ibid.). Increasingly in Meyerhold's practice imitative sound gave way to music in a more sophisticated background. After all, Meyerhold found in Chekhov himself the impetus to overcome realism. In the famous rehearsal incident which has become legend, thanks to Meyerhold's report of it, Chekhov objected to the croaking of frogs and barking of dogs which Stanislavsky had planned for *The Sea Gull,* insisting rather that such superfluous realism was contrary to the very nature of theater: "The theater is art, the theater reflects the quintessence of life" (*Articles,* 1:120). Of course, Stanislavsky, like Meyerhold, did not stand still with the Art Theater's early realism.

The Theater Studio of 1905, in which Stanislavsky invited Meyerhold to direct, was only one of several efforts made at the Moscow Art Theater to accommodate the mysticism which arose almost simultaneously with the renewal of realism. Apparently Meyerhold thought of the Moscow Art Theater as advancing in this channel too, for in an introduction he wrote for the 1905 venture he revealed the "other" Stanislavsky: "In the Moscow Art Theater there have always been two currents: a subtle realism, and lyricism. (And does not the latter carry with it the beginnings of mysticism?)" (*Articles,* 1:90). Both the realistic and the mystic currents were present in the repertory Meyerhold announced for the Theater Studio: Ibsen, Przybyszewski, Maeterlinck, Schnitzler, Strindberg, Hauptmann, Wedekind, and Hofmannsthal. How often the two elements struck a strange balance within a single work, not only in Chekhov, but also in such contemporaries as Ibsen and Hauptmann. Meyerhold likened the two tendencies at the Moscow Art Theater to the two pans of a scale with now one, now the other, in ascendancy, as indeed they ran parallel in the repertory of directors working elsewhere at the time: thus Otto Brahm in Germany produced both the early naturalistic Hauptmann and the early symbolist Hofmannsthal.

Later Meyerhold tried to identify Stanislavsky altogether with the second stream; in 1912 Golovin and he wrote to Stanislavsky:

*Here in St. Petersburg rumor has it that you alone bear the whole burden of an agonizing crisis in the struggle between two currents within the Moscow Art Theater: the old, represented by the adherents of naturalistic theater, and the new, which you represent along with the young people seeking a way out and new directions in theater art.*

*We are wholeheartedly with you in the struggle! We wish you victory! We wish you courage and strength! We are convinced that you will win out, for you have caught up in your strong hands the banner of the new art, fearless in your confrontation of all enemies.*

The half decade leading up to Meyerhold's and Golovin's letter justified the notion of the "other" Stanislavsky. Like the Meyerhold of 1906, Stanislavsky enjoyed a pause for contemplation which brought him to a reexamination of his course. The effect of external truth which he had thus far achieved through verisimilitude on stage seemed now to demand the addition of an inner truth, or "psycho-technique," to keep the actor's first vivid experience of his part from diminishing with repeated performance and to help him communicate this experience to an audience. As Stanislavsky's new insights took him away from outward realism, so the repertory of the Moscow Art Theater during these years moved somewhat out of the path of strict imitation. Simultaneously with Meyerhold at Komissarzhevskaia's theater, Stanislavsky staged at the Moscow Art Theater Leonid Andreev's symbolist play *The Life of Man* (1907); he also did a quite enchanting production of Maeterlinck's *Blue Bird* (1908), still current in the Moscow Art Theater repertory. And, per-haps most important of all, Stanislavsky invited Gordon Craig to design *Hamlet* (1911). These three productions showed the Art Theater's effort to make up for its deficiency in nonrealist repertory by embracing other dimensions of theater. Soon thereafter Meyerhold nevertheless branded the theater's production of Molière's *Imaginary Invalid* as Meiningenism.[17] Evidently Stanislavsky had again failed, as with the Theater Studio ten years earlier, to depart from his theater's original tradition and realize his "other" self.

Meyerhold, however, blamed the faults of the *Imaginary Invalid* not on Stanislavsky but on Alexander Benois, the actual director of Molière's comedy, and on the theater itself, calling Meiningenism "the most harmful phenomenon of all those which the Art Theater knew" (*Articles,* 1:272). Toward Stanislavsky personally Meyerhold often showed a pupil's veneration, and Stanislavsky in turn arranged for Meyerhold to succeed him as head of the Stanislavsky Opera Studio, though Meyerhold's arrest cut short his tenure. Indeed the personal relationship of the two men was more amiable than is commonly supposed.

If the two directors seemed closest at the end of the first decade of the century, surely the moment of their utmost divergence came in the first years after the Revolution. While Meyerhold turned his efforts to putting the Revolution into the theater, Stanislavsky remained professionally undistracted from his pursuit of beauty and truth. At the Bolshoi Theater (1918–22), in lectures central to his method, Stanislavsky not only dealt with the most unrealistic and aesthetically conventional of forms, the opera, but also concentrated on the artist's inner creative state of mind, that which appears oblivious to the outer world. Further, in the sharpest polemic Meyerhold launched against Stanislavsky, an article in collaboration with Valerii Bebutov entitled "The Isolation of Stanislavsky" (1921), Stanislavsky was ironically charged with teaching at the Habima Theater formalist methods close to Meyerhold's own: "In the ancient Hebrew and Armenian surroundings fanatics of the Moscow Art Theater's Third Studio [Vakhtangov's studio, later the Vakhtangov Theater] are always present when Stanislavsky gives his lessons: 'No living on stage! Clear resounding voices! Theatrical walk! Flexible bodies! Expressive language of gesture! Dance! Bow! Fencing with rapiers! Rhythm! Rhythm! Rhythm!' Stanislavsky resoundingly cries" (*Articles,* 2:33).

Despite Meyerhold's polemic it is clear that Stanislavsky was interested in Meyerhold's achievement. Stanislavsky, together with two leading members of the Art Theater, Olga Knipper-Chekhov and Vasilii Kachalov, saw at the Meyerhold Theater the success of the 1925 Moscow season, Nikolai Erdman's *Mandate,* and gave it highest praise, according to Pavel Markov, then head of play reading at the Art Theater: "I am completely taken with the director's whole conception," Stanislavsky said, ". . . especially his solution for the last act. . . . In this act Meyerhold has accomplished what I myself am dreaming of." [18] In 1926 Stanislavsky is known to have visited *The Magnanimous Cuckold,* and Lunacharsky stated in a report before the Communist Academy: "Gray-haired Stanislavsky, the great master of theater, is not afraid to move closer to the methods of Meyerhold as in *The Forest"* (*Articles,* 2:567).

Yet Stanislavsky never shot further from the mark than when he tried to approximate Meyerholdian methods in his production of Ostrovsky's *A Warm Heart* (1926). Two sets of this show used a flight of stairs and might technically therefore be called constructivist, though the stairs each time served chiefly as an apparatus for acting vulgar drunkenness. It is hard to understand why this production impressed Brecht favorably when he saw it in 1955, for by then it had a replacement cast. The play is still performed, though the second cast too is long since overage and the entire production is appalling evidence that the Moscow Art Theater became for a while a museum, even a mausoleum. Yet it is unfair to judge Stanislavsky's productions by the institutionalized few which survive at the Moscow Art Theater over thirty years after his death, nor is it possible to compare them with Meyerhold's, none of which survive at all.

Still, the quite opposite conceptions of theater art held by these two men exert great influence everywhere today. Stanislavsky took his departure from a hatred of theater and a love of truth. Magarshack quotes him as saying, "I know that scenery, make-up, costumes, and the fact that I have to perform my work in public is nothing but a barefaced lie." [19] Stanislavsky first sought to overcome the "lie" of theater by the truth of an historically exact stage picture and the valid portrayal of character, using idiosyncrasies of gait or gesture observed from real life. But as he developed his system, chiefly during the period 1906 to 1918, he sought more and more the inner truth of psychological experience. His famous method consisted in "psychic techniques" to give the actor concentration and a creative state of mind in which to relive the character's feeling and communicate it to the audience watching unseen beyond the invisible fourth wall. Meyerhold, on the other hand, dated from Blok's *Farce* his fascination with the theater as art, as the very lie Stanislavsky abjured; indeed, it was the art of the theater which Meyerhold tried to develop in every way, deriving it from traditions of other times and places. Similarly, he tried to teach acting as an art, leaving the actor inwardly free to exercise the utmost control of voice and body.

In basic principle, then, the two systems were antithetical. Officially Stanislavsky's was approved under Stalin as "realism" and Meyerhold's finally condemned as "formalism." Since Stalin's death and Meyerhold's rehabilitation, the process of restoring Meyerhold to his rightful place in the theater of the USSR has in part taken the peculiarly Soviet course of justification by authority. That is, it has seemed helpful to show how close Meyerhold always was to so established a figure as Stanislavsky. Capital evidence has been adduced from some of Meyerhold's own pronouncements made to Aleksandr Gladkov in the thirties and now published; for example, Meyerhold said: "It is a basic problem of the contemporary theater how to preserve a quality of improvisation in the actor's creativity within the framework of the complex and exact director's plan for the show. . . . I talked about this recently with Stanislavsky and he too is thinking about this. We approach the solution of one and the same problem like builders of a tunnel under the Alps. He comes at it from one side and I from the other, but somewhere in the middle we we are bound to meet." [20] Fevralskii too has surveyed the relations of the two directors in an excellent historical summary.[21] Finally, the actors Igor Ilinskii and Boris Zakhava, both of whom trained and acted with Meyerhold in addition to their experience outside the Meyerhold Theater, have testified to the closeness of the two directors' systems in actual practice. For us in the West, to whom legitimation of Meyerhold is irrelevant, Zakhava's comparison is doubtless the more interesting.

The point of tangency, as Zakhava shows, lies in the importance of physical action to both systems. Stanislavsky himself used his body most skillfully, and Meyerhold attributes to him certain exercises of the hands and wrists which Meyerhold in turn taught his pupils. Both considered physical action the starting point for psychological experience. By the early twenties Meyerhold cited in justification of his method the theory of William James: "Run and you will feel fear." But Stanislavsky too taught the "logic of physical action" as the road to "emotional memory." And none other than Meyerhold's wife, Zinaida Raikh, while Meyerhold was explicating pre-acting to the cast of *Bubus the Teacher,* asked, "Are not our 'pauses' like those at the Moscow Art Theater?" (*Articles,* 2:90). Meyerhold implied that his concept of pre-acting aimed merely at effective timing, the underlining of action, or the purely mechanical and physical headstart

toward it, whereas the Stanislavskian pause was needed for emotional preparation.[22] If the "pause" and pre-acting have, nevertheless, something in common, so too Stanislavsky's "through-action" toward the "ruling idea" may be compared to Meyerhold's notion of the "key idea."

Doubtless the final ineradicable difference between the two systems lay in the manner of communicating the key idea. For Stanislavsky the communication was always indirect and unconscious, an irradiation of feeling. Though the Meyerholdian actor could also feel his role, Meyerhold differed essentially from Stanislavsky in demanding the actor's conscious reserve of a last part of himself to judge his assumed character and his performance. That Meyerhold tried to place the artist's controlling reason at the service of the Revolution and to make of the actor an "actor-tribune," and that he identified political with artistic revolution—these were tragic errors, from the consequences of which not even Stanislavsky could save him in the end.

However authentic are the conversations with Meyerhold in the mid-thirties which Gladkov published in the sixties, at least Meyerhold's quoted remark on his two chief competitors surely reflects his sense of their relationship. According to Gladkov, Meyerhold said: "The Moscow Art Theater and my theater are not opposite poles; . . . my theater too is one of the Moscow Art Theater studios. . . . The opposite pole to me is the Kamerny." [23] How is one to explain so complete and bitter a rejection of the theater of Aleksandr Tairov, who first acted under Meyerhold's direction at Komissarzhevskaia's theater in 1906, who founded his Kamerny Theater in 1914 with aims close to Meyerhold's, and who came under pressure for "formalism," like Meyerhold, in the thirties? The first cause of hostility was evidently Tairov's giving less than due credit to Meyerhold for his collaboration in the staging of Paul Claudel's *Exchange* by the Kamerny (1918), which led to considerable resentment on Meyerhold's part. This was followed by a sharp debate between the two men toward the end of 1920. Meyerhold's at least oblique praise of Tairov's theater as one of bold innovation[24] had doubtless led to the invitation to Meyerhold to collaborate on Claudel's *Exchange,* but by 1922 each director was publicly deprecating the other's work.

At a later time Meyerhold recognized that Tairov's company along with the Moscow Art Theater's and his own must take the lead in the new five-year plan of 1929 (*Articles,* 2:185). But one such confession of unanimity hardly outweighs the more numerous hostilities. Tairov entitled his review of Verhaeren's play as produced by Meyerhold "The Twilight of *Dawns*" (1921).

Meyerhold, in turn, repeatedly attacked the Kamerny for the "aestheticism" of its repertoire and its mode of acting. In the last analysis the very closeness of the two theaters amounted to competition. For example, Vishnevskii, whose neophyte effort, *The Last Decisive Battle* (1931), had been sponsored by Meyerhold, gave his first mature play, *The Optimistic Tragedy* (1933), to Tairov, who scored a hit with it. Or again, Tairov gained a hearing abroad for his theory of theater art even before Stanislavsky and long before Meyerhold, by publishing *A Director's Notebook* (1921), shortly after its Russian appearance, in German as *Das entfesselte Theater* (1923). He also took his theater on tour abroad as early as 1923. Thus the younger of the two men enjoyed the older established repution in the West.

With his 1922 review of Tairov's book Meyerhold tried to accomplish two purposes: to demolish Tairov's ideas and to proclaim his own new system of biomechanics. Meyerhold called Tairov an amateur who taught not a "science" of acting but various acrobatic skills, ballet, fencing, and juggling, so that his all too lithe actors fell into overelegance and affectedness of pose and gesture. Meyerhold further accused him of cultural lag for repeating in 1921 the avant-garde ideas of 1905–17, including some of Meyerhold's own, now long since abandoned.

He denied Tairov's claim that showing naked bodies in movement represented an important innovation, pointing to the nudity used much earlier in costumes by Bakst and Fokine and to the transparent garments worn by Isadora Duncan. Above all, Meyerhold decried Tairov's neglect of that essential fourth dimension of theater, the audience.

In the same year, 1922, Meyerhold used the occasion of an obituary he wrote for Evgenii Vakhtangov to brand Tairov as a popularizer of the innovations devised by such other true avant-gardists as Vakhtangov: "The Kamerny Theater only watered down with its neo-stylization and always merely commercialized the results of the first experiments in *uslovnyi* theater" (*Articles,* 2:49). Citing the avant-garde directors Nikolai Foregger, Boris Ferdinandov, and Vadim Shershenevich as dissidents from the Kamerny method, he listed Kamerny faults which had caused their defection:

*The first left in order to create a popular theater in the vein of the French wandering troupes in the Middle Ages, in order to strengthen healthy traditions of market-place theater. The second and the third fled from Tairov's dilettantism, from the resounding banality, from the much-touted "nudity on stage," from the pseudo-acrobatic contortions, from the declaration of "neo-realism," from the sickly sweet little gestures, from the sentimental ravings;*

*fled in order to begin reinforcing through their own independent work the scientific bases of theater. (*Articles, 2:50.)

Polemical as Meyerhold's criticism assuredly was, it was nevertheless borne out by the reviews of bourgeois critics who saw Tairov's theater on its 1923 Western tour. It is unfortunate that many ideas closely resembling Meyerhold's first reached the West through the distortion of Tairov's theory and practice. Yet despite their differences the two men both belonged in the camp of nonrealism. And their repertories, as was also the case with Stanislavsky and Meyerhold, often nearly coincided. Tairov did a production of *Pierrette's Veil,* after Schnitzler (1916), six years after Meyerhold's version of the same work (*Columbine's Scarf*). Both staged the first plays of Vishnevskii. However, Tairov, not Meyerhold, produced Eugene O'Neill's *Hairy Ape* (1926) and, at Lunacharsky's request, Brecht's *Threepenny Opera* (1933). Bernhard Reich, the first architect of Brecht's reputation in the USSR, disappointedly condemned Tairov's version of the latter as a mere *"tänzerisches Musical* [song-and-dance show]";[25] one would have wished to see a production of it by Meyerhold.

Meyerhold not only shared with Stanislavsky and Tairov an emphasis on body movement; like them he sought to return to earlier traditions of theater.

After Meyerhold's success with the medieval miracle play adapted by Maeterlinck, *Sister Beatrice,* at Komissarzhevskaia's theater, Nikolai Evreinov did a season of medieval theater (1907–8), following it with one of Spanish Renaissance drama (1911–12). Meyerhold published a perceptive article in 1908 on Evreinov's medieval series in his book *On Theater.* "The Starinnyi Theater has fallen between two chairs," he commented (*Articles,* 1:190). While using the genuine texts, Evreinov had tried merely to re-create a medieval atmosphere with painted flats; he had not actually reconstructed the stage of the Coventry mystery plays. This contrast between genuineness and atmosphere had evidently produced a comic effect, causing the audience to laugh at unforeseen moments. For his part, Meyerhold held up his *Sister Beatrice* as an example of successfully re-created primitivism, achieved through a modern stylization of both stage picture and text. He drew the moral of Evreinov's failure: "So the lack of unified purpose was reflected in the audience's undesirable reaction: the producer had chosen genuine texts, the designer had not re-created the architectural features of primitive staging but had done stylized sets, and the director had neglected the technique of actors in ancient theaters. ... There was neither naïveté nor sincere athletism. No real subtlety. No real flexibility of movement. No real musicality of intonation" (ibid., 1:191).

Was it these lacks in Evreinov's Starinnyi Theater that prompted Meyerhold that very year to begin his first studio course, which he eventually expanded to offer training in all these missing techniques? He thus restored to acting a rich variety of earlier traditions that lay ready for use in such a modern mystery play as *Mystery-Bouffe.* Unfortunately, however, he could no more than Evreinov parallel his reuse of earlier acting techniques with the reuse of earlier staging practice, for the "total theater" with which he meant to break the frame of the conventional building was never completed. With Evreinov, as with the dramatist Andreev, Meyerhold shared the perception of the *uslovnyi* nature of theater art since ancient and medieval times; yet Meyerhold implemented his perception more completely than either, both qualitatively and quantitatively, in actual production.

Both Evreinov and another eclectic director, Fedor Komissarzhevsky, brother of the actress Vera, assisted Meyerhold in Komissarzhevskaia's theater and then briefly succeeded him in his post there; both then continued to produce plays independently until their emigration at the time of the Revolution. Just as Evreinov came close to Meyerhold with one side of his work, so Komissarzhevsky approached him with another, his belief in "synthetic theater," after Richard Wagner. Like Tairov, Komissarzhevsky trained each of his pupils (among them Igor Ilinskii) to be dramatic actor, singer, and dancer all in one. Yet however close Komissarzhevsky came in theory to Meyerhold, his largely musical productions could never in practice be mistaken for the works of Meyerhold's bolder genius.

Meyerhold's other slightly younger contemporary, Evgenii Vakhtangov, who might be compared with Meyerhold in genius, did not live long enough to fulfill his promise. As Meyerhold wrote in his obituary article on Vakhtangov, "In Memory of a Leader," the younger man had just completed his apprenticeship as the epigone of others, reaching an ever higher achievement with his productions. "But this was only the prologue. He had prepared himself to begin—and he died" (*Articles,* 2:50). Though the two met only in the year before Vakhtangov's death, when Meyerhold stopped to comment on Vakhtangov's show *The Miracle of St. Anthony,* by Maeterlinck, they had really, in the older man's opinion, been comrades in arms for years. By this Meyerhold meant that they had common aims in directing: "Vakhtangov was with us, of course, could not but be with us" (ibid.). At their first meeting after the performance Meyerhold praised both Vakhtangov and his cast for their "distinctness of form, sculptural expressiveness, the exactitude of staging and the exactitude of gesture (especially 'play with hands')" (ibid.,

2:525, n. 4). Their all too brief personal encounter had its sequel in Meyerhold's friendship for Vakhtangov's son Sergei after the father's death: Meyerhold dedicated his next show to the son and to the father's memory. And he later employed the son as architect of his new theater building and designer of three productions: *Bathhouse, The Last Decisive Battle,* and *A List of Assets.* Meyerhold's effort, undertaken together with Stanislavsky, to assure continuation of Vakhtangov's Third Studio after his death belongs, however, not to personal but to theater history.

But Vakhtangov brought Stanislavsky and Meyerhold together not just in death. Even before 1920 he had carried on a conversation with both about the possibility of their working together on the ground of his studio. Zakhava then tried unsuccessfully to realize this possibility.[26] When he appealed to the two directors in 1924, Stanislavsky felt himself unable to transfer to the ground of the Third Studio. Meyerhold, who had already worked in the studio as a visitor before Vakhtangov's death, undertook there a production long dear to his heart, Pushkin's play *Boris Godunov,* but, like two previous attempts, it remained uncompleted. Vakhtangov is regarded by Soviet theater historians, then, ideally and potentially, though not in fact, as the synthesizer of the two men's systems.

Vakhtangov began with Stanislavsky's teachings. After graduating from the drama school of a Moscow Art Theater actor, Aleksandr Adashev, he himself joined the theater in 1911. Soon after his admission to the company he noted in his diary (15 April 1911) the wish to organize a studio in order "to try out Stanislavsky's system on ourselves." [27] By January 1913 the younger people of the Moscow Art Theater had organized the First Studio, where Vakhtangov aroused the obvious consternation of his teachers with his first production, Gerhart Hauptmann's *Family Reunion*. Zakhava describes the perplexity of the Moscow Art Theater teachers at "their pupil's wholly uncompromising consistency, in which they were unable to recognize the fruits of their own teaching." [28] At first glance Vakhtangov might seem in *Family Reunion* to have realized Meyerhold's principles of baring the stage to give full play to the actors, rather than to have overdone Stanislavsky's method. But, Zakhava goes on:

*[From the steep amphitheater] I could see the actors full length, though there was no platform. The stage area was separated from the audience only by a small proscenium arch and, during intermission, by a modest curtain of gray cloth. But see, the curtain has opened. And what's this? Almost no set at all. . . . But then, more than this*

*is not necessary: all the rest is left to the art of the actor. . . . No, I've never seen such acting! The main thing which struck me was the complete absence of affectation in the actors. . . . Ideal simplicity and genuineness. One believed the people on stage had truly, that is in fact, had decidedly nothing whatever to do with the audience. Their "circle of attention" was firmly closed, their concentration within this "circle" was absolute.*[29]

The intensity of the acting with all its outward simplicity reached such heights that Zakhava even asks whether this was art or a psychiatric clinic. To answer, as Zakhava does, that it was both is really to make a statement as abstract and empty as the widely used cliché that Vakhtangov synthesized the two extremes of Stanislavsky and Meyerhold.

Rather, Vakhtangov seems to have been very much his own man and, while deeply interested in the work of both masters, steadfastly maintained his independence, until at last, threatened by illness, he sought protection for the promising studio he had to leave behind. He had refused an early offer from the other camp, the invitation to direct in what he called in a letter of 8 May 1912 "the theater of Blok, the poet," that is, the summer theater in Terioki, Finland, where Meyerhold directed.[30] In the same letter he negotiated for his own studio. And in diary entries of 12 and 13 April 1911 he proposed his own studio in order to test the method under conditions resembling a religious community, quite different from either Stanislavsky's or Meyerhold's systems. Thus Vakhtangov dreamed of an actors' company in which those playing the parts should open up their souls to each other in the play without falsehood. At another time he envisaged a collective which would be jointly administered; the requirements for admission: "to love art in general and theater art in particular. To seek joy in creativity. To forget the public. To create for ourselves. To enjoy for ourselves. To be our own judges." [31]

Vakhtangov's studio, with its aims of moral as well as aesthetic perfection, did come into being for a time among the students who rehearsed with him. But when he finally brought the Student Studio back into the fold as the Third Studio of the Moscow Art Theater, he surrendered his original position of independence. However, Gozzi's *Princess Turandot* (1922), on which recognition of the Third Studio as such depended, was very much Vakhtangov's own production, and in it he was by no means subservient to Stanislavsky. Indeed, by casting his vote in 1919 against the return of the First Studio into the Art Theater, Vakhtangov had already shown his considerable distance from the Stanislavsky of these years.

Nor was he, of course, Meyerhold's man either, though he had seen Meyerhold's production of *Columbine's Scarf* in 1911 and written in his diary: "What a genius is this director! Every one of his productions is new theater. Every one of his productions could launch a whole new trend." [32] In the end Vakhtangov was apparently tending more toward Meyerhold's manner of directing than Stanislavsky's. The production which Vakhtangov directed for the Habima Theater, *The Dybbuk* (1922), about the tragic love of two young people, contained with its satanic overtones moments close to *Columbine's Scarf*. And *Princess Turandot* in the Third Studio continued the enthusiasm for the *commedia dell'arte* evident in Meyerhold's *Love for Three Oranges*. Even Vakhtangov's last production for the First Studio, Strindberg's *Eric XIV* (1921), in which Michael Chekhov played the title role, partook more of the grotesque than of Stanislavskian psychological realism. Even so, it cannot be said that Vakhtangov synthesized the two great directors; rather, he stood his own ground, on which, given time, he would surely have made his own original contribution.

*Contemporary Theater Abroad: German, French, and Italian*

Meyerhold's theater art seems strikingly

close to the German theater of the Weimar period, the "Theater for the Republic" (1918–33), as it has been called since the retrospective show so entitled at the Berlin Academy of the Arts and since Günther Rühle's book on that theater (both 1967). The new spirit which became general everywhere in the arts after 1918 had made itself felt in Germany even before the war as negation of the past. Vasilii Kandinsky wrote in the avant-garde periodical *Sturm* in 1912: "The intellectual atmosphere is so charged in great moments with a precise will, a definite necessity, that one can easily be prophetic. . . . I believe there isn't a single critic who doesn't know that impressionism is finished." [33]

The same magazine published also in 1912 Marinetti's "Technical Manifesto," which could almost serve as a programmatic declaration for the new trends in language represented by Mayakovsky and the expressionists: in an aeroplane Marinetti felt the ineffectiveness of traditional grammar and made a new requirement of language, that it take on the dynamism of a motor. "Now that we can rise above the ground," he declared, the word must be freed from the trammels of solemnity.[34] Specifically this meant abandoning the sentence and punctuation, resorting to the infinitive and the ugly. The novelist Alfred Döblin in a piece in *Sturm* entitled "Dancers" demanded also that

exaggerated artiness in the dance be done away with: "We've had enough of bad lady dancers. . . . It would be all well enough if the lady dancers weren't so cultivated and so in love with nature and so on. I'd rather have a good strong obscenity." [35] This last might also have been quoted from Meyerhold or Brecht. But the *Sturm* contributors also relied on intuition and negated reason, thus marking themselves as "expressionists." Their exaltation and irrational faith divided them from the youth just returning from the war in 1918 to make a start as artists, writers, and directors.

*Neue Jugend* (New Youth) was the title of the war generation's magazine, published irregularly by Wieland Herzfelde. It introduced, among others, the youthful innovator in the theater Erwin Piscator, who marked his debut with a poem from the trenches. In the retrospect of his 1966 afterword for his two-volume *Works* Piscator viewed the youth of 1918 as somewhere between silly and serious. He recalled "when we tried in Berlin in 1918 to spread Dadaism among the people" and spoke wistfully of "plays such as I then had in mind as an ideal, plays such as those only now being written by [Rolf] Hochhuth, [Heinar] Kipphardt, or [Peter] Weiss, which adopt the factuality of documents, the severe exactitude of historical analysis." [36] A few years later (1924) the artist George Gross also saw Dada as a slap in the face of tradition, yet one given not lightly but in the name of reason: "The Dada movement had its roots in the realization, which came to me and my associates simultaneously, that it was perfectly nonsensical to believe the world was ruled by mind, any minds at all. . . . The approaching revolution brought clarity about this system [of the existing social structure]. . . . There were more important problems than those of art: those of the future, of the class struggle." [37] Thus serious purpose gradually came to dominate Dada's first youthful defiance.

The Meyerhold Theater also tried to present the world in the perspective of the class struggle, as in Mayakovsky's *Mystery-Bouffe* (1918). In the stage set for *Mystery,* according to a German specialist on Mayakovsky, Meyerhold realized ten years earlier than Piscator the latter's device known as the "global stage." [38] Not only in *Mystery* but also in *Earth Rampant* Meyerhold used trucks and motorcycles on stage, long before Piscator had an opportunity to realize his documentary spirit in a large theater. Actually, the strips which George Gross designed as background for Piscator's production of *The Good Soldier Schweyk* (1928) were less in Piscator's documentary spirit than in that of Meyerholdian caricature. Perhaps it was this congeniality of spirit which assured such a welcome in Moscow for the Gross album with which

Mayakovsky returned from Berlin in 1923.

Yet neither theater had direct acquaintance with the work of the other until later. Certainly the German encounter with the Meyerhold Theater on its 1930 tour to the West occasioned no liking on either side. The editor of Piscator's *Works*, Ludwig Hoffmann, testifies in his accompanying article: "The style of documentary analysis which Piscator developed found no sympathy in Moscow (even Meyerhold had not liked it on the occasion of his theater's tour in Germany)." [39] In turn, Meyerhold awakened but little sympathy in Berlin, for the opportunity to show his theater's work abroad came almost tragically late, when reaction against the "new spirit" had set in, all of seven years after Tairov had propagated the then new theater abroad, in theory with his book in German *Das entfesselte Theater*, and in practice with the Kamerny Theater's western tour. By the time Meyerhold's company first appeared in Germany the pendulum was already swinging back to realism. By then even Alfred Kerr, the antediluvia defender of realism, seemed almost right and up-to-date in saying of *The Forest:* "Quite lively. But wholly antimodern. . . . In the light of history Meyerhold is an interruption. A relapse." [40]

Except for Ilia Selvinskii's *Commander of the Second Army,* the plays which Meyerhold chose to represent his theater in Berlin all dated back four years or more in the repertory: *The Magnanimous Cuckold* (1922), *The Forest* (1924), and *The Inspector General* (1926); so it is no wonder his work seemed historic. *Roar China* (1926), strictly speaking the work of his pupil, Vasilii Fedorov, impressed the Berliners as elementary in its political propaganda. Herbert Jhering, doubtless the most perceptive among Meyerhold's critics, concluded his discussion of *The Forest*'s epic style and posterlike scene titles with a comment of true insight: "Meyerhold has nothing to do with Piscator. On the contrary: he depoliticalizes by the style of acting even *The Inspector General*. He builds *The Forest* on principles of form. Meyerhold's art is artistic theater. It has basically no connection with the masses." [41] Jhering perceived not only the true nature of Meyerhold's art but also his difficult position, for he spoke of Meyerhold's "isolation." From this Jhering drew a cruel conclusion: he predicted the "petrifaction" of Meyerhold's style. Indeed, all the German critics of the Berlin tour, including such "greats" as Kerr, Jhering, and Kurt Pinthus, recognized Meyerhold's historical eminence but conceded no possibility of his further influence.

But there was a plausible influence on Brecht, who himself was about to go under in the new wave of realism after 1933, only to emerge in the postwar years as the most influential single figure in contemporary theater. With the German avant-garde theater of Bertolt Brecht the theater of Meyerhold had had some contact beginning in the early twenties. More important than real contact, though, was the kinship of thought and method. It might be argued that Meyerhold's work has come to the West, if at all, chiefly as transformed by Brecht. The American director Norris Houghton says as much: "Brecht and Piscator had learned from Meyerhold, and the rest of us had learned from Brecht." [42]

Before setting Brecht up as the popularizer of revolutionary theater, one should specify the features of his art and its points of contact with Soviet theater, Meyerhold's in particular. At first there was virtually no contact. The common goal of a theater of world events in which personal psychologism has no place is explained by the common experience of war and revolution. Erwin Piscator, who, like Meyerhold, began his career as a proletarian director in 1920, wrote: "My aim was a political theater . . . a theater art sufficient to express our experience of the time and the world in a manner really suited to the time and encompassing the world." And he added: "Of course we all looked to Russia just then, of course we were all anxious to know about everything going on in the Soviet Union.

But must we just for that be stamped imitators of the Meyerholds and Tairovs? . . . The fact is that certain things in every era are in the air." [43]

Brecht's first work reflected an attitude widespread in the young generation, especially in the negative quality already remarked in George Gross's pronouncements. Brecht too took a negative stand in *Baal* (1922) against the exalted generalizations of expressionism. And in his adaptation of Marlowe's *Life of Edward II* (1924) he turned to an earlier theater tradition for fresh modes of rebellion against authority, illusions, morals. Two years before he had objected especially to established forms of acting when given his first opportunity to direct (Arnolt Bronnen's *Patricide*) at the Junge Bühne, Berlin. A lightweight and unknown, he pitted himself in this directorial assignment against two great heavyweights of the German stage, Agnes Straub and Heinrich George, and lost, as Meyerhold did at first against the Varlamovs and Davydovs of the Imperial Theaters.

Bernhard Reich knew Brecht only by the reputation of his losing fight with Straub and George and did not look forward, he recalled, to meeting this young upstart when both left Berlin to work at the Munich Kammerspiele in 1923. Yet the first chance meeting in the English Garden of Reich with his Latvian wife, Anna Lacis, and Brecht with his wife, Marianne, led to lasting friendship.

"Anna had studied in Moscow in the Studio of Komissarzhevsky," Reich remembered. "She knew all about the new Russian theater. Brecht questioned her. He was obviously interested in information on Soviet Russia and on the thinking there about the arts. Many more conversations followed this one." [44] Not only conversations: Brecht had no sooner met Anna Lacis, surely his best early informant on Soviet theater, than he enlisted her as his assistant in directing *Edward II* at the Kammerspiele (1924).

Lacis not only knew the Soviet theator in general but also had put to her own use a comparatively unknown work of Meyerhold's, as appears from her article, "Program for a Proletarian Children's Theater," on the use of theater art as therapy in the rehabilitation of homeless boys after the Russian Revolution; the play she used was Meyerhold's *Alinur* for children (1919). She attracted a band of such outlaw youths into the state school and foster home by getting them to improvise on a scene from Meyerhold's play in which "robbers are sitting around a fire in the forest and boasting of their deeds." [45] The boys so enjoyed rehearsing the play about the Tartar boy Alinur who defied his mother and terrorized his fellows that they stayed to stage a performance and finally to go to school.

Anna Lacis and Bernhard Reich remained both Brecht's friends and a co nection between him and the Soviet Union. The Reichs went to Russia in 1925, returning in 1928 to Berlin, where Brecht too had gone. In Berlin Lacis worked as representative for Soviet documentary films, arranging showings which Brecht sometimes attended. In the mid-thirties she published a book in Russia on the avant-garde theater, surely a contributing cause to her internment there under Stalin. After World War II Reich and she became major proponents of Brecht's work in the Soviet Union. (Lacis has produced his work in her Latvian home, Riga, and in 1962 published a book in Latvian on Brecht and Piscator.) Reich popularized Meyerhold in Germany (where he in 1967 provided the introduction for the Reclam anthology *Meyerhold, Tairow, Wachtangow: Theateroktober*); he has written an early and therefore basic book on Brecht for the Soviet Union; and Brecht himself asked his advice about the first post-war translation of Brecht's work into Russian (1956).

Besides the Reichs, another major informant for Brecht on the Soviet theater was the poet, playwright, and journalist Sergei Tretiakov, Meyerhold's collaborator, who first published Brecht in Russian translation. Tretiakov's *Epic Plays,* including translations of *St. Joan of the Stockyards, The Measures Taken,* and *The Mother,* appeared with an introductory essay on Brecht in 1936, and Brecht requested that Tretiakov's particularly vivid translations of these three plays be the ones used in the 1956 Soviet edition of his works. A slightly different version of the essay describing the friendship of the two men in Berlin in 1931 appeared in Tretiakov's *Liudi odnogo kostra* (People of Like Persuasion),[46] a series of literary portraits, including one on Piscator entitled "Six Bankruptcies." Unfortunately, the German avant-garde theater, which Tretiakov strove to make known in Russia, had been abruptly silenced by Hitler, and in 1938 Tretiakov himself was executed, allegedly as a spy, in Russia under sentence by the People's Court. Though it took the Russian "people," as Brecht referred to them, until Stalin's death to reverse the sentence and rehabilitate Tretiakov, Brecht immediately questioned the execution in a poem entitled "Is the People Infallible?" (1939), which asked in a refrain repeated in each of seven stanzas: "Suppose he isn't guilty?" In its opening line Brecht called Tretiakov "My teacher."

In return for his teaching Brecht adapted for the German stage Tretiakov's *I Want a Child,* a play which Meyerhold rehearsed and tried to get past party objections from 1927 to 1930.[47] Apparently the play was never performed in Germany either. Also significant for Brecht's relationship with the Meyerhold Theater is his defense of

Tretiakov's *Roar China* when it was given on the theater's 1930 tour in Berlin. Brecht noted his indignation at the critics' misunderstanding of Meyerhold's aims: concerned only for their "experience" of empathy, they failed to see "that there is here a real theory about the historic function of the theater (*werkausgabe*, 15:204).

Of course the Marxist view of the historic function of the theater had long been familiar to the Germans of Brecht's generation. But did the means of fulfilling it, the "alienation" which made possible the appeal to reason, come from the Russians? Self-conscious theater art and the duality of the actor and his role, both basic principles with Meyerhold, are the essence of Brecht's *V-effect,* or *alienation,* which under the Brechtian nomenclature has decisively influenced all thinking about the theater today. Though in the appendix to *Mahagonny* (1929), Brecht systematized this kind of theater art in a table headed "epic drama," he did not use the word *alienation* until after his second trip to Moscow (1935). John Willett suggests that Brecht got his term for the famous V-effect from the Russian *ostranenie,* and Victor Erlich in his book on Russian formalism explains in detail the use of the word, especially by the formalist critic Viktor Shklovskii, to describe the striking metaphor or unusual vision common to all great art.[48] Ilia Fradkin, a Soviet authority on Brecht,

protests taking *alienation* back to the Russians, largely because the term thus becomes *formalistic,* a word connoting utter condemnation according to Soviet ideology.[49] Indeed, Brecht first discussed alienation, or the V-effect, in connection with the Chinese actor Mei-lan-fang, who gave a demonstration in Moscow in 1935, introduced by Meyerhold. Reich reported a conversation with Tretiakov, with whom Brecht stayed on his second Moscow visit (1935) and who had worked both as a dramatist with Meyerhold and as an editor of *Lef* with Shklovskii. Reich attested that Tretiakov explained to Brecht alienation in the sense of the Russian formalist critics and of the theater, as demonstrated by such a master as Mei-lan-fang.[50] Käthe Rülicke-Weiler, too, senses in Brecht admiration for and affinity with Eisenstein, Mayakovsky, and Meyerhold.[51]

Brecht, in fact, seems particularly to have admired Nikolai Pogodin's *Aristocrats* (1935), the production of Meyerhold's pupil Okhlopkov at the Realistic Theater. Rülicke says that during Brecht's last visit to the Soviet Union, in 1955, to receive the Lenin Prize, he urged Okhlopkov to revive *Aristocrats.* The revival took place in 1957. Both the early and late productions used theatrical devices: in the early production the stage platform was placed in the midst of the audience, and in both the early show and the revival, stage assistants wearing dark tights and masks opened the performance with a snowstorm of white confetti which they tossed on audience and stage alike; later in the play they agitated canvas to simulate waves when the characters plunged in to swim. Meyerhold, who had used such devices of Oriental theater for snow in *The Unknown Lady* before World War I, never carried illusionistic realism so far as the waves in *Aristocrats*. And Brecht never resorted to the device of the stage assistants at all. Yet the affinity between Meyerhold and Brecht and that between Meyerhold's pupil Okhlopkov and Brecht, deeper than devices, go to the heart of the matter, theater as conscious art, epitomized in "alienation."

Brecht continued to follow the Russian theater, and many details of performances at the Berliner Ensemble are attributable to that source: for instance, published Berliner Ensemble programs, illustrated and designed to stimulate thought and discussion, were reminiscent of Meyerhold's 1926 publication of the first program of the Meyerhold Theater as the interesting and controversial pamphlet *Affiche No. 1*. Yet Brecht did not "borrow" from Meyerhold and indeed seems not to have been impressed by any particular production of his. In an unrealized project of 1937 for founding "a society for inductive theater," the Diderot Society, Brecht considered inviting to membership not Meyerhold, but only Tretiakov and the Meyerhold pupils Eisenstein and Okhlopkov, along with other international figures of the theater and literary world.

In a 1939 lecture he gave for student amateurs of theater in Stockholm Brecht showed himself superbly well informed on all the technical contributions made by avant-garde directors from Antoine to Piscator. And in his lecture "On Experimental Theater" he said, "Vakhtangov and Meyerhold took certain dancing forms from Asiatic theater and created a whole choreography for drama. Meyerhold practiced a radical constructivism . . ." *(werkausgabe,* 15:286). He went on without always citing names: "The barriers between stage and audience were removed. . . . The revolving stage and cyclorama were invented and light was discovered. In acting the dividing line between cabaret and theater and between revue and theater was eliminated. There were experiments with masks, cothurns, and pantomimes. Far-reaching experiments were attempted with the traditional repertory of the classics" *(werkausgabe,* 15:286–87). Of course many of the devices Brecht mentioned were used by both Meyerhold and himself, and even according to the same overall pattern of development: from radical devices, episodic structure, and impudent satire toward visual beauty and true pathos. In Meyerhold's case the quick succession of episodes essential to the dynamism of *Tarelkin* or apparatus for acting like the whirligig swing in *The Forest* eventually gave way to the elegance of *Camille*. In Brecht's case the irony of a king's messenger on a wooden horse in *The Threepenny Opera* or soldiers on stilts with clown-white faces in *Man is Man* yielded later to the sober beauty of *Galileo,* which astounded Moscow in 1957 as a truly classic production.

Within limits the two directors had certain basic causes in common. Brecht had his actors break the frame of the illusion by direct appeal to the audience, especially with "songs." Indeed, both directors fought the same neverending battle against empathy and the "hypnosis" of the audience. Granted, Brecht kept the proscenium frame from which Meyerhold hoped to be liberated in his new building, for Brecht wanted to frame the dramatic events for objective consideration by the audience. Like Meyerhold he believed in the political role of the theater, though he hoped it might be fulfilled primarily by reasonable demonstration. Here again he shared with Meyerhold the belief that the actor must show, not be, the character he plays. "Show that you are showing," Brecht urged in one of the "Messingkauf" poems written in 1939–40 (*werkausgabe,* 1:778).

The two directors shared other basic tendencies. Both were concerned to employ few but telling stage properties—the pretzel on the lapel of Khlestakov in Meyerhold's *Inspector General,* like Mother Courage's spoon appended to her quilted jacket, underlined the unrelenting appetite of both characters; similarly, both directors delighted in circus and folk theater—Brecht tried the ballad form of the Augsburg Fair in the narrative of Mack the Knife, just as Meyerhold made the *balagan* element pivotal in all his work; and both tried to make the theater compete with mass entertainment forms like cinema and sport. Both drastically adapted the classics to their time, and both assigned a function to music in the theater. To measure the genius of one against the other is scarcely relevant. If Meyerhold as director had larger scope, Brecht has undoubtedly had greater influence in the West, based on his writings as well as his directorial work. If Meyerhold was ahead of his time, so that Brecht could have derived much from him, Brecht handed on in his own way certain Meyerholdian achievements now generally accepted without recognition of their source. Indeed, Brecht furthered many of their common causes so effectively that the main stream of theater art is unthinkable today without their "show" of the illusion and without their activation of the audience.

That Brecht should have been the one to propagate the ideas of alienation and activation, and that Russian theatrical innovations should have been cultivated by the Germans, could hardly have been foreseen. Normally ideas are promulgated through broad cultural contact; one would suppose, for instance, that the furor created by Diaghilev's Paris seasons might have launched a new movement in French ballet. Instead, the Diaghilev ballet left its mark in England, and the Royal Ballet and the Ballet Rambert have become the direct heirs of the Russian dancers. Of course, unlike ballet, the art of theater must surmount an additional obstacle, the problem of language; perhaps because the French classic theater was born of the seventeenth century and its language, it required renewal from within itself before being susceptible to new ideas from without. Certainly it had its own innovators; indeed, France was the first source of symbolism and the first symbolist theater was staged there. Meyerhold's production of Maeterlinck, first in the Theater Studio of 1905 and later for Komissarzhevskaia, occurred in the wake of A. M. Lugné-Poe, the French proponent of symbolist theater who first staged Alfred Jarry and Crommelynck in the nineties and who produced nonrealistically not only Maeterlinck but also Ibsen, with backdrops by such painters as Pierre Bonnard, Odilon Redon, and Edouard Vuillard, and with "chanted diction." [52]

The bibliography of Meyerhold's early reading has shown him aware also of the pioneers of theatrical change in other countries, with whom, together with Stanislavsky, he made common cause: Appia, Craig, Reinhardt, and Georg Fuchs.[53] Appia used rhythm and movement, Craig cubist forms, Reinhardt traditional forms of Greek, medieval, and Shakespearean theater; Fuchs emphasized beauty in the theater and the artistry of the actor. The Russian contribution to the renewal of theater art, made at this early point through Diaghilev's Paris seasons of opera and ballet (1909–29), took the form of splendors of color and sensual movement and music. Diaghilev's Russian artists Bakst and Golovin and the choreographer Fokine, also Meyerhold's collaborators, were soon joined in their work for the Paris seasons by Picasso, Matisse, and Braque. The Diaghilev troupe took as an apprentice Jean Cocteau, whose ballet *Parade* (1917), written with the composer Eric Satie, then helped to incorporate the new spirit in the arts. The international character of the new movement shows perhaps most clearly in the sequence of works Igor Stravinsky composed for the Diaghilev Ballet: from *The Firebird* (1910) and *Petrushka* (1911), both in a Russian folk spirit, through *The Rites of Spring* (1913) and *History of a Soldier* (1918), both indicative of new directions. Stravinsky's opera *The Nightingale* (1914), after a Chinese fairy tale, was staged in Russia at his special request by Meyerhold at the former Mariinskii Theater, Petrograd (1918). It had little success, but it indisputably "connected with many further attempts to renew the art of opera" (Rudnitskii, p. 226).

In this way the work of art in the theater was transformed in a few years by an international cooperation of genius. From the stuffed-box model of reality current in the nineties it became with Lugné-Poe the perceived representation of an idea, with Craig an intellectual aesthetic construction, with Appia a three-dimensional rhythmic whole, and with Diaghilev at first a luxury of folk colors and movement and later abstraction and surrealism or simplistic constructivism.

Simultaneously with this international transformation occurring chiefly in Paris, perhaps the most important reform of the French stage as such, with a quite different intent, took place largely outside Paris. Jacques Copeau was "the main artisan of the return to integrity on the French stage." [54] After the first seasons of his Théâtre du Vieux Colombier (1913–14), Copeau continued his work at his studio and school, at first near Paris but later, during World War I, in New York, until it was possible to return to Paris in 1920. Like Meyerhold, Copeau bared the stage in order to present afresh works of the great tradition, and like Meyerhold he found the genuineness of theater in the

recognition of its artificiality. Stanislavsky, however, was the Russian director whom Copeau knew, thanks to the Moscow Art Theater's foreign tour (1922–23), and the Vieux Colombier's communal living resembled Vakhtangov's studio above all. By the mid-twenties the Vieux Colombier had centrifugally dispersed many major figures to other undertakings. Copeau himself resigned in 1924. Georges Pitoëff, a Russian actor-director who first acted professionally in Komissarzhevskaia's theater after Meyerhold's departure, then joined with two Copeau alumni, Louis Jouvet and Charles Dullin, and with a pupil of Firmin Gémier, Gaston Baty, to form the Cartel des Quatre (Cartel of the Four) in 1928. Among Pitoëff's first productions in the West had been Blok's *Farce* (Geneva, 1915), which Pitoëff must have known in the repertory of Komissarzhevskaia's theater. Baty at his Théâtre Montparnasse received Meyerhold's troupe on its 1930 tour abroad. Besides this actual contact, Baty came close to Meyerhold on theoretical points with his belief in subordinating the text of a play to the larger whole of its creation in the theater.

More important in the continuation of ideas related to Meyerhold's is the second generation of French directors to emerge since Copeau. Jean-Louis Barrault, for example, in his efforts to "stage the unreal" has sought overt means of expression especially in pantomime and movement. And like the Meyerhold of the immediate postrevolutionary years, Jean Vilar, director of the Théâtre National Populaire, long tried to bring the experience of theater to the masses, often in great outdoor spectacles, as at the Avignon Festival.

In calling Copeau an "artisan of the return to integrity on the French stage," Jacques Guicharnaud means by "integrity" both "concentration" and "wholeness," as opposed to the "disruption" and "unloosing" of forces in the "theater of cruelty" propagated by Antonin Artaud. Just as Marinetti had long ago proposed putting glue on the seats or making everyone run round the auditorium to shake up the audience, or as Meyerhold and Brecht strove to break the "hypnosis" of the audience, so Artaud rejected the notion of theater as relaxation and tried to give back the traditional revelatory seriousness of the theater. To shatter routine acceptance and penetrate to metaphysical truth, Artaud was ready to use "cruelty": "Dans l'état de dégénérescence où nous sommes, c'est par la peau qu'on fera rentrer la métaphysique dans les esprits" ("In the state of degeneration we have now reached, we must inject metaphysics through the skin, if it is to get into the mind").[55]

Surely it is a misunderstanding to make Artaud's "cruelty" into bloodcurdling physical horror alone, as occurs so frequently of late on stage and screen. Still, Artaud clearly meant by the term the use of strong means to shatter the spectator's indifference. As early as 1928 he advocated employing sound effects such as can be realized only now through modern sound equipment.[56] Meyerhold had anticipated him in *The Last Decisive Battle,* training upon the audience cannons from which blanks were fired, though this all too direct assault had to be given up after the first few performances. Among the total means of theater for activating the audience, including sound, light, music, and movement, Artaud found the carefully regulated movements of the actor particularly effective for reaching the organism—or, as he hypothesized, even the potential cannibalism—of the audience; he therefore called the actor "an athlete of the heart." [57] Though Artaud in 1922 mentioned work by the Russians on improvisation to "exteriorize" profound sensibilities, he surely meant Stanislavsky, not Meyerhold. Yet what a fitting designation is his "athlete of the heart" for the biomechanical actor!

Among such diverse trends in French twentieth-century theater, many of which are comparable to the diversity of ideas in the theory and practice of Meyerhold alone, "one tendency seems to dominate the French theater of today," according to Guicharnaud: "a clear movement toward anti-realism and its growing acceptance by the public." [58]

Which European theatrical tradition the leading Italian director Giorgio Strehler might claim as his own is open to question. Strehler began his professional career as a director with the *Compagnie des Masques,* a group he formed, which included Sascha Pitoëff, in Switzerland, where all were interned during the Second World War. (The tenuous connection of Pitoëff père with Meyerhold's work at Komissarzhevskaia's theater has already been mentioned.) Earlier, as a student in Italy, Strehler had opposed establishment and boulevard theater, and upon his return there he continued to work in new directions with plays by dramatists from Shakespeare to Brecht. The latter saw in him his Italian disciple. Above all, Strehler has revived the native tradition of the *commedia dell'arte* in his quarter of a century's work at the Piccolo teatro, Milan. His production of Carlo Goldoni's *Arlechino; or, The Servant of Two Masters* (revived with the Piccolo teatro company for the 1973 Salzburg Festival) exemplifies numerous Meyerholdian principles. Set on a small stage upon the stage, with the curtain pulled and footlight candles lighted in view of the audience, the action of *Arlechino* is not confined to the small stage alone. The players' covered wagons (Blok's and Meyerhold's *balagan*), standing one on each side of the large stage, shelter the actors' preparations and their practice exercises before entrances and their plaudits to their fellows upon exits. Actors off stage also engage in play with those on stage when, in the function of Meyerhold's stage assistants, they hand up needed properties to those on stage, such as a handkerchief for weeping, which they then take back to wring out and return to receive more tears; or they offer properties not needed, as when a stage assistant in comic pantomime tries to press a sword on a reluctant duelist. A high point is reached with the stage assistants hurling to Harlequin at jugglers' speeds platters of food for the dinner he finds himself obliged to serve to two masters at once. When his duplicity is discovered, the whole cast overflows in tumultuous pursuit of him, not just onto the off-stage borders of the stage itself, but also through the whole auditorium, until at last in a moment of supreme play with the illusion a child in the audience cries, "See, there he is!" and all the players climb with hue and cry and lanterns after Harlequin, who, once discovered on high, swings down to safety on a rope. Thus Strehler uses devices with superb effectiveness in *commedia dell'arte* which together amount almost to a historic panorama of Meyerhold's successive experiments from *Farce* to *The Bedbug.* However, to stage Shakespeare with the help of these devices, as Strehler does in his rewrite of the chronicle plays, *Das Spiel der Mächtigen* (Salzburg, 1973) is a more doubtful undertaking. At any rate, Meyerhold's methods in the hands of talented directors continue to yield interesting theater.

*Meyerhold's Legacy: Eisenstein and the Theater Today in Russia and the West*

Meyerhold's legacy has been indirect, at best. The almost quarter-century repression of his theater art in the Soviet Union has meant that no theater there today carries on his work in direct succession, as is the case for productions of Stanislavsky and Vakhtangov. Nor did his work during his lifetime attract followers from the West, as did Stanislavsky's, though Western disciples, Jay Leyda, Herbert Marshall, and Ivor Montagu, did study with Eisenstein, undoubtedly Meyerhold's most illustrious pupil. The pupil relationship was determined by more than the single year (1921–22) which Eisenstein spent as a member of the Meyerhold Workshop. Eisenstein in an autobiographical sketch ascribed his first sense of an artistic calling to an earlier encounter with the master's work, "some especially vivid theater experiences" at *Masquerade, Don Juan,* and *The Constant Prince,* all of them Meyerhold productions at the Alexandrinskii, which Eisenstein saw in postrevolutionary Petrograd.[59] And in a revision of the same sketch, "How I Became a Director"

(1946), Eisenstein called two shows, Fedor Komissarzhevsky's production of Gozzi's *Turandot* and Meyerhold's production of Lermontov's *Masquerade,* the "thunder claps" which made him an artist.

Eisenstein came to Petrograd to study civil engineering, joined the Red Army in March 1918 and, assigned to military construction not far away, there began work in the theater. He organized a drama club, for which he wrote, directed, and acted in the first play, a satiric adaptation to the Soviet era of Gogol's *Inspector General.* He was then sent by the army to Minsk with a professional actor to organize a provincial theater. Though assigned to Minsk as a designer, Eisenstein was as much an amateur in this as in directing and acting, though he had made sketches on his own for Mayakovsky's *Mystery-Bouffe,* which according to Fevralskii he probably did not even see in Petrograd in 1918. After leaving the army he worked in the Proletkult Theatre in Moscow in 1920, again as a designer. He began acting and directing professionally with Meyerhold and for a year studied stage direction at the Meyerhold Workshop. His "season with Meyerhold," as Eisenstein called it in yet another autobiographical sketch (1933), caused him to pay generous tribute to his teacher. And in the autobiographical notes with which he busied himself during his last illness in the

Kremlin hospital (1946) he named Meyerhold as his spiritual father and said of him, "I never loved anyone, never adored or worshipped anyone as I did my teacher. . . . For I am not worthy to untie his shoe laces, though he didn't wear shoes but leggings in the unheated workshop for stage directors on Novinsky Boulevard." [60]

Along with such almost abject worship Eisenstein uttered the criticism that at least during the first two terms at the workshop Meyerhold never came to grips with essentials but made his instruction a kind of strip tease, removing one veil after another without betraying the secret of his stage direction. Not until the last spring term, when Meyerhold staged Ibsen's *Doll's House,* did Eisenstein receive what he called the most important lesson of his life in directing. He even listed this show among all the memorable performances he experienced in a lifetime of travel and acquaintance with the performing arts —from Chaliapin and Stanislavsky, Yvette Guilbert and Mistinguett, to Chaplin and Gershwin—and concluded: "But not one of these impressions can ever eradicate from my memory the impressions I received from those three days of rehearsal of *Doll's House* in the high school on Novinsky Boulevard." [61] Rudnitskii attests the fact that it was Eisenstein who saved the Meyerhold archive, now preserved in the Central State Archive of Literature and Art; indeed, at the moment Eisenstein was thus praising *Doll's House* Meyerhold's name was unmentionable, and his archive was hidden at the Eisenstein dacha (Rudnitskii, p. 259). To the overwhelming experience of *Doll's House* Iutkevich adds as highly instructive for Eisenstein and him—both then workshop students—Meyerhold's conduct of rehearsals for *The Magnanimous Cuckold*.

Because no scholarships were available in the early Soviet years the two workshop students Iutkevich and Eisenstein had to earn their living by doing odd jobs for other theaters. Accordingly they submitted plans for a revival of Meyerhold's pantomime *Columbine's Scarf* to the director Foregger, with a dedication to Meyerhold and the subtitle "a montage of attractions." Though the subtitle as a whole was used there for the first time, the term *attraction* had already acquired the meaning of aggressive theater through Eisenstein's work in the Proletkult Theater (1921) on *The Mexican,* after Jack London. Meyerhold paid this show the unique tribute of taking the whole workshop to see it early in 1922: "Indeed this was the first time," Iutkevich points out, "that the 'master' agreed to look at his pupil's work" (Iutkevich, p. 232). Though Eisenstein was credited merely as designer of the production, at least one directorial idea had been his as well: to show on stage a boxing match which was to have taken place behind the scenes. "This was in essence," Iutkevich comments, "the first realization of that theory of 'attractions' which he later developed in his productions of *Even a Wise Man Stumbles* (often called *The Sage*) after Ostrovsky and *Listen Moscow* and *Gas Masks* by Tretiakov" (ibid., 233). If *The Mexican* carried into effect the attraction of the boxing match, another attraction—having a character enter on tightrope from the audience, which Eisenstein planned for *Scarf*—was not realized, as the latter show was never staged. Eisenstein did, however, put the entry on a tightrope into his outrageous *Sage,* of which some scenes were given at the Bolshoi Theater in honor of Meyerhold's twenty-fifth professional anniversary (1923).

A "montage of attractions" truly came into being in the cinematographic episodes of Meyerhold's *Death of Tarelkin,* on which Eisenstein worked as assistant director. After the "cinematification" of the 1922 *Tarelkin* and a first brief film, "Glumov's Diary," which Eisenstein made for *The Sage,* he turned to film making for good. It appears that Eisenstein first conceived the notion of "a montage of attractions" as the subtitle of the unrealized *Scarf* plan, then helped put it into practice in Meyerhold's *Tarelkin,* and applied it himself in the political revue *The Sage*. At any rate he defined it in connection

with *The Sage* in an article of 1923. Rudnitskii, though, feels that the technique itself had been realized five years earlier by Mayakovsky and Meyerhold in the first version of *Mystery-Bouffe;* they derived it, in turn, from best theatrical traditions of the past, on which they based their revolution of the theater. However, in the introductory sentences to his English translation of "A Montage of Attractions," in *The Film Sense* (1942), Jay Leyda writes that Eisenstein's early concept was realized only later in the film medium.

It is true that Eisenstein achieved mature realization of his concepts only in the motion pictures which constituted his major work. Yet in the present cinematic era of unplotted action and the hand-held camera, Eisenstein's major canon of films seems historic and momentarily irrelevant to today's trends. In contrast, his early theory and practice of theater in Meyerhold's sense has become relevant to much recent avant-garde theater. Eisenstein's 1923 definition of the concept of attraction reads: "Attraction (in the crosscut of the theater) is any aggressive moment of theater, that is any element of it which subjects the spectator to emotional or psychological experience proved in practice and mathematically calculated to produce in him a definite emotional shock, which in turn and in its entirety is aimed solely at making it possible for the spectator to grasp the show's idea content—its final ideological conclusion." [62] This shock treatment, with its attack upon the audience in order to shake, and perhaps activate it is wholly relevant to present theater practice in the West, even if the ultimate aim of communicating idea content is still largely undeveloped here, despite the work of the Living Theater, or "guerrilla" theater.

"Montage," in Eisenstein's early definition, meant little more than the putting together of attractions, or attacks upon audience sensibility. Later he understood far more by "montage": an extremely subtle art of composition, the counterpoint of sound and color, and finally even his entire sense of form. Perhaps it is Eisenstein's theory of form—the unity of form and content —that most deserves renewed study today. Eisenstein's theories show him not simply the heir of Meyerhold. Neither was he the heir of Meyerhold alone: perhaps it is Eisenstein, not Vakhtangov, who accomplished the synthesis of Stanislavsky's and Meyerhold's methods. Brecht remarked that the attribution of such synthesis to Vakhtangov was based on a misconception: "Vakhtangov represents the Stanislavsky-Meyerhold complex before it is torn asunder" (*werkausgabe,* 15:386). If Vakhtangov was thus the predecessor, then Eisenstein might well be seen as the successor, the proponent of their synthesis. For while

Eisenstein sought the "real thing" by casting amateurs who looked the part —"typage," as he called it—thus proving himself a realist and Stanislavsky's heir, at the same time he was unceasingly preoccupied with the formal implications of "montage," thus proving himself an artist of form and a disciple of Meyerhold. A genius in his own right, he brought together the inheritance of both Russian masters of theater art.

While Eisenstein's films have become "classic" in both the best and worst senses of the word, his early theater productions have remained virtually unknown, even though the two genres in which he did theater work have again come to the fore. The political fantastic and "formalistic" revue, as in *The Sage* or an unrealized project with Meyerhold in 1921, *Puss-in-Boots* (see fig. 3.11), represents one style; and the nearly documentary *Gas Masks,* by Tretiakov, which in 1923 he staged with the author on the scene at the gas works, represents the other. Both furnished precedents for recent avant-garde work at diverse locations: off-Broadway, at the Royal Court, at the Taganka in Moscow, in Stuttgart, in Amsterdam.

The revue form has become almost a specialty of the Theater on the Taganka. A few of the revues there are based on history (*Ten Days That Shook the World,* after the autobiography of

John Reed, and *Pugachev*); others, on a poet's work (*Listen!* on Mayakovsky; *Watch Your Faces,* on Andrei Voznesensky; *Under the Cloak of the Statue of Liberty,* on Evtushenko). *Ten Days* was advertised as a popular presentation "with pantomime, circus, buffoonery, and shots fired," recalling Mayakovsky's designation for *Bathhouse:* a drama "with circus and fireworks." B. Galanov likens the dialectic of *Ten Days,* the revolutionary message contrasted to the horseplay of the circus form, to the antithesis "mystery" and "bouffe" of Mayakovsky's first Soviet play. The slogan "Back to Meyerhold," used by the Taganka Theater in connection with its production of *Ten Days* and cited by Galanov in his article on the play,[63] might point back further than 1918 to Meyerhold's treatment of the mystics in Blok's *Farce:* indeed the United States senators at John Reed's hearing, four in a row across the stage, are soon discovered, like the four mystics, to be mere empty gowns and mortarboards. In another scene, as if to recreate the atmosphere of a political meeting for Meyerhold's "October in the Theater," Red sailors march to accordion music through the Taganka audience (awaiting admission in the lobby), which has already been pinned with red badges. After the show, ballots are distributed to be cast for or against the performance in ballot boxes at the exits, recalling the question-

naire used with Meyerhold Theater audiences.

Though portraits of four spiritual ancestors—Stanislavsky, Vakhtangov, Meyerhold, and Brecht—occupy a place of honor in the Taganka lobby, Iurii Liubimov, the theater's director, looks forward on his own as well as back to them. At one moment in *Ten Days* he uses a new device, a sheet of projected light like rain, to curtain off actors from audience, thus taking a step beyond Meyerhold, who long before tried single projectors instead of a curtain. And quotations from Lenin delivered over the loudspeaker at the Taganka, though reminiscent of Meyerhold's screen projections, now wholly envelop the audience in an aura of electronic sound. Liubimov has carried biomechanics perhaps furthest of all from the point of departure: in a prison scene in *Pugachev* a dance drama is enacted in which a central figure is propelled now to one side, now to another, against a circular chain held inexorably against him by his torturers. The rhythmic ritual of the torment compounds the experience of suffering to an extreme surely inaccessible to realism.

Other Soviet directors continued Meyerhold's ideas, having received them firsthand. Two Meyerhold Workshop alumni and Meyerhold Theater actors became directors of leading Moscow theaters: Okhlopkov and Pluchek. Okhlopkov as director put into practice

Meyerhold's unrealized concept of an arena-type flexible playing space. At his tiny Realistic Theater (1930–37) he rebuilt the stage anew for each production. An English visitor, André van Gyseghem, describes how he found his way to a seat for Okhlopkov's production of Aleksandr Serafimovich's *Iron Stream* (1933) by ducking under a clothes line and stepping over a bawling baby, both part of the action which had already begun by the time the audience was admitted. The audience was again "included" in Pogodin's *Aristocrats* (1935, revived 1957) when snow fell on onlookers and actors alike; the stage assistants who threw out the snow and pushed branches past a stationary skier to give the illusion of motion had been borrowed from Kabuki by Meyerhold as early as *Farce*. Not only such devices of nonrealism but the whole concept of *uslovnyi* theater was finally defended by Okhlopkov in a series of articles in *Teatr* (1959).

Since the thaw in Soviet art Pluchek, the younger alumnus of the Meyerhold workshop and theater, director of the Moscow Theater of Satire, has revived all three plays of Mayakovsky's canon, *The Bathhouse* (1953), *The Bedbug* (revived, together with Iutkevich, in 1955), and *Mystery-Bouffe* (1957). To be sure, some of Pluchek's solutions in the revivals seem all too realistic; for instance, in *The Bedbug,* the only one of the three plays still running, the world of 1979 is shown not futuristically but against the background of the actual Moscow University skyscraper; and in *The Bathhouse* the Phosphorescent Lady, delegate of the year 2030, is represented, not as Meyerhold showed her, in a space costume, but as a present-day model Soviet woman. Still, many of Pluchek's own shows have been as refreshingly inventive as his witty production of Aleksandr Tvardovskii's *Terkin in the Other World*. And more recent productions of Max Frisch's *Don Juan* and Beaumarchais's *Marriage of Figaro* have kept faith with the theater's professed satiric bent.

Naturally, Tvardovskii's satiric subject, the daring return from the other world of the rank-and-file soldier Terkin, who prefers earth to paradise, is unthinkable without the precedent of Mayakovsky's *Mystery-Bouffe*. And so in a larger sense the inheritance of Meyerhold is felt in many interesting productions of recent Soviet theater which derive from the satiric tradition. Furthermore, in the inventive productions which have been given Evgenii Shvarts's fairy-tale satires, by the late director-designer Nikolai Akimov (*The Shadow,* 1940), at the Leningrad Theater of Comedy, and by director Oleg Efremov (*The Naked King,* i.e., *The Emperor's New Clothes,* 1960) at the Contemporary Theater, Moscow, one may trace a direct descent from Vakhtangov's *Turandot* as well.

It is again relevant to ask how much Vakhtangov and Meyerhold shared in common.

The reuse of Meyerholdian devices appeared concrete and specific in two Soviet productions of Griboedov's *Woe from Wit* in the sixties. One, by Evgenii Simonov (1963) at the national classical theater, the Malyi in Moscow, revived Meyerhold's idea of adding as silent roles the group of young revolutionaries, the Decembrists, from whose midst Chatskii emerged. And in the other, by Georgii Tovstonogov (1962) at the Bolshoi Dramatic Theater, Leningrad, the conclusion of act 3 extended Meyerhold's treatment of the silent scene at the end of *The Inspector General*. In the moment it took for a curtain to pass announcing the advent of the real inspector, Meyerhold had replaced the society surrounding the mayor with mannequins in horrified poses. Similarly, Tovstonogov suddenly switched to strobe lighting, and the eerie flashes revealed a transformed society threatening Chatskii with the rumor of his madness: the actors had rapidly donned rubber masks and then circled round Chatskii on the band of the rotating stage with seemingly mechanized gestures and grotesque grins on their inhuman masks.

Of course, a precedent for such emphasis of the director's intent may be found as much in Artaud as in Meyerhold's *Woe to Wit,* for in the same year

(1928) as Meyerhold's production Artaud had written: "Mise en scène: les personnages seront systématiquement poussés au type" ("Staging: the characters will be systematically pushed toward the typical").[64] But the intent need not be ascribed to the director at all; it may be quite as much the author's. Griboedov, after the model of eighteenth-century comedy, typified his characters even by name: the heroine's father, Famusov, might be called in English Mr. Prominent, his secretary, Molchalin, Mr. Taciturn, and so on. Still, theater as it is tending today needs to invoke no authority for shattering audiences with many of the means Meyerhold explored.

In the early twenties Eisenstein and Meyerhold embarked in the opposite direction from the revue-type "montage of attractions" to the documentary inclusion of reality. In retrospect it is plain that the flirtation of the two directors with *littérature trouvée* (as when Meyerhold made room for the news of Perekop in *Dawns*), or with staging *sur place* (as when Eisenstein produced Tretiakov's *Gas Masks* at the gasworks), occurred in response to the excitement of outward events. For the genius of both lay not just in appropriating the material of reality but in organizing it, that is, forming it artistically. Certainly Meyerhold later repudiated the Proletkult (proletarian culture) movement for its naive rendering of the raw stuff of every day. Interestingly, a proletkultish trend toward "Living Newspaper" and *agitprop* (agitation-propaganda) recurs today with such "documentaries" as *Life Price,* by Michael O'Neill and Jeremy Seabrook, at the Royal Court, London (about child rape), or with such historical pseudodocumentaries as *The Deputy,* by Rolf Hochhuth; *In the Matter of J. Robert Oppenheimer,* by Heinar Kipphardt, in Germany; or the Soviet play *The Truth, Nothing But the Truth,* by D. Al, at the Leningrad Gorky Theater, where a United States congressional hearing on the Russian Revolution is reenacted with the prosecutor in the audience's midst as if at a political meeting.

At least in the West such documentary realism often goes hand in hand today with satiric surrealism, as in Jakov Lind's *Ergo* or Sam Shepard's *La Turista,* in both of which acrobatics and work on multiple levels recall Meyerholdian devices of the twenties. In the USSR the genre of satiric fantasy seems temporarily quiescent; it is represented only by earlier classics, the works of Brecht, Mayakovsky, or Evgenii Shvarts. The simultaneous occurrence of documentary and fantasy today should not astonish us; these were concurrently features of the early Soviet period of Meyerhold and Eisenstein's collaboration. And both have the same bite of political tendentious-

ness, despite the pretense of objectivity in the first.

As already noted, the influential contemporary director Jerzy Grotowski of the Polish Laboratory Theater counts Meyerhold among the "fathers." Another director, Peter Brook, then of the British Royal Shakespeare Society, called for his second coming, at least in the United States: "In America today the time is ripe for a Meyerhold to appear, since naturalistic representations of life no longer seem to Americans adequate to express the forces that drive them." [65] Not even a Meyerhold, though, could play savior to the many nonnaturalistic directions of contemporary theater. Despite his chameleon-like changeability, he clearly said no to certain current tendencies of theater art. Grotowski's emphasis on the "trance," for example, comes closer to Stanislavsky, and experiments with communal living by the now defunct Living Theater of Julian Beck or Richard Schechner's Performance Theater look rather to Vakhtangov or Jacques Copeau.

Nor are all the Meyerholdian trends worth saving. Surely the mannered pictorialism of *Sister Beatrice* with Komissarzhevskaia is no longer viable. Yet beautiful stage pictures of the elegance of *Don Juan* or *Masquerade,* integrated with a key idea, have come into vogue again, as witness a number of productions around the world in 1968 alone:

Beaumarchais's *Figaro* at the Theater of Satire, Moscow, Shakespeare's *Winter's Tale* by the Royal Shakespeare Society, Stratford, and Lind's *Ergo* at the Public Theater in New York, to name three.

Still other Meyerholdian impulses seem inevitably right today. The direct actor-audience contact of Meyerhold-Pierrot sitting on the edge of the bare stage to speak the last lines of Blok's *Farce* was a precedent for the naive immediacy almost half a century later of the two tramps seated on the ramp, showing us their shoe soles, in Beckett's *Godot*. The cannons trained on the balcony in Tretiakov's *Roar China* threatened the audience just as do the asylum inmates advancing upon us in Peter Weiss's *Marat/Sade*. It was Meyerhold who broke through the fourth wall of mimetic illusion to establish such audience contact, whether amicable or hostile.

Equally important for the avant-garde today is Meyerhold's early example in giving the theater political purpose. Meyerhold's slogan "Put the October Revolution into the Theater" encompassed the doubly political thrust of Verhaeren's *Dawns,* which tried both to include the reality of Perekop in the performance and to achieve audience participation as at a political meeting. True, Meyerhold stopped short of the conclusion *ad absurdum* at which the Living Theater aimed in *Paradise Now*

(1968) when it attempted to send the audience into the street to get arrested. Complete activism is as preposterous an aim for political theater as the complete reproduction of reality on stage is for the mimetic theater. Neither extreme, of course, invalidates the substance of its doctrine, and both propaganda and imitation rightly continue to be part of theater today. Political theater, to which Meyerhold contributed so greatly, is successfully influencing contemporary attitudes, whether in the West with the vague antiorthodox message of love in the American musical *Hair* or in the USSR with the aggressive antibourgeois ideology of *Ten Days That Shook the World* at the Taganka Theater, Moscow. But today's effort to influence the audience is often ritualistic, as in Jean-Claude Van Itallie's *Serpent* at Joseph Chaikin's Group Theater in New York, which uses movement according to a "score," as Meyerhold did.

Nor did Meyerhold, for all his much-decried text revision, abandon the word or collectively create new words in quite the modern manner. Often his adaptation of classics amounted to cleansing them of the darkened varnish of time and "contemporizing" them, as in his production of Gogol's *Inspector General,* or restoring them to their original intent, as in Pushkin's *Queen of Spades.* But the trend begun with Meyerhold's revision of the classics has led to much abuse in our time. Indeed, the actor's attitude of conscious objectivity toward his role, on which Meyerhold insisted throughout and which reached its peak recently with the worship of Brechtian alienation in the West, seems again to be going out of style today.

If some items of the rich Meyerholdian inheritance are unusable, still others may yet prove fruitful. Perhaps Artaud's misunderstood catchword "theater of cruelty" may enable the dark melodramatic strain of a play like *Masquerade* again to come to the fore in the West, as it has done in two Soviet revivals, one at the Malyi and the other at Iurii Zavadskii's Mossoviet Theater in Moscow. Or the multi-level acrobatics pioneered in *Woe to Wit* may beget more productions than Benno Besson's *Peace* at the Deutsches Theater, Berlin, and Peter Brook's *Midsummer Night's Dream* at the Royal Shakespeare Society, London. (The program of this last invokes Meyerhold by name.)

Whether or not Meyerholdian tendencies and devices recur, the same moot questions of theater art, most of which Meyerhold raised, still concern the avant-garde. Often Meyerhold's answers still seem right today. He urged the inclusion of the audience, though he stopped short of total audience participation. He abolished the curtain and the fourth wall of the theater illusion, and he often used the whole auditorium, though he never got the adaptable theater he had planned, convertible for use either as an arena or with the audience in the center, viewing a production on all sides around it. He gave plays in places other than the theater, though, unlike Stanislavsky, he did not put untrained people in the parts, for he believed in the professional actor. He schooled actors in movement and in devices from other acting traditions, since he strove for the conscious use and adaptation of expressive means where he found them. He revised the classics and created shows while working closely with an author in the theater, for he aimed to achieve relevant theater art, though he never created a show solely in collective collaboration or, as a rule, produced works without words. He tried to make theater art part of the October Revolution, but he stopped short of subordinating it to politics. Indeed, the one consistent principle essential in the many trends of his work is the refusal to subordinate theater art to any other art, whether literature or politics, or even to reality itself. If the avant-garde were given to looking backward, instead of by definition forward, it would surely recognize one of the fathers of modern theater in Vsevolod Meyerhold.

# Appendix 1: Table of Meyerhold's Productions (1905-39)

Table of Meyerhold's Productions (1905–39), beginning with the Theater Studio of 1905. List compiled by Aleksandr V. Fevralskii with the assistance of Maia M. Sitkovetskaia.

## 1. COMPLETED PRODUCTIONS

| Author | Play | Designer | Composer | Theater | Date |
|---|---|---|---|---|---|
| | | | | | 1905 |
| M. Maeterlinck | Death of Tintagiles | Acts 1–3, S. Iu. Sudeikin, Acts 4–5, N. N. Sapunov | I. A. Sats | Theater Studio, Moscow | Summer—no opening date |
| G. Hauptmann | Schluck and Jau (co-director V. E. Repman) | N. P. Ulianov | R. M. Glier | " | " |
| S. Przybyszewski | Snow | V. I. Denisov | | " | " |
| H. Ibsen | Comedy of Love | V. I. Denisov | | " | " |
| | | | | | 1906 |
| H. Ibsen | Hedda Gabler | N. N. Sapunov (set), V. D. Miliutin (costumes) | | Theater of V. F. Komissarzhevskaia, St. Petersburg | 10 Nov. |
| S. Iushkevich | In the City | V. K. Kolenda | A. K. Liadov | " | 13 Nov. |
| M. Maeterlinck | Sister Beatrice | S. Iu. Sudeikin | | " | 22 Nov. |
| S. Przybyszewski | Eternal Fairy Tale | S. Iu. Sudeikin | | " | 4 Dec. |
| H. Ibsen | Doll's House | V. I. Denisov | | " | 18 Dec. |
| A. Blok | Farce | N. N. Sapunov | M. A. Kuzmin | | 30 Dec. |
| M. Maeterlinck | Miracle of St. Anthony | V. K. Kolenda | | " | |
| | | | | | 1907 |
| G. Heiberg | Tragedy of Love | V. Ia. Sureniants | | " | 8 Jan. |
| H. Ibsen | Comedy of Love | V. I. Denisov | | " | 22 Jan. |

| Author | Play | Designer | Composer | Theater | Date |
|---|---|---|---|---|---|
| H. von Hofmannsthal | Marriage of Zobeida | B. I. Anisfeld | | Theater of V. F. Komissarzhevskaia | 12 Feb. |
| L. Andreev | Life of Man | V. E. Meyerhold (plan), V. K. Kolenda | | " " | 22 Feb. |
| L. Andreev | To the Stars | | | Casino, V. R. Gardin's company, Terioki | 27 May |
| | Evening of "New Art," readings by the poets A. Blok, S. Gorodetskii, V. Piast, et al.; dramatization of two songs by P. I. Tschaikovsky | N. N. Saven | | " " | 13 June |
| | Evening of excerpts and dances from R. Strauss, Salomé | N. N. Saven | | Music Studio, Ollila | 20 June |
| F. Wedekind | Awakening of Spring | V. I. Denisov | | Theater of V. F. Komissarzhevskaia | 15 Sept. |
| M. Maeterlinck, trans. V. Briusov | Pelleas and Melisande | V. I. Denisov | V. A. Spiess von Eschenbruck | " " | 10 Oct. |
| F. K. Sologub | Victory of Death | V. E. Meyerhold (plan), N. A. Popov (execution) | | " " | 6 Nov. |
| M. Maeterlinck | Sister Beatrice | K. K. Kostin | | Company under direction of V. E. Meyerhold and R. A. Ungern, Vitebsk (Also Minsk, Kherson Poltava, Kiev, and | 1908 17 Feb. |

| Author | Play | Designer | Composer | Theater | Date |
|---|---|---|---|---|---|
| A. Blok | Farce | K. K. Kostin | | Kharkov until 4 May 1908) | 17 Feb. |
| F. Wedekind, trans. V. E. Meyerhold; prologue trans. S. Gorodetskii | Vampire (Spirit of Earth) | K. K. Kostin | | " | 19 Feb. |
| H. von Hofmannsthal | Electra | K. K. Kostin | | " | 20 Feb. |
| H. Ibsen | Hedda Gabler | K. K. Kostin | | " | 21 Feb. |
| F. K. Sologub | Victory of Death | K. K. Kostin | | " | 22 Feb. |
| L. Andreev | Life of Man | K. K. Kostin | | " | 23 Feb. |
| G. Hauptmann | Hostage of Charlemagne | K. K. Kostin | | " | 24 Feb. |
| H. Ibsen | Master Builder | K. K. Kostin | | " | 12 Mar. |
| K. Hamsun | At the Imperial Gates | K. K. Kostin | | " | 13 Mar. |
| K. Hamsun | At the Imperial Gates | A. Ia. Golovin | | Aleksandrinskii, St. Petersburg | 30 Sept. |
| O. Wilde | Salomé (choreographer M. Fokine) | L. S. Bakst | A. K. Glazunov | Mikhailovskii, St. Petersburg | Opening set for 3 Nov., but forbidden in October |
| P. Potemkin | Petrushka | M. V. Dobuzhinskii | V. F. Nuvel | Lukomore, St. Petersburg | |
| E. A. Poe, adapted by V. Trakhtenberg | Fall of the House of Usher | M. V. Dobuzhinskii (sets), V. Ia. Chembers (costumes) | V. G. Karatygin | | 6 Dec. |
| F. L. Sollogub | Honor and Revenge | I. Ia. Bilibin | | | |
| N. Gogol | Trial | A. K. Shervashidze | | Aleksandrinskii | 1909 19 Mar. |

| Author | Play | Designer | Composer | Theater | Date |
|---|---|---|---|---|---|
| R. Wagner | Tristan and Isolde | A. K. Shervashidze | | Mariinskii, St. Petersburg | 30 Oct. |
| D. Merezhkovskii | Paul I (two scenes) | A. K. Shervashidze | | Private house, St. Petersburg | 1910, early |
| E. Hardt | Fool Tantris | A. K. Shervashidze | M. A. Kuzmin | Aleksandrinskii | 9 Mar. |
| P. Calderón de la Barca, trans. K. Balmont | Adoration of the Cross | S. Iu. Sudeikin | | "Tower Theater," apartment of V. Ivanov, St. Petersburg | 19 Apr. |
| A. Schnitzler; Dr. Dapertutto (V. E. Meyerhold) | Columbine's Scarf (pantomime) | N. N. Sapunov | P. Donanyi | House of Interludes, St. Petersburg | 12 Oct. |
| Molière | Don Juan | A. Ia. Golovin | J.-F. Rameau | Aleksandrinskii | 9 Nov. |
| E. Znosko-Borovskii | Transformed Prince | S. Iu. Sudeikin | | House of Interludes | 3 Dec. |
| M. Mussorgsky | Boris Godunov | A. Ia. Golovin | | Mariinskii | 1911 6 Jan. |
| Iu. Beliaev | Red Tavern | A. Ia. Golovin | | Aleksandrinskii | 23 Mar. |
| L. N. Tolstoy | Living Corpse (codirector A. L. Zagarov) | K. A. Korovin | M. A. Kuzmin | " " | 28 Sept. |
| Volmar Liustsinius (V. N. Solovev) | Harlequin, the Marriage Broker | K. I. Evseev | V. A. Spiess von Eschenbruck, Iu. L. de Bur | Nobles' Assembly, St. Petersburg | 8 Nov. |
| C. W. Gluck | Orpheus (choreographer M. Fokine) | A. Ia. Golovin | | Mariinskii | 21 Dec. |
| Dr. Dapertutto | Lovers (pantomime) | V. I. Shukhaev, A. E. Iakovlev | C. Debussy (2 preludes) | N. P. Karabchevskii's house, St. Petersburg | 1912 Jan. |
| K. Balmont | Three Dawns | | E. Grieg | Tenishevskii audi- | 5 Mar. |

| Author | Play | Designer | Composer | Theater | Date |
|---|---|---|---|---|---|
| Dr. Dapertutto | Lovers | N. I. Kulbin | C. Debussy | Cooperative of artists, Terioki | 9 June |
| Volmar Liustsinius | Harlequin, the Marriage Broker | N. I. Kulbin | Iu. L. de Bur | " | |
| P. Calderón de la Barca, trans. K. Balmont | Adoration of the Cross | Iu. M. Bondi | | " | 29 June |
| A. Strindberg | Crimes and Crimes | Iu. M. Bondi | | " | 14 July |
| G. B. Shaw, adapted by V. E. Meyerhold | You Wouldn't Have Said That for Anything | Iu. M. Bondi | | " | 15 July |
| F. K. Sologub | Hostages of Life | A. Ia. Golovin | | Aleksandrinskii | 6 Nov. |
| | | | | | 1913 |
| R. Strauss, trans. M. Kuzmin | Electra | A. Ia. Golovin | | Mariinskii | 18 Feb. |
| G. D'Annunzio | Pisanella (choreographer, M. Fokine) | L. S. Bakst | I. da Parma | Châtelet, Paris | 11 June |
| F. Nozière, G. Muller | Tavern in Seville | K. A. Veshilov | M. V. Vladimirov | Suvorin's Theater, St. Petersburg | 16 Dec. |
| | | | | | 1914 |
| A. Pinero | Mid-Channel | A. Ia. Golovin | | Aleksandrinskii | 30 Jan. |
| A. Blok | Unknown Lady, Farce (codirector Iu. M. Bondi) | Iu. M. Bondi | M. A. Kuzmin | Tenishevskii Auditorium | 7 Apr. |
| G. de Maupassant, adapted by O. Métenier | Mlle. Fifi | S. Iu. Sudeikin | | Suvorin's Theater | 15 Aug. |
| E. Wolf-Ferrari | Secret of Suzanna | S. Iu. Sudeikin | | L. Ia. Lipkovskaia production at Mariinskii | 20 Sept. |

| Author | Play | Composer | Theater | Designer | Date |
|---|---|---|---|---|---|
| | | | | | **1915** |
| A. Bobrishchev-Pushkin | *Triumph of the Nations* (apotheosis) | | Mariinskii | S. Iu. Sudeikin | 11 Oct. |
| M. Lermontov | *Two Brothers* | | Aleksandrinskii | A. Ia. Golovin | 10 Jan. |
| | Demonstration evening of the Meyerhold Studio | | Meyerhold Studio | A. V. Rykov | 12 Feb. |
| Z. Gippius | *Green Ring* | V. G. Karatygin | Aleksandrinskii | A. Ia. Golovin | 18 Feb. |
| P. Calderón | *Constant Prince* | V. G. Karatygin | " | A. Ia. Golovin | 23 Apr. |
| G. B. Shaw | *Pygmalion* | | " | P. B. Lambin | 26 Apr. |
| O. Wilde, scenario by V. E. Meyerhold | *Picture of Dorian Gray* (motion picture) | | Thiemann and Reinhardt | Camera man: A. A. Levitskii, Designer: V. E. Egorov | First run: 1 Dec. |
| | | | | | **1916** |
| A. Ostrovsky | *The Storm* | | Aleksandrinskii | A. Ia. Golovin | 9 Jan. |
| M. Glinka, scenario by M. Fokine | *Jota Aragonesa*, ballet (choreographer M. Fokine) | | Mariinskii | A. Ia. Golovin | 29 Jan. |
| A. Schnitzler, Dr. Dapertutto | *Columbine's Scarf* | | Actor's Rest (Prival Komediantov), Petrograd | S. Iu. Sudeikin | 18 Apr. |
| S. Przybyszewski, scenario by V. Akhramovich | *Strong Man* (motion picture) | | Thiemann and Reinhardt | Camera man: F. Benderskii, Designer: V. E. Egorov | First run: 9 Dec. |
| | | | | | **1917** |
| D. Merezhkovskii | *Romantics* (codirector Iu. L. Rakitin) | | Aleksandrinskii | A. Ia. Golovin | 21 Oct. |

| Author | Play | Designer | Composer | Theater | Date |
|---|---|---|---|---|---|
| A. Sukhovo-Kobylin | Marriage of Krechinskii (codirector A. N. Lavrentev) | B. A. Almedingen | | Aleksandrinskii | 25 Jan. |
| A. Dargomyzhskii | Stone Guest | A. Ia. Golovin | | Mariinskii | 27 Jan. |
| M. Musorgsky | Wedding | | | Auditorium of the Petrovskii Institute, Petrograd | 24 Feb. |
| M. Lermontov | Masquerade | A. Ia. Golovin | A. K. Glazunov | Aleksandrinskii | 25 Feb. |
| O. Wilde | An Ideal Husband | A. Ia. Golovin | | School of dramatic art, Mikhailovskii Theater, Petrograd | 24 Apr. |
| A. Sukhovo-Kobylin | Affair (codirector A. N. Lavrentev) | B. A. Almedingen | | Aleksandrinskii | 30 Aug. |
| A. Sukhovo-Kobylin | Death of Tarelkin | B. A. Almedingen | | " | 23 Oct. |
| N. Rimsky-Korsakov | Snow Maiden | K. A. Korovin | | Mariinskii | 14 Dec. |
| H. Ibsen | Lady From the Sea (co-director N. A. Stravinskaia) | A. Ia. Golovin | | Aleksandrinskii | 15 Dec. |
| | | | | | 1918 |
| L. N. Tolstoy | Peter the Baker | A. Ia. Golovin | R. A. Mervolf | " | 8 Apr. |
| I. Stravinsky | Nightingale | A. Ia. Golovin | | Mariinskii | 30 May |
| H. Ibsen | Doll's House | V. E. Meyerhold (plan), V. Dmitriev (execution) | | Theater of the Workers' Club, Petrograd | 7 June |
| D. Ober | Fenella (codirector S. D. Maslovskaia) | P. B. Lambin | | Mariinskii | 7 Nov. |

| Author | Play | Designer | Composer | Theater | Date |
|---|---|---|---|---|---|
| V. Mayakovsky | Mystery-Bouffe (codirector V. Mayakovsky) | K. S. Malevich | | Theater of Musical Drama, Petrograd | 7 Nov. |
| | | | | | 1920 |
| H. Ibsen | Doll's House | | | First Soviet Theater in the name of Lenin, Novorossiisk | 6 Aug. |
| E. Verhaeren, trans. G. Chulkov, adapted by V. E. Meyerhold, V. Bebutov | Dawns (codirector V. M. Bebutov) | V. V. Dmitriev | | Theater RSFSR I, Moscow | 7 Nov. |
| | | | | | 1921 |
| V. Mayakovsky | Mystery-Bouffe, 2nd version | V. P. Kiselev, A. M. Lavinskii, V. L. Khrakovskii | | " | 1 May |
| H. Ibsen, adapted by V. E. Meyerhold, V. Bebutov, O. Zhdanova | League of Youth (codirectors V. M. Bebutov, O. P. Zhdanova) | V. E. Meyerhold, V. M. Bebutov, O. P. Zhdanova (plan) | | " | 7 Aug. |
| | | | | | 1922 |
| H. Ibsen, revised by V. E. Meyerhold | Doll's House; or, How a Lady of Bourgeois Background Opted for Independence and a Job | | | Actor's Theater Moscow | 20 Apr. |
| F. Crommelynck, trans. I. Aksenov | Magnanimous Cuckold | L. S. Popova, V. V. Liutse | N. N. Popov Jazz Band | Meyerhold Workshop, Actor's Theater | 25 Apr. |
| A. Sukhovo-Kobylin | Death of Tarelkin | V. F. Stepanova | | Meyerhold Workshop, GITIS Theater, Moscow | 24 Nov. |

| Author | Play | Designer | Composer | Theater | Date |
|---|---|---|---|---|---|
| M. Martinet, trans. S. Gorodetskii, adapted by S. Tretiakov | Earth Rampant (adapted from Night) | L. S. Popova | | Meyerhold Theater, Moscow | 1923<br>4 Mar. |
| A. Ostrovsky | Profitable Post (codirector A. B. Velizhev) | V. A. Shestakov | | Theater of the Revolution, Moscow | 15 May |
| A. Faiko | Lake Liul (codirector A. M. Room) | V. A. Shestakov | | " " | 7 Nov. |
| A. Ostrovsky adapted by V. E. Meyerhold | Forest | V. E. Meyerhold (plan), V. F. Fedorov (execution) | | Meyerhold Theater | 1924<br>19 Jan. |
| I. Ehrenburg, B. Kellermann, adapted by M. Podgaetskii | D. E. | V. E. Meyerhold (plan), I. Iu. Shlepanov (execution) | | " " | 15 June (Leningrad) |
| A. Faiko | Bubus the Teacher | " | Chopin, Lizst | " | 1925<br>29 Jan. |
| N. Erdman | Mandate | " | | " | 20 Apr. |
| N. Gogol, adapted by V. E. Meyerhold, M. Korenev | Inspector General | V. E. Meyerhold (plan), V. P. Kiselev (execution) | M. F. Gnesin, songs by Russian composers | " | 1926<br>9 Dec. |
| F. Crommelynck | Magnanimous Cuckold | L. S. Popova, V. V. Liutse | | " | 1928<br>26 Jan. |

| Author | Play | Designer | Composer | Theater | Date |
|---|---|---|---|---|---|
| A. Griboedov, compilation of versions by V. E. Meyerhold, M. Korenev | Woe to Wit (Woe from Wit) | V. A. Shestakov N. P. Ulianov (costumes and makeup) (construction), | B. V. Asafev, choice and arrangement of classical music | Meyerhold Theater | 12 Mar. |
| V. Mayakovsky | Bedbug (directorial assistant V. Mayakovsky) | Sc. 1–4, V. E. Meyerhold (plan), Kukryniksy (execution); Sc. 5–9, A. M. Rodchenko | D. D. Shostakovich | " | 1929 13 Feb. |
| I. Selvinskii | Commander of the Second Army | V. E. Meyerhold (plan), E. Vakhtangov (execution) | V. Ia. Shebalin | " | 24 July (Kharkov) |
| V. Mayakovsky | Bathhouse (directorial assistant V. Mayakovsky) | V. E. Meyerhold (plan), S. E. Vakhtangov, A. A. Deineka (execution) | V. Ia. Shebalin | " | 1930 16 Mar. |
| I. Ehrenburg, B. Kellermann, adapted by M. Podgaetskii, N. Mologin, et al. | D. S. E. (new version of D. E.) | V. E. Meyerhold (plan), I. Iu. Shlepanov, et al. (execution) |  | " | 7 Nov. |
| Vs. Vishnevskii | Last Decisive Battle | V. E. Meyerhold tangov (execution) (plan), S. E. Vakh- | V. Ia. Shebalin | " | 1931 7 Feb. |
| Iu. Olesha | List of Assets | V. E. Meyerhold (plan), S. E. Vakh- | G. N. Popov | " | 4 June |

| Author | Play | Designer | Composer | Theater | Date |
|---|---|---|---|---|---|
| | | tangov, I. I. Leistikov, K. K. Savitskii (execution) | | | 1932 |
| Molière | Don Juan | A. Ia. Golovin | J.-F. Rameau | Pushkin Theater, Leningrad | 26 Dec. |
| Iu. German | Prelude (after the novel Professor Kelberg) | I. I. Leistikov | V. Ia. Shebalin | Meyerhold Theater | 1933 28 Jan. |
| A. Sukhovo-Kobylin | Marriage of Krechinskii | V. A. Shestakov | M. L. Starokadomskii | " | 14 Apr. (Leningrad) |
| M. Lermontov | Masquerade | A. Ia. Golovin | A. K. Glazunov | Pushkin Theater | 25 Dec. |
| A. Dumas fils, trans. G. Shpet, Z. Raikh, M. Tsarev | Camille | V. E. Meyerhold (plan), I. I. Leistikov (execution) | V. Ia. Shebalin | Meyerhold Theater | 1934 19 Mar. |
| P. Tschaikovsky, scenario and text, after the A. Pushkin story, by V. E. Meyerhold, V. Stenich | Queen of Spades | L. T. Chupiatov | | Malyi Opera, Leningrad | 1935 25 Jan. |
| A. Chekhov | 33 Fainting Fits ("Jubilee," "The Bear," and "The Proposal") | V. E. Meyerhold V. A. Shestakov | | Meyerhold Theater | 25 Mar. |

| Author | Play | Designer | Composer | Theater | Date |
|---|---|---|---|---|---|
| A. Pushkin | Stone Guest (radio play) | | V. Ia. Shebalin | All-Soviet Radio Committee, Moscow | 17 Apr. |
| A. Griboedov, compilation of versions by V. E. Meyerhold, M. Korenev | Woe to Wit (Woe from Wit) | V. E. Meyerhold, V. A. Shestakov (properties), N. P. Ulianov (costumes and makeup) | B .V. Asafev, choice and arrangement of classical music | Meyerhold Theater | 25 Sept. (Leningrad) |
| A. Pushkin | Stone Guest (concert reading) | | V. Ia. Shebalin | " " | 1937<br>10 Feb. |
| A. Pushkin | Mermaid (radio play) | | V. Ia. Shebalin | All-Soviet Radio Committee, Moscow | 24 Mar. |
| L. Seifulina | Natasha | F. V. Antonov | V. Ia. Shebalin | Meyerhold Theater | Apr.—never opened |
| N. Ostrovskii, adapted by E. Gabrilovich | Tempering of Steel | V. A. Stenberg | G. N. Popov | " " | Nov.—never opened |
| M. Lermontov | Masquerade | A. Ia. Golovin | A. K. Glazunov | Pushkin Theater | 1938<br>29 Dec. |
| | Presentation of the Lesgaft Institute of Physical Culture, Leningrad, at All-Soviet Physical Culture Parade | V. E. Meyerhold with organizers of the presentation L. P. Orlov, N. P. Seryi | S. S. Prokofiev | Palace Sq., Leningrad; Red Sq., Moscow | 1939<br>6 July<br>18 July |

## 2. PRODUCTIONS NOT COMPLETED

| Author | Play | Designer | Composer | Theater | Date |
|---|---|---|---|---|---|
| L. Mei | Girl from Pskov | D. S. Steletskii | | Aleksandrinskii | early 1902 |
| A. K. Tolstoy | Czar Fedor Ioannovich | A. Ia. Golovin | | " | 1908–9 |
| C. W. Gluck | Queen of the May | | | " | 1913 |
| F. K. Sologub | Enchantments of the Shades (motion picture) | V. E. Tatlin | | Thiemann & Reinhardt | 1917 |
| W. Shakespeare | Hamlet | | | RSFSR I, Meyerhold Theater | 1920–38 |
| I. Aksenov | Struggle for Victory (pageant) | A. A. Vesnin, L. S. Popova | | Khodynskoe Field, Moscow (plan only) | 1921 |
| G. B. Shaw | Heartbreak House | S. M. Eisenstein | | Actor's Theater (plan only) | 1922 |
| P. Mérimée, adapted by N. Loiter | Jacquerie | | | Meyerhold Theater | 1923 |
| G. Bizet | Carmen | | | Meyerhold Theater (plan only) | 1925 |
| A. Pushkin | Boris Godunov | S. P. Isakov | | Vakhtangov Studio | 1925–26 |
| S. Tretiakov | I Want a Child | V. E. Meyerhold, El Lissitzky | | Meyerhold Theater | 1927–30 |
| P. Hindemith | Latest News | | | Malyi Opera | 1931–32 |
| N. Erdman | Suicide | V. E. Meyerhold (plan), I. I. Leistikov, N. V. Grigorovich, S. V. Kozikov (execution) | M. L. Staroka-domskii | Meyerhold Theater | 1932 |

| Author | Play | Designer | Composer | Theater | Date |
|---|---|---|---|---|---|
| V. Mayakovsky, adapted by V. E. Meyerhold, A. V. Fevralskii | *Bedbug* | V. E. Meyerhold (plan) | D. D. Shostakovich | Meyerhold Theater | 1936 |
| A. Pushkin | *Boris Godunov* | V. A. Shestakov | S. S. Prokofiev | " | 1936 |
| S. Prokofiev, libretto by V. Kataev | *Semen Kotko*, completed by S. G. Birman (23 June 1940) | A. G. Tyshler | | Stanislavsky Opera Theater | 1939 |

## 3.  COLLABORATION WITH OTHER DIRECTORS IN THEIR PRODUCTIONS

| Author | Play | Designer | Composer | Theater | Date |
|---|---|---|---|---|---|
| P. Claudel | *Exchange* (plan with A. Ia. Tairov) | G. B. Iakulov | | Kamerny Theater, Moscow | 1918 |
| R. Wagner, adapted by V. Bebutov, V. Shershenevich | *Rienzi* (pantomime scenes; overall supervision of V. M. Bebutov's production) | G. B. Iakulov | | RSFSR I | 1921 |
| Meyerhold Workshop | *Paris Commune* (supervision of group directing) | Meyerhold Workshop | | Krasnopresnenskii Club of the Trekhgornaia factory, Moscow | 1922 |
| E. Toller | *Machine Wreckers* (revision of P. P. Repnin's production) | V. P. Komardenkov | | Theater of the Revolution | 1922 |
| E. Toller | *Man and the Masses* (revision of A. B. Belizhev's production) | V. A. Shestakov | | " | 1923 |

| Author | Play | Designer | Composer | Theater | Date |
|---|---|---|---|---|---|
| S. Tretiakov | Roar, China! (supervision and revision of V. F. Fedorov's production) | S. M. Efimenko | | Meyerhold Theater | 1926 23 Jan. |
| V. E. Meyerhold (plan), R. Akulshin (text) | Through a Village Window (a collective production) | V. A. Shestakov | R. I. Mervolf | " | 1927 |
| A. Bezymenskii | The Shot (supervision of the directors V. F. Zaichikov; S. V. Kozikov; A. E. Nestroy; F. P. Bondarenko, assistant) | V. V. Kalinin, L. P. Pavlov | R. I. Mervolf | " | 1929 |
| G. Verdi | Rigoletto (completion of production prepared by K. S. Stanislavsky) | M. P. Bobyshov | | Stanislavsky Opera Theater | 1939 10 Mar. |

# Appendix 2: *Amplua aktera*
# The Set Roles of the Actor's Art

[Translator's Note]
*Biomechanics, in its original meaning, is that subdivision of physiology concerned with the motions of animals and humans. Applying the data of anatomy, physiology, and theoretical mechanics, it weighs the rationality and economy of movements in order to perfect them (sport), to replace amputated limbs (military medicine), and to cure pathological conditions (orthopedics and neurology). Leonardo da Vinci was a pioneer in this field of study.*

*Meyerhold adopted the term for his system of training the actor in movement. He distinguished the actor's conscious will, which dictates the task to be executed in space and time, from the physical instrument at his disposal, his body, which has been schooled in routines for executing the assignment. The actor's "reflex sensitivity," that is, his apprehension of the task and his capacity for its execution, is both heightened and quickened by exercises Meyerhold used for this purpose. He laid the foundation for his system in the course in movement which he taught in his prerevolutionary Petersburg studio (1914–16), using the word* biomechanics *and popularizing it through his teaching in his Moscow workshop after 1922.*

*Explications of biomechanics were published in Meyerhold's review of Aleksandr Tairov's book* Zapiski rezhissera (*A Director's Notebook), in* Pechat' i revoliutsiia, *no. 1 (1922), pp. 305–9; the report of a lecture by Meyerhold entitled "Akter budushchego" (The Actor of the Future),* Ermitazh, *no. 6 (1922), pp. 10–11; and finally in the brochure which follows,* Amplua aktera (*The Set Roles of the Actor's Art), by V. E. Meyerhold, V. M. Bebutov, and I. A. Aksenov (Moscow, 1922).*

Amplua aktera *was commissioned by the Research Department of GVYRM (Gosu-*

*darstvennye vysshie rezhisserskie masterskie, State Graduate School for Theater Directors —the Meyerhold Workshop).*

## *Amplua aktera*

*Who should become an actor.*
The indispensable qualification of the actor is a capacity for sensitivity of the reflexes. A person lacking this capacity cannot be an actor.
*Reflex Sensitivity.*
Reflex sensitivity is the capacity to recreate in emotional experience [*chuvstvovaniakh*], in movement and in words a task assigned from without.
*The communication of reflex sensitivity.*
The coordinated communication of reflex sensitivity constitutes the ART OF ACTING. Each element of acting is necessarily composed of three essential moments:

      1. INTENTION
      2. REALIZATION
      3. REACTION

The intention is the intellectual apprehension of a task assigned from outside (by author, dramatist, theater director or on the initiative of the actor himself).
The realization consists of a cycle of voluntary [*volevoi*],[1] mimetic and voice reflexes.[2]

---

1. The term "emotional experience" [*chustovovanie*] is used in the technical scientific sense without admixture of popular or sentimental coloration.

The same must be noted concerning the term "voluntary" [*volevoi*], for the voluntary reflex must be differentiated, on the one hand, from the system of acting dependent on "inspiration" (without the systematic use of narcotics) and likewise, on the other hand, from the method of "experiencing" (the hypnotic training of the imagination).

Of the two systems mentioned, the first which forces upon the feelings, relaxed in preparation for the assault, an artificially willed stimulus and the

Reaction is the reduction of the impulse of will after the realization of mimetic and vocal reflexes, preparatory to receiving a new intention (transition to a new element of acting).

The actor must control his capacity for reflex sensitivity. Reflex sensitivity means reducing to a minimum the process of conscious awareness ("the time of simple reaction").

A person who has noted in himself the presence of this indispensable capacity for reflex sensitivity may be or may become an actor. In accordance with certain native physical qualifications, he may take in the theater one of the set roles, depending on the dramatic functions peculiar to it (see gloss 3).

---

second which forces upon the feelings a hypnotic expansion of the will, relaxed in preparation for this purpose—both must consequently be rejected for their unsuitability and danger for the physical health of those subject to their action.

A more detailed analysis of these phenomena is reserved for special investigation in *The Art of Acting* (no. 3 in the series scheduled for publication by the GVYRM Publishing House). [Authors' note.]

2. "Mimetic reflexes." This term designates all movements occurring on the periphery of the actor's body, and likewise the movements of the actor himself in space. [Authors' note.]

## Tables: The Set Roles (Male and Female)

| Set role | Necessary qualifications of the actor | Examples of the role | Dramatic function |
|---|---|---|---|
| *Male* | | | |
| **I  HERO** | | | |
| First | Male<br>1 Greater-than-average height. Long legs. Two types of face: broad (Mochalov, Karatygin, Salvini) & narrow (Irving). Average size of head is desirable. Neck long & round. With broad shoulders, average waist & hip line. Great expressiveness of the hands & wrists. Large eyes, especially in width, preferably light in color. Voice of great strength, range and richness of timbre. Medium baritone, tending to bass. | Oedipus Rex, Karl Moor, Othello, Macbeth, Leontes, Angelo, Brutus, Hippolytus, Lantenac, Don Garcia, Don Juan (Pushkin), Boris Godunov. | The overcoming of tragic obstacles[1] on the plane of pathos (irrationality). |
| Second | 2 May have less height, a higher voice, less insistence on the requirements for the first hero. | Edgar, Laertes, Vershinin, Lopakhin, Kolychev, Shakhovskoi, Ford, Erenien, Friedrich von Telramund, Dmitrii Karamazov. | Overcoming of dramatic obstacles on the plane of self-renunciation (rationality). |
| **2  LOVER** | | | |
| First | 1 Height no less than average, long legs. Expressive eyes & mouth. Voice may be high (tenor). No excess weight. Middle height. | Romeo, Molchalin,[2] Almaviva, Calaf. | Active overcoming of obstacles to love on the lyric plane. |
| Second (naive) | 2 Less insistence on the requirements. May be less than average height. No excess weight. | Parsifal, Tikhon (Ostrovsky's *Storm*), Tesman, Karandyshev, Oswald, Treplev, Czar Feodor, Alyosha Karamazov. | Overcoming of obstacles to love on the ethical plane. |

| Set role | Necessary qualifications of the actor | Examples of the role | Dramatic function |
|---|---|---|---|
| **3 MISCHIEF MAKERS** | | | |
| First | Male<br>1 Height not above average. Voice unimportant. Slender figure. Great mobility of eyes & face muscles. Aptitude for mimicry. | Khlestakov, Petrushka, Pulcinello, Harlequin, Iashalackey, Punch, Benedick, Gracioso, Stensgor, Glumov. | Play with non-catastrophic obstacles of their own making. |
| Second | 2 Great overweight is permissible, as is a poorly proportioned figure. Mimicry requirement still higher. An unusual timbre of voice is possible. | Epikhodov, Sancho Panza, Lamme-Goedzak, Tartarin, Firs, Chebutykin, Arkashka, The Boarder, Waffles, Leporello, Sganarelle, Raspliuyev, Peniculus. | Play with obstacles not of their own making. |
| **4 CLOWN, FOOL, SIMPLETON, ECCENTRIC** | | | |
| | Capacity for "exaggerated parody" (grotesque,[3] fantasy). Talent for juggling and acrobatics. | Trinculo, Clarin, both Gobbos, gravediggers, fools, clowns and simpletons of the English & Spanish theater, stage assistants. | Intentional retardation of the development of the dramatic action by means of breaking the illusion (exceeding the frame). |
| **5 VILLAIN INTRIGUER** | | | |
| First | 1 Either a low voice (the spy in *Angelo* [Pushkin's play after *Measure for Measure*]) or a high one (Wagner's Melot). Preferably medium height. Eyes unimportant (even crossed eyes are permissible). Mobility of face muscles for the play between two persons. Poor proportions of figure possible. | Iago, Franz Moor, Salieri, Claudius, Antonio (*Tempest* & *Julius Caesar*), Edmund, Gessler. | Play with catastrophic obstacles of their own making. |

| Set role | Necessary qualifications of the actor | Examples of the role | Dramatic function |
|---|---|---|---|
| Second | 2 Less insistence on the requirements than for the first villain. | Vasilii Shuiskii, Smerdiakov, Shprikh, Zagoretskii, Rosencrantz & Guildenstern, Kazarin. | Play with destructive obstacles not of their own making. |

6 MYSTERIOUS STRANGER (as if from "other world")

| | | | |
|---|---|---|---|
| | Requirements approximately the same as for the first hero; great magic & significance of stage presence. Voice of an exceptional timbre and rich in modulations. | Mysterious stranger (*Masquerade* & *Lady from the Sea*), Count of Monte Cristo, Flying Dutchman, Lohengrin, Petruchio, Pierre Bast, Graf Trast, Napoleon, Julius Caesar, ·Neschastlivstev, Kean, Fool Tantris. | Concentration of the plot by its transfer to another personal plane. |

7 OUTSIDER, RENEGADE, UNBELIEVER

| | | | |
|---|---|---|---|
| | Requirements of voice as for the hero, less insistence on requirements of a physical nature than for the hero. | Onegin, Arbenin, Pechorin, Stavrogin, Paratov, Krechinskii, Prince Hal, Flaminio, Protasov, Solenyii, Hamlet, Jacques (Shakespeare), Kent, Sigismund, Ivan Karamazov, Careno. | Concentration of the plot [4] by its transfer to another extra-personal plane. |

8 FOP

| | | | |
|---|---|---|---|
| | Height unimportant. Legs long in proportion. Voice preferably high. Ability to use falsetto. | Lucio, Osric, Mozart, Mercutio, Repetilov, Baron. | Unintentional retardation of the plot development by its transfer to the personal plane. |

| Set role | Necessary qualifications of the actor | Examples of the role | Dramatic function |
|---|---|---|---|
| **9 MORALIST** | | | |
| | Deep bass. Figure unimportant. | Duval senior, Gloucester, Priest (Pushkin's *Feast in Time of Plague*), Ivan Shuiskii, Clotaldo. | Intentional acceleration of plot development by the introduction of the moral norm. |
| **10 GUARDIAN** (Pantalone) | | | |
| | Height and voice with the exception of tragic figures (Lear, Miller) unimportant. | Shylock, Covetous knight (Pushkin), Famusov, Polonius, Arnolphe, Lear, Miller, Rigoletto, Triboulet. | Active application of personally established norms of conduct to a situation not of their own making. |
| **11 FRIEND** (Confidant) | | | |
| | Figure and voice unimportant. Height should not exceed that of his friend. | Horatio, Artemida (cf. #16) Banquo. | Support, sympathy, and encouragement of friend to explain his actions. |
| **12 BRAGGART** (*Miles gloriosus*) | | | |
| | Excess weight permissible. Deep bass voice. Ability to use falsetto. | Falstaff, Bobadil, Skalozub, *miles gloriosus* (Plautus). | Complication in the development of the action because of misappropriation of the dramatic functions of others (notably of the hero). |
| **13 GUARDIAN OF THE LAW** | | | |
| | | Kliukva, all the Pompeys of Shakespeare, brothel keeper (*Pericles*), Scribe's prefect, Pliushkin, Medvedev (*Lower Depths*). | Introduction of police norms for an unyielding circumstance and complication in development of action. |

| Set role | Necessary qualifications of the actor | Examples of the role | Dramatic function |
|---|---|---|---|
| 14 SCIENTIST (Learned doctor, wise man) | | | |
| | No general qualifications. | Molière's doctors, Bologni, B. Shaw, Krugosvetlov, Stockman, Don Quixote. | Enchantment of action by the introduction of discussions foreign to it. |
| 15 MESSENGER | | | |
| | No general qualifications. | Soldier in *Antigone,* Stable boy in *Hippolytus,* Patriarch (*Boris Godunov*), ghost (*Hamlet*). | Communication of events which have occurred offstage. |
| 16 MEN IN WOMEN'S PARTS | | | |
| | No general qualifications. | Washwoman (Sukhovo-Kobylin, *Death of Tarelkin*). | |
| 17 WALK-ONS | | | |
| | No general qualifications. | Murderers, passersby, soldiers, courtiers, guests. | Fulfillment of those functions of the main characters, which the latter cannot carry out for the sake of the economy of the dramatic action. |

| Set role | Necessary qualifications of the actor | Examples of the role | Dramatic function |
|---|---|---|---|

*Female*

**1  HEROINE**

| First | 1 Greater-than-average height, long legs, small head, exceptional expressiveness of wrists. Large almond-shaped eyes. Two types of face: Duse, Sarah Bernhardt. Long rounded neck. Width of hips should not greatly exceed width of shoulders. Voice of great strength & range, conversational pitch tending to contralto, wealth of timbres. | Princess Turandot (Schiller) Electra (Sophocles), princess of Russian fairy tale, Cleopatra, Infante Fernando (Kovalenskaia), Phaedra, Joan of Arc, Hamlet (Sarah Bernhardt), L'Aiglon, Medea, Lady Macbeth, Mary Stuart, Fru Inger, Iordis. | The overcoming of tragic obstacles on the plane of pathos (irrationality). |
| Second | 2 Less height permissible, higher voice, less insistence on the requirements than in #1. | Portia, Imogene, Magda, Nora, Amalia, Lady Milford, Cordelia, Sophia Pavlovna, Kupava, Rosalind. | Overcoming of dramatic obstacles on the plane of self-renunciation (rationality). |

**2  YOUNG GIRL IN LOVE**

| First | 1 No less than average height, long legs for change of clothes, expressive eyes & mouth. Voice may be high (soprano). Bust not too much developed. | Desdemona, Juliet, Phaedra (Euripides), Ophelia, Julia (Ostrovsky), Nina (*Masquerade*). | Active overcoming of obstacles to love on the lyric plane. |
| Second | 2 Less insistence on the requirements. Shortness permissible. No excess weight. | Aksiusha, Sonia, (Chekhov), Celia, Bianca (*Taming of the Shrew*), Thea, Dagni (Ibsen), Eliza, Angélique (Molière), all lovers. | Overcoming of obstacles to love on the ethical plane. |

| Set role | Necessary qualifications of the actor | Examples of the role | Dramatic function |
|---|---|---|---|
| **3 MISCHIEF MAKER** | | | |
| First | 1 No greater than average height, voice unimportant, slender figure. Great mobility of eyes & face muscles. Capacity for mimicry. | Betsy (Tolstoy), Toinette, Dorine, Turandot (Gozzi), Larissa, Helen (Euripides), Liza, Beatrice, Praxagora, Mirandolina, Liza Doolittle, Lysistrata, Katherine, Mistress Ford. | Play with non-catastrophic obstacles of their own making. |
| Second | 2 Not too plump. Less strict requirements than for the "first mischief maker." | Mistress Page. Certain characters from Aristophanes' *Praxagora* and *Lysistrata,* servants carrying on a parallel plot. | Play with obstacles not of their own making. |
| **4 FEMALE FOOL, SIMPLETON, ECCENTRIC** | | | |
| | Capacity for exaggerated parody, grotesque, fantasy. Talent for gymnastics and acrobatics. | Fools in love, clowns, simpletons and eccentrics, some of Ostrovsky's and Gogol's old women in love from the *commedia dell'arte,* stage assistants. | Intentional retardation of the dramatic action by means of breaking the illusion (exceeding the frame). |
| **5 VILLAINESS, INTRIGUER** | | | |
| First | 1 Low voice of great range & strength. Greater-than-average height. Large, mobile eyes (cross eyes permissible). Extreme skinniness and boniness permissible. | Regan, Clytemnestra, Kabanikha, Herodias, Ortrud. | Play with catastrophic obstacles of their own making. |
| Second | 2 Voice not important. No set requirements for height & figure. | Goneril, wicked fairies, stepmothers, young witches, Cinderella's sisters, sis- | Play with catastrophic obstacles not of their own making. |

| Set role | Necessary qualifications of the actor | Examples of the role | Dramatic function |
|---|---|---|---|
| | | ters in Pushkin's "Fairy Tale of Czar Saltan." | |
| 6 STRANGER (as if from another world) | | | |
| | Requirements approximately the same as for the first heroine. Great magic and significance of stage presence. Voice of exceptional timbre and rich in modulations. | Anitra, Anna Mahr, Cassandra, Princess Adelma, Esmeralda, Miss Erlynne. | Center of action. |
| 7 OUTSIDER, RENEGADE, UNBELIEVER | | | |
| | Same requirements of voice as for the first heroine. Less insistence on requirements of a physical nature. | Electra (Hofmannsthal), Tatiana, Nina Zarechnaia, Katerina, Irina (Chekhov), Hedda Gabler, Griselda (Boccaccio), Marguerite Gautier, Nastasia Philippovna. | Concentration of plot by its transfer to another extrapersonal plane. |
| 8 COURTESAN | | | |
| | Height unimportant. Good physical proportions. Voice unimportant. | Laura (Pushkin), Erotia (Plautus), Catherine (Shaw), Queen (*Hamlet*), Bianca (*Othello*), Froken Diana (Ibsen), Acroteleutia, Mistress Quickly. | Unintentional retardation of dramatic action by the transfer of it to the personal plane. |
| 9 MATRON | | | |
| | Excess weight is possible. Preferably low voice & preferably great height. | Khlestova, Catherine the Great (Pushkin's *Captain's Daughter*), Ogulova (Ostrovsky's *Dowerless Daugh-* | Intentional acceleration of the dramatic action by the introduction of moral norms. |

| Set role | Necessary qualifications of the actor | Examples of the role | Dramatic function |
|---|---|---|---|
| | | *ter*), ladies of high degree, certain queens, Volumnia. | |
| **10 GUARDIAN** | | | |
| | Height, figure & character of voice are unimportant. | Muravetskaia, Frau Hergentheim (Sudermann), Nurse (*Phaedra*), mother of Balladina, abbess, mother of Crown Prince Dmitrii, Volokhova (*Czar Feodor*). | Active application of personally established norms of conduct to a circumstance not of their own making. |
| **11 CONFIDANTES** | | | |
| | No general qualifications. | Emilia, servants, friends not conducting intrigues of their own. | Support & encouragement of the heroine friend to explain her actions. |
| **12 MATCHMAKER** | | | |
| | No general qualifications. | All matchmakers with the exception of those who are clowns. | Moral support for immoral undertakings. |
| **13 GUARDIANS OF THE LAW** | | | |
| | No general qualifications. | Mrs. Pierce (Shaw) & the majority of housekeepers, aunts, old maids, mothers-in-law (preferably eccentrics). | Application to an unmastered circumstance of police norms, which thus complicate the action. |

| Set role | Necessary qualifications of the actor | Examples of the role | Dramatic function |
|----------|---------------------------------------|----------------------|-------------------|
| **14 SCHOLAR, SUFFRAGETTE** | No general qualifications. | These parts should preferably be given to eccentrics or mischief makers. | Enhancement of the action by the introduction into it of a foreign interpretation. |
| **15 MESSENGER** | No general qualifications. | | Communication of events which have occurred off-stage. |
| **16 BOYS IN GIRLS' PARTS** | No general qualifications. | Boys, pages, Conrad (*Jacquerie*) Cherubino (*Figaro*), Fortunio (Musset). | |
| **17 WALK-ONS** | No general qualifications. | Guests, passers-by, friends, etc. | Fulfillment of those functions of the main characters which they themselves cannot fulfill while preserving economy of the action. |

## Glosses 1–4

[Meyerhold's Notes to Tables of Set Roles]

### 1. Tragic obstacles.

Obstacles arising on the way to the realization of an idea inspired in the hero by reason of his tragic guilt. This fault, which is not in essence, but all the more in particular, an offense against human ethical norms, means the acceptance by one or another protagonist of a task exceeding the bounds of human possibility and the rights thereof. The obstacles met by the tragic hero derive not from the ill will of interested persons but from the very manner of the task's execution, which leads the protagonist beyond the pale of human actions and feelings.

### 2. Paradoxical composition.

In order to get the audience's attention for the effect they have set out to achieve, dramatists sometimes resort to a mixture or complete reversal of composition. Thus they develop the traditionally comic situation on the tragic plane and vice versa, or they transpose generally accepted criteria of the dramatic perspective. A common phenomenon of nature, the sunset, gives a sufficiently full notion of the manner of such an effect. The observer has become so accustomed to see warm tones in the foreground and to count on their graduation into cold ones proportionate to the distance away toward the horizon that he is generally inclined to identify the concept of distance with this distribution of colors. Therefore he is unavoidably struck to see red-orange on the horizon and blue in the foreground.

The most primitive use of paradoxical composition is simple parody, hence its widespread employment in comic compositions.

### 3. Grotesque.

Intentional exaggeration and distortion of nature and the combination of objects which neither nature nor our daily experience combine, along with the insistent underlining of the material and ordinary sense of the form thus created. The absence of such insistence transfers the manner of distorting and combining into the realm of surrealist play of fantasy, thus transforming the grotesque into the fantastic. In the realm of the grotesque when ready-made composition is replaced by its exact opposite or when known and esteemed methods are applied to the representation of objects the opposite of that which established these methods—this is called parody.

The theater, which is an unnatural combination of natural, temporal, spatial and numerical phenomena such as necessarily contradict our daily experience, is by its very essence an example of the grotesque. Arising from the grotesquerie of the masquerade of ceremony, it is unavoidably destroyed by any attempt to remove the grotesque from it and base it on reality. As the basic characteristic of the theater, the grotesque demands for its realization the inevitable transposition of all elements introduced into the theater from without, among these the transformation also of the human being so indispensable to the theater, transforming him from an ordinary person—an individual—into a protagonist. This transformation, which has the purpose of preparing the emotionally material element in the surrealist combination of the grotesque, discards from the stage whole series of the actor's capacities in favor of one cluster only, designed to make the protagonist occupy a specific theatrical place and normalize a strictly qualified assignment. The SET ROLE is the assignment of the actor, which he takes on when he possesses the necessary qualifications for the most complete and exact fulfillment of the role's dramatic functions.

*4. Plot.*

The plot is the reciprocal and consequential concatenation of outward obstacles and outward means of overcoming them, consciously introduced into the action of the play by the interested characters.

Development of the Actor's Native Gifts

The native gifts essential to the actor are inevitably insufficient and must therefore be developed and trained.

This development, according to the above, must take two directions:
a) development of the capacity for reflex sensitivity and b) development of the physical qualifications for the set role by means of acting methods relevant to it.

*Chief subjects of training for a)* will be:
1) Development of the sense of one's body in space (movement with a conscious center, balance, transition from large to small movements, consciousness of gesture as a result of movement even in static moments).
2) Acquiring the capacity to convert the musical instinct into a conscious directing of oneself like a musician.
3) Acquiring the capacity to orient oneself in the system of acting.

*for group b):*
Once one knows with geometric clarity all the positions of biomechanics, which takes its departure from a single law of mechanics in all manifestations of force and from the similarity of all animal limbs, then these motions peculiar to animals are applied to certain types of roles by assimilating the roles characterized by these motions.

All this work must be done by one's devoting oneself to acting, quite apart from one's personal wishes or theoretic convictions. Usually this is done by trial and error and is three-fourths unconscious. However, such a process wastes an immeasurable amount of effort, nerve sensibility and time. The task of theater education is the systematization of such labor.

The following titles are planned for publication by GVYRM:
1. The Set Roles of the Actor's Art.
2. Analysis of the Dramatic Text.
3. The Art of Acting.
4. The Stage.
5. The Director's Art.
6. Political Action. *(Agitatsionnoe deistvie)*
7. The Grotesque.
8. The Fable. *(Fiabesco/ Fiabesque)*
9. Biomechanics.
10. The Process of Creating the Play on Stage. *(Put' K Cozdaniiu Spektaklia),* v. 2.

# Appendix 3: Program of Biomechanics, Meyerhold Workshop (1922)

*The following Program of Biomechanics is the unabridged translation of nine previously typewritten pages from TsGALI [Central State Archive of Literature and Art] USSR, Fond 963, Unit 1335, 1922. Photographs of biomechanical exercises are presented in the Spring 1973 issue of* Drama Review *(vol. T57), on the cover and in "Lee Strasberg's Russian Notebook," pp. 106–21.*

## Program of Biomechanics: First year of instruction.

1. Training in various kinds of sport and gymnastics. The actor must know and study all phases of movements without dwelling on any one for long, so as not to develop heavy muscles which hinder lightness and freedom of motion. (Example: the Japanese actor.)
2. Biomechanical gymnastics have the purpose of developing in the actor;
    a) Fluid and easy movements (legato).
    b) Sharp, quick, distinct movements (staccato), aimed at achieving the greatest possible diapason of motion.
3. Biomechanical exercises have the purpose of teaching the actor how to have:
    a) A feeling of balance and a center of gravity within himself and within the frame of his surroundings;
    b) Coordination with the stage space, one's partner, and the stage properties;
    c) A state of physical alertness or "reflex sensitivity," quick reaction to the task assigned by the director without loss of psychic balance and calm;
    d) A director's consciousness, an outside perspective on the material in its coordination with the stage space, partner, costume, and properties.

## Biomechanical Gymnastics.

Positioning of the body and the extremities.
   a) Positioning of the body.
       1) Bending and raising, fast and slow, in all directions.
       2) Deep-knee bends with attention to erect posture.
       3) Work on the abdomen and diaphragm.
       4) Work on the shoulders.
   b) Positioning of the head and arms and legs.
       1) Work on the neck. Balancing a ball. Quick and slow turns.
       2) Hands and fingers. Juggling wands.
       3) Legs: extending the legs. Rapid formation in groups, running. Deep-knee bends. Charleston; heels. Balancing a ball, a wand with the foot.

## The Elements of Biomechanical Exercises.

Practice of exercises alone.
   1) Standing.
   2) Walking.
   3) Running.
   4) Falling.
   5) Group formations.
   6) Throwing of the disc, the spear, the shot put.

7) Touching hands and head to legs.
8) Positioning from the side angle [*rak-kurs*, i.e., *raccourci*]

## Biomechanical Exercises.  ✓

Development of attention, coordination, and reflex sensitivity.
1) The bow.
2) The stone.
3) Fall, recovery.
4) Blow with a dagger.
5) Blow from knee-bent position.
6) Slap.
7) From the play *D. E.*

## The Actor.

A. Material (A₂)

   1. THE BODY
     a) The trunk without the extremities, en masse.
     b) The extremities, arms and legs.
     c) The head and face: eyes, mouth.
   2. VOICE AND DICTION, cf. the special course in the word.

B. Biomechanics
   1. a) The human organism as an auto-motive mechanism.
     b) Doubly automatic actions.
     c) Mimetism and its biological significance (Bekhterev).*
   2. d) Motor action of the human being.
     1) Movements of single organs, the trembling or stimulation of

* Bekhterev, Vladimir (1857-1927), psychologist, author of a system of reflexology.

muscles, turning of the eyes, mimetic movement of the head, arms, legs, and single groups of muscles;
2) Complex of movements of the whole organism or chain of movements, movements of the whole organism: walking, running, act of reading, writing, transporting loads, the most complex movements in work of one kind or another, acts of doing.

3. Acts of inhibition (not doing), outwardly devoid of motion or showing motion to an only slightly noticeable degree: the patient tolerance of blows, abstention from active resistance, etc.
   e) Play as an outlet for superfluous energy.
   f) Receivers, conductors, dispatchers.
   g) Study of the mechanism of reaction in the nervous system.
   h) Psychic reactions as the object of scientific study.
   i) Psychic phenomena, simple physico-chemical reactions in the form of tropism, taxis* or purely physiological reflexes.
   j) Reflex instinct.
   k) Reflexes, their connection, sequence, mutual dependence.
   l) Mechanization, subconsciously habitual acts.
   m) Physical and reflexive normalization.
   n) The influence of sound stimuli, the role of a sharp cry in a moment of tense action.
   o) Action and musical background,

* "Taxis" means the movement of simple-cell organisims, for example spermatozoids, in response to a stimulus; thus phototaxis means such movement occasioned by light.

the choreographing in written form of movements set to a given piece of music according to the laws of counterpoint, or the composing of music for a given "score" of movements according to the same laws of counterpoint.

p) Meter and rhythm.

# Mimetism.

a) Study by the actor of muscular movements, the direction, force pressure, or traction produced by a movement, extent or length of its trajectory or speed.
b) Movement of the trunk, the arms, the legs, the head (center of balance), pose from side angle [rakkurs, i.e., raccourci].
c) Rationalization of movements.
d) Sign of refusal [otkaz].
e) Rates of movement.
f) Legato and staccato.
g) Gesture as a result of movement.
h) The large and the small gesture.
i) Laws of coordinating the body and objects outside oneself, of coordinating the body and objects in the actor's hands—juggling, the body and costume.
j) Laws of coordinating time and space.
k) Geometrization.
l) Laws of even and uneven numbers.
m) Laws of construction.
n) Dance.
o) Acrobatics.
p) Antics appropriate to the theater.
q) Eccentricity.
r) Hand manipulations.
s) Word movement.

# Acting.

1. Three systems of acting: temperament, the method of re-living, motor skills.
2. $N = A_1 + A_2$
3. $A_1 = n \curlywedge r$ *
4. Set roles [amplua]; native gifts, stage functions.
5. The grotesque.
6. Improvisation.
7. Actor and audience.
8. Ensemble.
9. Log book of the production.

# Summary of Experience, Study.

1. Study of theme according to sources.
2. Study of schools and trends, styles.
3. Study of the methods of acting of various schools.

# Organization of Work.

1. Workshop of the actor.
2. Work clothes [prozodezhda].
3. Textbooks.
4. The actor's musical score.
   a) Intended meaning.
   b) Finished form.
5. Log book.
6. Schedule: rehearsals, performances.
7. Creating a role.

* n = namerenie (intention); o = osushchestvlenie (execution, fulfillment of intention); r = reaktsiia (reaction, return to initial position).

## Laboratory of Biomechanics.

The task of the biomechanical laboratory is to work out through experimentation a biomechanical system of acting and of actor's training. The work of the laboratory is conducted on two levels: a) the theoretical and b) the practical.

To the theory of biomechanics belongs the study of the biological and social bases of the actor's art.

1. Study of the animal organism.
2. Study of individual and collective reflexology.
3. Establishment of general principles of organized movement.
4. Establishment of laws concerning the actor's movement in stage space.

To the practice of biomechanics belongs the working out of a series of exercises from the simplest forms of individual movement to the most complex coordinated movements of masses. Training the "new high-velocity man" (A. Gastev's formulation*) with his quick reaction, his capacity to be always on the alert for ways of building socialism, his ability to save his strength and expend a minimum of nervous energy. Development of a passion for design. Care of the body and nerves. Sense of the body. Sense of poses from side angle [*rakkursy*]. Constant persistent training in all phases of this complicated system.

BIOMECHANICS or the BIOMECHANICAL SYSTEM of Vs. Meyerhold attempts to establish laws of movement for actors in stage space; by experimentation it devises set exercises for training and works out methods of the actor's art based on exact calculation and regulation of the actor's conduct on stage.

Vsevolod Meyerhold

## Biomechanics.

Plan 1) Single portion of the body. 2) Poses from the side angle [*rakkursy*]. 3) The hands. 4) The face.

## List of Exercises.

1. Shooting a bow.
2. Forward jump, landing on back, shift of weight.
3. Fall, catching oneself and throwing one's weight.
4. Blow on the nose.
5. Slap.
6. Leg thrusts from squat position.
7. Play with a wand.
8. Throwing someone a ball.
9. Throwing a stone.
10. Leap onto the chest of partner.
11. Play with a short dagger.
12. Quadrille.
13. Rope jumping.
14. The horse.
15. Four ice-skaters.
16. Tripping-up.
17. The bridge (body bent backwards, only soles of feet and palms touching ground).
18. The handsaw.
19. The scythe.
20. Funeral.
21. The jester.
22. Leapfrog.

---

* A. K. Gastev (1881-1941), poet and pioneer of cybernetics.

*A sense of the complexity of these exercises can be derived from an elaboration of the ninth, the stone exercise, provided by André van Gyseghem, an Englishman who visited the Meyerhold Workshop in the thirties and described the exercise in his* Theatre in Soviet Russia *(London, 1943), pp. 39–40:*

1) To concentrate the attention of the pupil—the hands are clapped twice together in a downward movement, the arms hanging loosely.

2) Preparing to run—with a jump, turn and face the right, landing with the left foot in front.

3) Preparing to run—knees bent, right hand in front, left hand behind.

4) Running.

5) To arrive where the stone lies—stop running with a jump, landing on the left foot and with the left shoulder in front.

6) Return to normal position.

7) Prepare to get the stone—rise on the toes and drop on to the right knee. Lean the body backward and then forward.

8) Lifting the stone—pick up the imaginary stone with the right hand, rise, swing the right arm round in a wide circle—swing it round to the left—front and back again to behind the body, where it hangs. The left shoulder is high, the right low, the right hand at about knee level. The knees are bent slightly.

9) Preparing to run with the stone—move backward a few steps.

10) Running with the stone—the stone still in the right hand held behind the body, left shoulder being raised.

11) Arriving at the place from which to throw—stop running, always with a slight jump, landing with the left shoe in front.

12) Preparing to throw the stone—swing the stone over to the left front and grip the right wrist with the left hand.

13) Swinging the stone—swing the body weight on to the right foot—sweep the right arm back and swing it in a circular motion, still clasped by the left hand. Release the left hand and the circle widens until the whole right arm is swinging in a huge circle from the shoulder.

14) Looking for the object to be hit—the circular movement stops, the right arm (and stone) held out in front while the student looks.

15) Rejudging the distance—run a few steps forward, jump and stop.

16) Preparing to throw—swing the stone back, and the right leg.

17) Throwing—swing the right arm forward and the left back.

18) What is the result? Preparation—kneel on the right knee, clap the hands and listen with the right hand cupping the ear.

19) The mark is hit—point forward with the left arm, lean back with the right arm on the right hip.

20) Finish—rise, facing inward and clap twice as at the beginning.

# Appendix 4: Curricula of the Meyerhold Workshop

*The following curricula, previously unpublished, are taken from TsGALI USSR, Fond 963, Units 1284 and 1331, and Fond 998, Unit 793.*

## Program of Studies for GVYTM

[Gosudarstvennye vyshie teatral'nye masterskie—State Graduate Institute of Theater, i.e., the Meyerhold Workshop] in the Academic Year 1922–1923.

A. FIRST-YEAR STUDENTS.

| Names of courses and subjects: | First, second or third quarter: | Hours: |
|---|---|---|
| *I. Course in Movement* | | |
| 1. Anatomy and the fundamentals of biology | I | 2 |
| 2. Dance | 1, 2, 3 | 2 |
| 3. Training in movement through physical culture | 1, 2, 3 | 6 |
| 4. Biomechanics | 1, 2, 3 | 6 |
| 5. Word movement | 3 | 2 |
| *II. Course in the Word* | | |
| 1. Placing of the voice and breathing | 1, 2, 3 | |
| 2. Diction and correction of defects | 1, 2, 3 | 6 |
| 3. Poetics | 2 | 2 |
| 4. System of prose | 3 | 2 |

*III. Course in Dramatic Literature*

| | | |
|---|---|---|
| 1. Introduction to poetics | I, 2 | 2 |
| 2. Analysis of dramatic literature | 3 | 2 |
| 3. Logic. Biomechanism [*sic*] | I, 2, 3 | 2 |

*IV. Course in Elementary Technology*

| | | |
|---|---|---|
| 1. Elementary mathematics, descriptive geometry, and projectional drawing | 1, 2, 3 | 2 |
| 2. Technology of materials | I, 2 | 2 |
| 3. Plastic anatomy | I | 2 |
| 4. Analysis of the material elements of staging | 1, 2, 3 | 4 |

*V. Course in Music*

| | | |
|---|---|---|
| 1. Rhythmic gymnastics | I, 2, 3 | 4 |
| 2. Elementary theory of music | I, 2, 3 | 2 |

*VI. Technical Course*

| | | |
|---|---|---|
| Fundamentals of staging | 1, 2, 3 | 2 |

*VII. Course in Social Sciences*

| | | |
|---|---|---|
| Required subjects | I, 2, 3 | 2 |

Pro-Rector Beria

B. SECOND-YEAR STUDENTS, DEPARTMENT OF STAGE DIRECTING

*I. Course in Movement*

| | | |
|---|---|---|
| 1. Dance | I, 3 | 2 |

2. Training in physical
culture                   I, 2, 3        2
3. Biomechanics and
word movement         I, 2, 3        6
4. The gesture of music
and pantomime            2, 3        2

*II. Course in the Word*

1. The word on stage     I, 2, 3        2
2. Poetics                  2           2
3. System of prose          2           2

*III. Course in Dramatic Literature*

1. Logic and bio-
mechanism            I, 2          2
2. Analysis of dramatic
literature           I,    3        2
3. Russian theater       I, 2, 3        2
4. Chinese theater       I             2
5. Japanese theater          3         2

*IV. Course in Elementary Technology*

Mathematics
1. Descriptive geometry
and projectional
drawing              I, 2, 3        2
2. Optics and lighting
on stage             I, 2, 3        2
3. Technology and
study of materials   I, 2, 3        2
4. Analysis of elements
of plastic staging   I, 2, 3        4

*V. Course in Music*

1. Harmony               I, 2, 3        2
2. Theory of forms       I, 2, 3        2

*VI. Technical Course*

Fundamentals of
staging                  I, 2, 3        6

*VII. Course in Social Sciences*

Required subjects         I, 2, 3        4
Pro-Rector Beria

## GEKTEMAS

(Gosudarstvennye eksperimental'nye masterskie) im. Meierkhol'da [Meyerhold State Institute of Technology, Theater Workshop], Course of Study for the Academic Year 1927–1928.

I.

1. Saravianov, V. N.    Historical
materialism     2
2. Gnesin, M. F.        Analysis and history of musical
forms           2
3. Gnesin, M. F.        Literature of
music           I
4. Grigoriev, M. S.     Analysis and history of literary
forms           2
5. Tarabukin, N. M.     Analysis of
form in the
fine arts       2
6. Andrei Belyi         The literary
word            2
7. Bebutov, D.          Dramatic
literature      2
8. Stepanov, V. Ia.     Bibliography of
theater         I

II.

1. Vsevolod Meyerhold    Technology
of directing ⎫
⎬ 6
2. Seminar for participants in
the course of Vs. Meyerhold ⎭

TOPICS

a) Creating the play on stage.
b) The director's "score" of the production.
c) Mounting the play.
d) The director's promptbook.
e) Musical setting of the production.
f) Properties for the production.
g) Technical equipment of the stage.
h) Mise en scène (blocking).
i) Work of the director with the actor.
j) Art of the actor.
k) Biomechanics.
l) Method of evaluating the production.
m) Estimate of audience reaction.
n) The problem of the theater building.
o) Motion pictures.

III. TECHNICAL WORK IN THE MEYERHOLD THEATER

All students of the class in stage directing at the Meyerhold Workshop directly participate in the technical work of the Theater under the supervision of Master Craftsman Vs. Meyerhold. They work as 1) directorial technicians, 2) directorial assistants, 3) foremen and 4) managers of various parts of the production. In addition, almost all the students of the class in stage directing participate in the production as actors.

3. Study of the type character roles of the theater and of stage function.
4. Theory of the art of acting (How to create a role).
5. Education of the actor.
6. Daily schedule of the actor and the organization of his work.
7. Professional selection in the theater.
8. The actor's copyright for the type character role.

II. THE DIRECTOR: *Laboratory for the analysis of stage directing.*

1. Analysis of especially significant productions in the history of styles in the theater (theater history).
2. Analysis of systems of directing.
3. Stage management.
4. Internal order of work in the theater.
5. Creating the play on stage.
6. Mounting the play.
7. Daily schedule of the director and organization of his work.
8. Categories of directing.
9. Professional selection in the theater.
10. The director's copyright.

# The Actor, the Director

I. THE ACTOR: *Laboratory for the analysis of acting.*

1. Analysis of the art of actors in the past (memoirs, journals, letters, criticism).
2. Analysis of the art of contemporary actors.

# Notes

## Introduction

1. See Oskar Schlemmer et al., *Die Bühne im Bauhaus*, Bauhausbücher, vol. 4 (Frankfurt, 1925); also Mikhail Barkhin and Sergei Vakhtangov, "A Theater for Meyerhold," trans. Edward Braun, *Theatre Quarterly* 2, no. 7 (July–September 1972): 69–73.

2. Nora Beeson first published excerpts of her English translation of Meyerhold's 1913 book *O teatre* [On theater]: "Farce," *Tulane Drama Review* 4, no. 1 (1959): 139–49; "On Theater," ibid. 4, no. 4 (1960):138–48.

3. Three basic Soviet publications are: *Vstrechi s Meierkhol'dom* (Moscow, 1967); V. E. Meierkhol'd, *Stat'i; Pis'ma; Rechi; Besedy*, 2 vols. (Moscow, 1968); K. L. Rudnitskii, *Rezhisser Meierkhol'd* (Moscow, 1969).

4. The considerable interest in Soviet theater after 1917 is reflected in such publications as those by Oliver Sayler, Huntly Carter, and Norris Houghton noted in the bibliography below.

5. Nick Worrall, "Meyerhold Directs Gogol's *Government Inspector*," *Theatre Quarterly* 2, no. 7 (July–September 1972): 75–95.

6. Quoted in N. D. Volkov, *Meierkhol'd* (Moscow, 1929), 2:220.

## Chronological table

1. K. S. Stanislavsky, *Moia zhizn' v iskusstve* (Moscow, 1962), p. 344. Retranslated here is what Stanislavsky earlier rendered in English as, "The time for the unreal on the stage had come." *My Life in Art* (Boston, 1924), p. 434.

## Chapter 1. The New Theater

1. Chekhov gave his advice to Meyerhold in a letter to Olga Knipper of 2 January 1900. A. P. Chekhov, *Polnoe sobranie sochinenii i pisem* (Moscow, 1949), 18:292.

2. Meyerhold's sense that Nemirovich-Danchenko's play *V mechtakh* [In dreams], produced by the Art Theater in 1901, was superficial and the consequent worsening of his relations with one director of the theater are described in an article by E. A. Polotskaia, "Chekhov i Meierkhol'd," in *Literaturnoe nasledstvo* (Moscow, 1960), 68:428–29.

3. K. S. Stanislavsky, *Sobranie sochinenii* (Moscow, 1959), 6:426.

4. B. N. Bugaev [Andrei Belyi], *Mezhdu dvukh revoliutsii, 1905–11* (Leningrad, 1934), pp. 64–67.

5. Ibid.

6. Alexander Blok, *Sobranie sochinenii* (Moscow, 1962), 5:98.

7. Ibid., pp. 96–97.

8. *The Theater in Soviet Russia*, trans. Edgar Lehrman, Columbia Slavic Studies (New York, 1957), p. 80.

9. The stand taken in my article "V. E. Meyerhold: A Russian Predecessor of Avant-Garde Theater," *Comparative Literature*, Summer 1965, pp. 234–50, that *uslovnyi* might serve as an abstract term for nonrealistic theater in general, unfortunately proves untenable. For *uslovnyi* seems to be inevitably associated with symbolist theater at the turn of the century.

10. London, 1927, p. 150.

11. *Teatr kak takovoi*, 2nd ed. (Moscow, 1923), p. 18.

12. Ibid., p. 19.

## Chapter 2. Petersburg Productions (1908–18)

1. Quoted in Volkov, 2:12, from a press interview for the Moscow *Russkoe slovo*.

2. *Articles,* 1:160; Meyerhold was quoting from Peter Altenberg.

3. *Protiv techeniia* (Leningrad and Moscow, 1962), p. 501.

4. Ibid., pp. 408–9.

5. *Aleksandr Iakovlevich Golovin: Vstrechi i vpechatleniia; Pis'ma; Vospominaniia o Golovine* (Leningrad and Moscow, 1960), pp. 187–88.

6. Ibid., p. 330.

7. Volkov called the journalists Apollinaire and Kervilly Meyerhold's "constant companions" and cited Meyerhold's letter home in which he praised all that Apollinaire had done in his little book *Le Théâtre italien* (1910) to make Gozzi known. Volkov, 2:285.

## Chapter 3. The Meyerhold Method

1. *Sovremenniki: Vakhtangov, Meierkhol'd* (Moscow, 1969), p. 350.

2. Anna Fedorovna Geints, who in 1927 sacrificed herself to save a drowning child, wrote to Volkov her recollections of the studio of 1908–9; the sessions evidently took place at Meyerhold's apartment on Zhukovsky Street. Besides Gnesin's course in musical reading and Meyerhold's in plastic gymnastics, voice and diction were taught. The repertory consisted of Sophocles' *Antigone,* Hofmannsthal's *Electra,* the contemporary dramatists Ibsen, Maeterlinck, Chekhov, and Peter Altenberg; the class also took part in the cabaret productions at Lukomore. Volkov, 2:40–41.

3. See note 2 above.

4. "Realismus und Stilisierung" [Realism and stylization], signed "b," in the theater program of the Berliner Ensemble, Brecht's company, for *The Caucasian Chalk Circle* (1954), p. 6.

5. Jerzy Grotowski, *Towards a Poor Theatre* (New York, 1969).

6. Guillaume Apollinaire, *Oeuvres complètes en 4 vols.* (Paris, 1966), 3:900.

7. *Teatral'nyi oktiabr'* (Leningrad and Moscow, 1926), p. 177.

8. *Teatr sotsial'noi maski* (Moscow and Leningrad, 1931), p. 42.

9. Alpers, p. 33.

10. TsGALI (Tsentral'nyi Gosudarstvennyi Arkhiv Literatury i Iskusstva, Central State Archive for Literature and Art), f. 963, op. 1, ed. khr. 1335 (1922), 11; see Appendix 3.

11. See p. 310 of this volume.

12. The aim Meyerhold envisaged with his biomechanical training for actors was very like the goal of Grotowski's work with actors today, though the first couched his formulation in scientific language and the second in mystical terms. Meyerhold aimed at "reflex sensitivity," the actor's capacity for "reducing to a minimum the time of conscious awareness of 'time of simple reaction.' " *Amplua aktera,* p. 4. Grotowski calls his way "a via negativa" or "eradication of blocks": "The education of an actor in our theatre is not a matter of teaching him something; we attempt to eliminate his organism's resistance to this psychic process. The result is freedom from the time-lapse between inner impulse and outer reaction." *Towards a Poor Theatre,* p. 16.

13. V. V. Maiakovskii, *Polnoe sobranie sochinenii v 13 tt.* (Moscow, 1959), 12:18.

14. See especially Appendix 3.

15. Some of Temerin's photographs, as well as Liutse's sketches, are reprinted in *Encounters,* and others have been published

in the Spring 1973 number of *Drama Review*.

16. *Protiv techeniia,* pp. 219–20.

17. *Il trucco e l'anima* (Turin, 1965), p. 294.

## Chapter 4. Soviet Productions (1918–39)

1. Juri Jelagin, *Temnyi genii* [Dark genius] (New York, 1955). Until the publication in 1969 of Rudnitskii's biography Jelagin's was the only one to cover Meyerhold's entire career.

2. *Dnevnik moikh vstrech* (New York, 1966), 2:44.

3. Ibid., p. 45.

4. *Oeuvres complètes,* 3:937.

5. Ibid.

6. *Izbrannye stat'i v 2 tt.* (Moscow, 1958), 1:788.

7. A. V. Fevral'skii, "Misteriia-buff," in *Spektakli i gody,* eds. A. Anastas'ev and E. Peregudova (Moscow, 1969), pp. 13–14.

8. *Teatr sotsial'noi maski,* p. 22.

9. Ibid.

10. *Maiakovskii v vospominaniiakh sovremennikov* (Moscow, 1963), p. 308.

11. B. Rostotskii, *O rezhisserskom tvorchestve V. E. Meierkhol'da* (Moscow, 1960), p. 31.

12. A. A. Gvozdev, *Teatr imeni Meierkhol'da, 1920–1926* (Leningrad, 1927), p. 29.

13. Ibid., pp. 30–31.

14. Rostotskii, pp. 41–42.

15. "Ostrovskii v postanovkakh Meierkhol'da," *Teatr* (April 1937):30–45.

16. V. Maksimova, " 'Dokhodnoe mesto' v Teatre revoliutsii," in *Voprosy teatra* (Moscow, 1967), p. 41.

17. Ia. O. Boiarskii et al., eds., *Moskovskii Teatr Revoliutsii, 1922–1932* (Moscow,

1933), p. 141.

18. Ibid., pp. 5, 49–50.

19. See note 15 above.

20. Alpers, *Teatr sotsial'noi maski,* p. 43.

21. *Teatr imeni Meierkhol'da,* p. 47.

22. See note 5 to Introduction above.

23. Translated under the title *Wit Works Woe* by Sir Bernard Pares in *Masterpieces of Russian Drama,* ed. George Rapall Noyes (New York, 1961), 1:85–155.

A year before Meyerhold staged Griboedov's play, at a party in his honor (27 January 1927), a message was read as a joke directed at his "contemporization" of *The Inspector General.* Purportedly from the "Local Committee of Dead Authors" its actual authors were the satirists Evgenii Zamiatin and Mikhail Zoshchenko. They proposed a list of titles for future contemporization, among which were:
*L. N. Tolstoy,* The Electrification of the Village *(The Power of Darkness).*
*A. S. Griboedov,* Roar Griboedov (Woe from Wit) [*This was an allusion to the Meyerhold Theater's successful play* Roar China, *by Tret'iakov*].
Annenkov, *Dnevnik moikh vstrech* 2:77.

24. *O teatre i dramaturgii,* 2 vols. (Moscow, 1958), 1:622.

25. Productions by G. A. Tovstonogov at the Leningrad Gorky Theater (1962) and by E. R. Simonov at the Moscow Malyi Theater (1963).

26. The scenes in the 1928 production were as follows; the asterisked scenes, all added inventions of Meyerhold, were omitted in his revival of 1935:

* 1  The pub
  2  The antechamber
  3  The antechamber
* 4  The dancing class
  5  The portrait gallery
  6  Lounge

* 7 Billiard room and library
  8 The white room
  9 At the door
 10 At the door
*11 The shooting gallery
 12 Upstairs vestibule
 13 Library and dancing room
 14 Dining room
 15 Music room
 16 Before the fireplace
 17 On the stairs

*Articles,* 2:543; see especially Meyerhold's
1935 speech "Printsipy spektaklia," *Articles,*
2:323.

27. That I was fortunate enough to see
the 1935 revival is another reason for
choosing to discuss that production here.

28. *Izbrannye proizvedeniia,* vol. 4,
*Rezhissura* (Moscow, 1966), p. 97.

29. A. V. Lunacharskii, *"Gore ot uma* v
Malom teatre." *Literaturnoe nasledstvo,*
vol. 82, *Neizdannye materialy* (Moscow,
1970), 432–33.

30. Ibid., 82:436.

31. *Polnoe sobranie sochinenii,* 12:189,
199.

32. See Meyerhold's letter of 1930 to
Golovin, *Articles,* 2:214.

33. *P'esy* (Moscow, 1967), p. 265.

34. *Théâtre complet* (Paris, 1878), 1:20.

35. *Izbrannye proizvedeniia,* vol. 4,
*Rezhissura,* pp. 597–98.

36. Ibid., pp. 603–4, 597.

37. *Vestnik teatra,* no. 85–86 (15 March
1921), p. 7.

## Chapter 5. Meyerhold and Other Arts and Artists

1. London, 1962, p. 252.

2. *Lef* 2 (April–May 1923):66.

3. Quoted in Sophie Küppers-Lissitzky,
*El Lissitzky* (London and Greenwich,
Conn., 1968), p. 354.

Here El Lissitzky, not Aleksei Gan, who
is usually cited as theorist of constructivism,
speaks for the new art. Gan, however, criticized Meyerhold's *Tarelkin* as insufficiently
abstract to be representative. Stepanova too
felt that biomechanics predominated over
constructivism in the way the actors used
her apparatus. Meyerhold considered her
expression of this view in an interview
(1922) a stab in the back and never again
employed her as designer. See Rudnitskii,
p. 276.

4. Quoted in Küppers-Lissitzky, *El Lissitzky,* pp. 372–73.

5. Ibid., p. 326.

6. See the article by Mikhail Barkhin in
the special number on constructivist architecture in the USSR (1917–32) of the
British periodical *Architectural Design,*
February 1970, pp. 88–90.

7. "A Theatre for Meyerhold," trans. Edward Braun, *Theatre Quarterly,* July–Sept.
1972, 69–73 (*Encounters,* 570–78).

8. Ibid., p. 70.

9. Edward Braun, trans., *Meyerhold on
Theatre* (New York, 1969), p. 267.

10. Translated in Braun, pp. 311–24.

11. Jay Leyda, *Kino* (London, 1960),
pp. 81–82.

12. Ibid., p. 81.

13. Ibid.

14. *Istoriia sovetskogo kino* (Moscow,
1969), 1:375.

15. In *Sergei Prokofiev: Stat'i i materialy*
(Moscow, 1965), pp. 94–120.

16. Introduction to Konstantin Stanislavsky, *Stanislavsky on the Art of the Stage,*
ed. David Magarshack (London, 1950),
p. 33.

17. "Benois as Director," *Articles,* 1:271.

18. *Pravda teatra* (Moscow, 1965), p. 43.

19. Introduction to *Stanislavsky on the Art of the Stage*, p. 23.

20. A. Gladkov, "Repliki Meierkhol'da," *Teatral'naia zhizn*, no. 5 (1960), p. 19.

21. "Stanislavskii i Meierkhol'd," *Tarusskie stranitsy* (Kaluga, 1961), pp. 289–91.

22. Meyerhold made his point not by abstract statement but by an example meant to show the impracticality of experiencing the role: Mariia Zhdanova, a member of the Art Theater, appeared before the camera as Lucy in a scene of the motion picture *The Strong Man* (*Mocny czlowiek* [Homo sapiens]), by Przybszewski, which Meyerhold directed in 1917; when, however, the camera man stopped the machine at the end of the predetermined footage for the scene, saying, "I've finished," she exclaimed, "But I haven't yet begun" (*Articles*, 2:90).

23. S. V. Zakharev and Sh. Sh. Bogatyrev, eds., *Stanislavskii: Pisateli, artisty, rezhissery o velikom deiatele russkogo teatra, 1863–1963* (Moscow, 1963), p. 71.

24. "Benois as Director," *Articles*, 1:271.

25. Bernhard Reich, *Im Wettlauf mit der Zeit* (Berlin, 1970), p. 369. Note also Reich's monograph in Russian, *Brekht* (Moscow, 1960).

26. Zakhava, *Sovremenniki: Vakhtangov, Meierkhol'd*, p. 364.

27. *Materialy i stat'i*, ed. L. D. Vendrovskaia (Moscow, 1959), p. 25.

28. *Sovremenniki: Vakhtangov, Meierkhol'd*, p. 83.

29. Ibid., p. 81.

30. *Materialy i stat'i*, p. 30.

31. Ibid., p. 25.

32. Quoted in Boris Zakhava, *Vakhtangov i ego studiia*, 2nd ed. (Moscow, 1930), p. 138.

33. *Der Sturm* 3, no. 129 (1912):157.

34. Ibid., no. 132, pp. 194–95.

35. Ibid., no. 129, p. 162.

36. *Schriften*, ed. Ludwig Hoffmann, 2 vols. (Berlin, 1968), 2:264, 267.

37. "Abwickelung," *Das Kunstblatt*, ed. Paul Westheim (Berlin, 1924), pp. 37–38.

38. Hugo Huppert, "Und diese bahnbrechend konstruktive Theatertat (die 1918 verwirklichte Massenrevue-Inszenierung) geschah fast ein Jahrzehnt vor Piscators zwingender Erdball-Vision. (This pioneer deed of reshaping the theater [which was the staging of a mass spectacle, realized in 1918] occurred almost a decade before Piscator's compelling vision of the planet Earth)." Introduction to *Mysterium buffo*, Reclams Universalbibliothek 135 (Leipzig, 1969), p. 11.

39. Piscator, *Schriften*, 2:357.

40. *Berliner Tageblatt*, no. 171 (10 April 1930). For this and other quotations from press criticism of the Meyerhold Theater during its 1930 tour thanks are due to the Wilhelm Richter Archive of Theater Criticism, Akademie der Künste, Berlin.

41. *Börsen-Courier*, 10 April 1930.

42. *Return Engagement* (New York, 1962), p. 17.

43. *Schriften*, 2:266.

44. *Im Wettlauf mit der Zeit*, p. 239.

45. Anna Lazis, "Das Programm eines proletarischen Kindertheaters," *Alternative* 11, no. 50/60 (April–June 1965): 65.

46. 1936; reprint ed., Moscow, 1962.

47. The German translation exists in an undated mimeograph. The translation by Ernst Hube was revised by Brecht; the publisher is Max Reichard Verlag, Freiburg.

48. John Willett, *The Theatre of Bertolt Brecht* (London, 1967), p. 178; Victor Erlich, *Russian Formalism* (The Hague, 1965), pp. 176–80.

49. "B. Brekht: khudozhestvennye mysli," *Teatr* (January 1956), p. 147.

50. Reich, *Im Wettlauf mit der Zeit*, p. 371.

51. *Die Dramaturgie Brechts* (Berlin, 1968), p. 110. In her article "Brecht in der USSR," *Neue Deutsche Literatur* 16, no. 2 (February 1968): 7–28, she accounts not only for his relations with the Soviet Union but also for his trips there in 1932, 1935, 1936, 1941, and 1955. Reich, who omits the 1936 trip, is the better authority.

52. Jacques Guicharnaud, *Modern French Theater* (New Haven, 1961), p. 240.

53. See Meyerhold's article on Craig, *Articles*, 1:167–69.

54. Guicharnaud, *Modern French Theater*, p. 224.

55. "Le théâtre de la cruauté," Premier manifeste, 1932, in Artaud, *Oeuvres complètes* (Paris, 1961–   ), 4:118.

56. *Oeuvres complètes*, 1:47.

57. "Le théâtre de la cruauté," Second manifeste, 1933, in *Oeuvres complètes*, 4:134.

58. *Modern French Theater*, p. 15.

59. *Izbrannye proizvedeniia*, 1:88.

60. Ibid., 1:82, 305–6.

61. Ibid., 1:310.

62. Ibid., 2:270.

63. In *Spektakli i gody,* eds. A. Anastas'ev and E. Peregudova (Moscow, 1969), p. 501.

64. *Oeuvres complètes,* 2:46.

65. *The Empty Space* (London, 1968), p. 27.

# Glossary

*agitprop*, department of "agitation" and "propaganda," authorized by the Central Committee of the Communist party; also local departments for the same purpose of propagating communist causes; dissolved in 1930.

*alienation*, description of a phenomenon from a naive point of view, as if seen for the first time. Viktor Shklovskii began directing attention to the concept, *ostranenie,* as he called it, in 1914, exemplifying it in the work of Leo Tolstoy. Brecht used the device in his work for the theater in the twenties, though he first called it *Verfremdung,* a translation of the Russian, after 1935 when he encountered it in Russian theater practice on his second trip to Moscow.

*amplua (emploi) (see also* Appendix 2), a set role of the actor's art, such as ingénue or soubrette.

*annihilation*, the relationship of Sergei Eisenstein and Sergei Tretiakov to a classic original, as when, disregarding tradition, they produced Alexander Ostrovsky's *Even a Wise Man Stumbles* (1923) in the form of a political satiric revue, consisting in acrobatics, film, and topical caricature.

*balagan* (from the Persian *bālāhānä,* balcony), a movable structure for a dramatic presentation at a fair; hence popular theater on a primitive level. Meyerhold wrote two articles titled "Balagan," one included in *On Theater,* the other in *Love for Three Oranges,* in both of which he urged a return to simpler forms of theater. *Balagan* has been here translated *farce,* as has been also the title of Blok's play *Balaganchik,* which, properly speaking, refers to the proprietor of such a show booth at a fair. Alexander Benois used *balagan* to disparage Meyerhold's *Don Juan,* calling it

*nariadnyi balagan,* a farce in fancy dress.

*Bauhaus,* a school of architecture and design, founded in Weimar by Walter Gropius (1919), moved to Dessau (1925), and dissolved in Berlin (1933) after the advent of Hitler. At various times Mies van der Rohe, Vasilii Kandinsky, Paul Klee, Lyonel Feininger, and Oskar Schlemmer, among others, taught and worked there.

*biomechanics,* literally the study of mechanics as applied to living beings, pioneered by Leonardo da Vinci and much furthered in our time by work done in military medicine, orthopedics, and zoology. After 1922 Meyerhold so called his system of exercises, taken from sport, industry, and acting traditions of the past; the actor trained in these movements was consciously to use them in creating his role on stage.

*cinematification,* imitation in the theater of devices, situations, and, above all, the tempo and chase typical of the silent films of the twenties, as, for example, in *The Death of Tarelkin* (1922).

*commedia dell'arte,* derived from Greek and Roman comedy; it used stock characters, situations, costumes and conventions of blocking and movement, from which its actors improvised a performance. After enjoying great popularity in the fifteenth and sixteenth centuries, it declined thereafter, despite efforts by Carlo Gozzi to revive it in the eighteenth century; nevertheless, it influenced the plays of Molière, Marivaux, Tieck, Blok.

*constructivism,* a movement in twentieth-century art which used industrial materials to create abstractly geometric works. Constructivist artists also made functional designs for useful objects, architecture, and typography; for the Meyerhold Theater the constructivists Liubov Popova and

Varvara Stepanova built sets using also the vertical dimension and incorporating machines for acting.

*contrary effect*, so called in the unfinished handbook on directing *Rezhissura*, begun in the mid-thirties by Sergei Eisenstein. This reversal of the tradition coincided with Meyerhold's "paradoxical composition" (see below) and his exemplification of it notably in *Woe to Wit* and *33 Fainting Fits*.

*Duncanism. See* Duncan, Isadora, in the index.

*formalism*, the separation in philosophical theory of content and form usual with the ancient Greeks. In the second decade of this century Max Scheler in Germany so named his new ethics, and in the early twenties in Russia a group of gifted critics —among them Viktor Shklovskii and Roman Jakobson, the latter a founder of structuralism, influential today—so called their new stylistics. In Soviet aesthetics the term connotes condemnation.

*futurism*, first launched by the manifesto (1909) of the Italian Filippo Marinetti, who urged total abrogation of the past and tradition. The Russian futuristic manifesto "A Slap in the Face of Public Taste" (1912), signed by Mayakovsky among others, revealed rather the romantic need to shock, "épater le bourgeois." After the Revolution Russian futurism, as propagated in Mayakovsky's magazine *Lef*, advocated a utilitarian art and a journalistic literature dedicated to the betterment of life for the masses.

*GEKTEMAS* (Gosudarstvennye eksperimental'nye teatral'nye masterskie, State Experimental Theater Workshop), designation of the Meyerhold Workshop for the longest period of its existence (1923–31).

*grotesque*, usually meaning strange, incongruous, monstrous, designated in Meyerhold's parlance a sense of quick, unexpected shifts from one extreme to another.

*GVYRM* (Gosudarstvennye vysshie rezhisserskie masterskie, State Graduate School for Theater Directors), designation of the director's courses in the Meyerhold Workshop (1921–22).

*GVYTM* (Gosudarstvennye vysshie teatral'nye masterskie, State Graduate School of Theater), designation of the Meyerhold workshop in 1921–22.

*House of Interludes*, cabaret or intimate theater in Petersburg, at which Meyerhold staged *Columbine's Scarf* (1910), designed by Nikolai Sapunov.

*Kabuki*, Japanese folk theater of the seventeenth century.

*Kamerny Theater* of Aleksandr Tairov, opened with Kalidasa's *Sakuntali* (1914) and continued until its director's death in 1950. Though Tairov began his career with Meyerhold, whom he invited to collaborate on Paul Claudel's *Exchange* (1918), and though they stood for similar principles, Meyerhold considered the Kamerny antipodal to his own theater. Their quarrel is documented in Meyerhold's adverse review of Tairov's *Notes of a Director* (1922) (*Articles*, 2:37–43) and in Tairov's attack on Meyerhold's biomechanics, "Fokusnichestvo v teatre" (A Bag of Tricks in the Theater), which, though not republished in the Soviet anthology by Tairov, *Zapiski rezhissera*, may be found in German translation in Ludwig Hoffman and Dieter Wardetzky, eds., *Meyerhold, Tairow, Wachtangow, Theateroktober*, pp. 293–302.

*Lukomore*, Petersburg cabaret or intimate theater, in which Meyerhold produced

*Petrushka* as a play, designer Mstislav Dobuzhinskii (1908).

*Meiningenism*, the emphasis on historical authenticity of detail and individuality of portrayal, even of minor characters, achieved by the Duke of Saxon-Meiningen's theater (1866–91). Abuse of the theater's principles often by other theaters led to bad associations with the word, which later meant a clutter of historic detail for its own sake, or frantically distinctive acting by extras in crowds.

*moderne*, close in Soviet literary terminology to meaning decadent, though such gifted writers as Yeats, Eliot, Joyce, and Proust are categorized under "modernism."

*naturalism*, in principle, a renewed striving toward the exact imitation of nature in art, even the scientific study of it, as formulated in Emile Zola's *Le roman expérimental* (1880); in practice, a preoccupation with misery and often superfluous accumulation of its details. Among its great practitioners were, as well as Zola, Leo Tolstoy, Gerhart Hauptmann, and Theodore Dreiser.

*Noh-plays*, the oldest form of Japanese theater, portraying aristocratic Samurai warriors with dance, chorus, and song (fourteenth and fifteenth centuries), surviving in strict stylization of mask and pantomime (seventeenth century).

*paradoxical composition*, the device of reversing the tradition (*see also* contrary effect). Meyerhold defined this in a gloss to *Amplua aktera* (p. 309 above), citing as an example the avoidance of an acting stereotype: for instance, in Gogol's *Inspector General* Bobchinsky and Dobchinsky, who traditionally stutter by reason of all too rapid speech, were made to speak, instead, very slowly. Eisenstein in

*Iskusstvo kino* (1940) again elucidated the phenomenon, called "opposite solution" in Jay Leyda's translation (*Film Essays*, pp. 92–108).

*perekliuchenie*, sudden changeover of mood, tempo, and lighting, doubtless most effectively used by Meyerhold in *The Inspector General*.

*pictorialism*, the carefully stylized grouping of actors on a shallow stage in an effort to restore pictorial beauty to an age weary of naturalism. Enunciated in principle in part in Georg Fuchs's *Stage of the Future* (1904), pictorialism was successfully practiced by Meyerhold in *Sister Beatrice* with Komissarzhevskaia (1906).

*pre-acting* (*predygra*), Meyerhóld's theory that the actor should prepare an important moment of performance by a sign or gesture to the audience in advance, even a pause, as practiced in *Bubus the Teacher* (1925).

*Proletkult*, the totality of proletarian cultural organizations (1917–32), which staged theater for and by the workers, reaching a membership of some 400,000 around 1920.

*Proun*, synthetic word coined by El Lissitzky (1919) from the Russian words *proekt utverzhdeniia novogo* (project for the affirmation of the new). A year later Lissitzky gave to his artists' workshop in Vitebsk the slogan *Unovis* (*utverzhdeniie* —or *ucherezhdenie*—*novogo v iskusstve:* affirmation—or establishment—of the new in art), and the two words are sometimes joined to read *Prounovis*.

*prozodezhda* (*proizvodstvennaia odezhda*, factory clothes), costumes simulating workers' overalls, such as Liubov Popova designed for the actors in *The Magnanimous Cuckold* (1922).

*raccourci*, the foreshortening which a figure suffers when seen in perspective, i.e., half- or side-view on stage.

*risunok* (drawing, outline), in Meyerhold's usage the shape or design of a role, also the silhouette or pose of a figure in a single moment of that role on stage.

*samozerkalenie. See* zerkalenie.

*Starinnyi teatr* (antiquarian theater), two Petersburg seasons, one of medieval theater (1907–8), the other of Renaissance and seventeenth-century plays (1911–12), produced by Nikolai Evreinov and N. V. Drizen.

*suprematism*, system of painting in combinations of simple abstract geometric forms, first proclaimed by Kazimir Malevich in 1915 and exemplified the same year in his painting *Black Square.*

*symbolism*, in antithesis to naturalism the transcendency of reality to the pure idea, conveyed by a sign or symbol and the music of language, rather than in the ordinary meaning of words. Among the symbolist dramatists produced by Meyerhold were Maurice Maeterlinck, Emile Verhaeren, Konstantin Balmont, Stanislav Przybyszewski, and Alexander Blok.

*Taganka*, the Moscow Theater of Drama and Comedy located on Taganka Square, founded in 1946, famous for the notable productions of Brecht and the poets Mayakovsky, Andrei Voznesenskii, and Evgenii Evtushenko staged there by Iurii Liubimov, director of the theater since 1964.

*Taylorization*, the American Frederick Winslow Taylor's system of rationalizing work motions in industry, in which Meyerhold found support for his rationalization of actors' motions in biomechanics.

*uslovnyi* (conditional), in general, an agreed-upon condition or assumption; in particular, the assumption that the theater is an art in its own right, not dependent upon reality as its point of reference. Historically *uslovnyi* has come to mean symbolist theater around the turn of the century by such writers as Maeterlinck and Verhaeren, though sometimes Meyerhold's productions as late as the twenties are classified under *uslovnost* or *uslovnyi teatr*, in contrast to the realism of other Soviet theaters.

*World of Art*, a group of Russian artists, including Leon Bakst, Alexander Benois, and Sergei Diaghilev, which from the nineties to 1924 strove to renew appreciation of the Russian artistic past and to create new beauty in Russian art.

*zerkalenie* (mirroring), or *samozerkalenie* (self-mirroring), Meyerhold's word for the actor's awareness of self as both directing will and executive instrument of his artistic intent.

# Selected Bibliography of Meyerhold's Own Works

## Books, Articles, Speeches

Nine articles in *Liubov' k trem apel'sinam*
[Love for three oranges]. 9 issues, 1914–
16. Some of these pieces were coauthored
with others; some were signed with Meyerhold's pseudonym, Dr. Dapertutto.

*O teatre*. Petersburg, 1913. Included fourteen
articles, excerpts from four of which are
translated in Edward Braun, *Meyerhold
on Theatre*, pp. 80–107, 119–43.

" 'Portret Doriana Greia.' " In *Iz istorii kino:
dokumenty i materialy*, pp. 15–24. Moscow, 1965.

*Rekonstruktsiia teatra*. Leningrad, Moscow,
1930. Translated in Braun, pp. 253–74.

[Speech at conference on issues confronting
the theater (May 1927)]. In *Ezhegodnik
instituta istorii iskusstv 1959*, pp. 130–34.
Moscow, 1959.

*Stat'i; Pis'ma; Rechi; Besedy*. 2 vols. Moscow, 1968. [Cited in the text as *Articles*.]

"Teatr: K istorii i tekhnike ego." In *Teatr:
kniga o novom teatre*, pp. 123–76. Petersburg, 1908. This anthology without editor
included articles by Lunacharskii and
Belyi, among others, along with the Meyerhold article cited. Translated (under
various headings) in Braun, pp. 23–64.
Republished in *O teatre*.

and Bebutov, V. M.; Aksenov, I. A. *Amplua
aktera*. Moscow, 1922. See Appendix 2.

and Derzhavin, Konstantin, eds. *"Boris
Godunov" A. S. Pushkina*. Materialy k
postanovke. Petersburg, 1919.

## Anthologies of Meyerhold's Articles and Speeches in Translation

Braun, Edward, ed. *Meyerhold on Theatre*.
London, 1969.

Crino, Giovanni, ed. *La rivoluzione teatrale*.
Rome, 1962.

*Ecrits sur le théâtre*. Vol. 1. *1891–1917*. Collection "Théâtre années 20." Lausanne,
1973.

Gourfinkel, Nina, ed. *Le théâtre théâtral:
V. E. Meyerhold*. Paris, 1963.

## Plays by Meyerhold

and Bondi, Iu. M. *Alinur*. Petrograd, Moscow, 1919. Fairy-tale play in three acts.

and Bondi, Iu. M.; Solov'ev, V. N. *Ogon'*
[Under fire]. *Love for Three Oranges*, no.
6–7 (1914), pp. 19–55. Melodrama.

and Vogak, K. A.; Solov'ev, V. N. *Liubov' k
trem apel'sinam*, after Gozzi. *Love for
Three Oranges*, no. 1 (1914), pp. 11–19.
Performance scenario.

## Periodicals (dates in parentheses indicate Meyerhold's editorship)

*Afisha TIM* (1926).

*Liubov' k trem apel'sinam* [Love for Three
Oranges]. (9 issues, 1914–16).

*Zhizn' iskusstva* (Leningrad, 1924–25).

*Zrelishcha* (weekly, 1922–24).

# General Bibliography

Abensour, Gérard. "Meyerhold à Paris." *Cahiers du Monde Russe et Soviétique* 5 (1964): 5–31.

Alpers, B. " 'Gore ot uma' v Moskve i Leningrade." *Teatr* (June 1963): 28–38.

———. Ostrovskii v postanovkakh Meierkhol'da." *Teatr* (April 1937):30–45.

———. *Teatr sotsial'noi maski.* Moscow and Leningrad, 1931.

Annenkov, Iu. *Dnevnik moikh vstrech.* 2 vols. New York, 1966.

Apollinaire, Guillaume. *Oeuvres complètes en 4 vols.* Vol. 3. Paris, 1966.

Appia, Adolphe. *Die Musik und die Inszenierung.* Monaco, 1899. Translated by Robert W. Corrigan and Mary Douglas Dirks as *Music and the Art of the Theatre.* Coral Gables, Fla., 1969.

Artaud, Antonin. *Oeuvres complètes.* Paris, 1961– . Vol. 4, 1964.

*Art in Revolution: Soviet Art and Design Since 1917.* Catalogue of exhibit, Hayward Gallery, 26 February–18 April 1971, London.

*Avantgarde Osteuropa, 1910–30.* Catalogue of exhibit, Deutsche Akademie der Künste, October–November 1967, Berlin. Tübingen, 1967.

Barkhin, Mikhail, and Vakhtangov, Sergei. "A Theatre for Meyerhold." Translated by Edward Braun. *Theatre Quarterly* 2 (1972): 69–73.

Bessekhes, A[l'fred Iosifovich]. *Teatr i zhivopis' Golovina.* Moscow, 1970.

Belyi, Andrei. *See* Bugaev, B. N.

*Biografii studentov pervogo vypuska (1926) teatral'nykh masterskikh im. Meierkhol'da.* Moscow, 1926.

Blok, Aleksandr. *Sobranie sochinenii.* 8 vols. Moscow, 1960–63.

Boguslavskii, A. O.; Diev, V. A.; and Karpov, A. S. *Kratkaia istoriia russkoi sovetskoi dramaturgii.* Moscow, 1966.

Boiarskii, Ia. O.; Zubtsov, I. S.; Popov, A. D.; Cherniak, Ia. Z.; and Shchagin, A. I., eds. *Moskovskii Teatr Revoliutsii, 1921–32.* Moscow, 1933.

Bowlt, John. "Artists of the World, Disunite." Introduction to *Russian Avantgarde (1908–22).* Catalogue of exhibit, Leonard Hutton Galleries, pp. 10–14. New York, 1971.

Bradshaw, Martha, ed. *Soviet Theaters, 1917–41.* New York, 1954.

Braun, Edward. "Constructivism in the Theatre." In *Art in Revolution: Soviet Art and Design Since 1917.* Catalogue of exhibit, Hayward Gallery, 26 February–18 April 1971, London, pp. 60–81.

———, ed. *Meyerhold on Theatre.* London and New York, 1969.

Brecht, Bertolt. *Gesammelte Werke.* 20 vols. werkausgabe edition suhrkamp. Frankfurt, 1967. [Cited in the text as *werkausgabe.*]

———. "Realismus und Stilisierung." In Theater Program of the Berliner Ensemble for *The Caucasian Chalk Circle.* 1954.

———. trans., *Ich will ein Kind haben. See* Tret'iakov, Sergei M.

Briusov, Valerii. "Nenuzhnaia pravda." *Mir iskusstva* 7 (1902): 67–74.

Brook, Peter. *The Empty Space.* London, 1968.

Brukson, Ia. *Teatr Meierkhol'da.* Leningrad and Moscow, 1925.

Bugaev, B. N. [Andrei Belyi]. *Mezhdu dvukh revoliutsii, 1905–11.* Leningrad, 1934.

Carter, Huntly. *The New Spirit in Russian Theatre, 1917–28.* London, 1929.

Chekhov, A. P. *Polnoe sobranie sochinenii i pisem.* Vol. 18. Moscow, 1949.

"Chekhov i Meierkhol'd." In *Literaturnoe nasledstvo. See* Polotskaia.

Chulkov, Georgii, ed. *Fakely.* No. 1. Petersburg, 1906.

Coquelin, C. *The Art of the Actor.* Translated by Elsie Fogerty. London, 1932.

Craig, Gordon. *Art of the Theater.* Edinburgh and London, 1905. Translated into Russian in 1908.

Derzhavin, Konstantin. *Epokhi Aleksandrinskogo teatra.* Leningrad, 1932.

Diderot, Denis. "Paradoxe sur le comédien (1770)." In *Diderot's Writings on the Theater.* Edited by F. Green. Cambridge, 1936.

*Drama Review* T57 (Spring 1973). Special Russian issue with cover photographs of Meyerhold's biomechanical exercises and further photographs in "Lee Strasberg's Russian Notebook," pp. 106–21.

Dumas fils, Alexandre. *Théâtre complet.* Vol. 1. Paris, 1878.

Efros, Nikolai. *MXT 1898–1923.* Moscow, 1924.

Ehrenburg, Il'ia. *Liudy, gody, zhizn'.* Moscow, 1961.

Eisenstein, Sergei. *Film Essays.* Translated by Jay Leyda. New York, 1970.

———. *Film Form; Film Sense.* Translated by Jay Leyda. New York, 1957.
*See also* Eisenshtein

Eisenshtein, Sergei. *Izbrannye proizvedeniia.* Vol. 4. Moscow, 1966.

———. *Teatral'nye risunki.* Moscow, 1970.

Elagin, Iu. *See* Jelagin.

Erlich, Victor. *Russian Formalism.* The Hague, 1965.

Eventov, I. *Maiakovskii v Petrograde.* Leningrad, 1963.

Evreinov, N. N. *Pro scena sua.* Petersburg, 1913.

———. *Teatr dlia sebia.* Petrograd, 1915.

———. *Teatr kak takovoi.* 2nd ed. Moscow, 1923.

———. *The Theater in Life.* London, 1927.

*Fakely. See* Chulkov, Georgii.

Fevral'skii, A. V. *Desiat' let teatra Meierkhol'da.* Moscow, 1931. [Cited in the text as *Desiat let.*]

———. "Maiakovskii v bor'be za revoliutsionnyi teatr." In *Maiakovskii i sovetskaia literatura,* pp. 291–350. Moscow, 1964.

———. "Meierkhol'd i Shekspir." In *Vil'iam Shekspir,* pp. 374–402. Moscow, 1964.

———. "Misteriia-buff." In *Spektakli i gody.* Edited by A. Anastas'ev and E. Peregudova, pp. 12–24. Moscow, 1969.

———. *Pervaia sovetskaia p'esa "Misteriia-buff."* Moscow, 1971.

———. "Prokof'ev i Meierkhol'd." In *Sergei Prokof'ev: Stat'i i materialy,* pp. 94–120. 2nd ed. Moscow, 1965.

———. "Stanislavskii i Meierkhol'd." In *Tarusskie stranitsy,* pp. 289–91. Kaluga, 1961.

Fokin, M. *Protiv techeniia* (Leningrad, Moscow, 1962).

Fokine. *See* Fokin, M.

Fradkin, I. "B. Brekht: khudozsestvennye mysli." *Teatr* (January 1956): 142–55.

Fuchs, Georg. *Die Schaubühne der Zukunft.* Munich, 1906.

———. *Revolution des Theaters.* Munich, 1909.

Gassner, John. *Form and Idea in the Modern Theater.* New York, 1956.

Gladkov, A[leksandr]. "Iz vospominanii o Meierkhol'de." In *Moskva teatral'naia,* pp. 347–76. Moscow, 1960.

———. "Repliki Meierkhol'da." *Teatral'naia zhizn'* (May 1960): 19–21.

Gnesin, M. F. *Stat'i, vospominaniia, materialy.* Moscow, 1961.

*Gogol' i Meierkhol'd. See* Nikitina, E. F.

Golovin, A. Ia. *Aleksandr Iakovlevich Golovin: Vstrechi i vpechatleniia; Pis'ma; vospominaniia o Golovine.* Leningrad and Moscow, 1960.

——. *Maskarad Lermontova v eskizakh Golovina.* Moscow and Leningrad, 1946.

Gorchakov, Nikolai A. *The Theater in Soviet Russia.* Translated by Edgar Lehrman. Columbia Slavic Studies. New York, 1957.

Gorelik, Mordecai. *New Theatres for Old.* 1940. Reprint. New York, 1962.

Gray, Camilla. *The Great Experiment: Russian Art (1863–1922).* London, 1962.

Gross, George. "Abwicklung." In *Das Kunstblatt.* Edited by Paul Westheim. No. 2. Berlin, 1924.

Grotowski, Jerzy. *Towards a Poor Theatre.* New York, 1969.

Guicharnaud, Jacques. *Modern French Theater.* New Haven, 1961.

Gvozdev, A. A. *Teatr imeni Meierkhol'da, 1920–26.* Leningrad, 1927.

Hoffmann, Ludwig, and Wardetzky, Dieter, eds. *Meyerhold, Tairow, Wachtangow: Theateroktober.* Reclam-Universalbibliothek 349. Leipzig, 1967.

Hoover, Marjorie L. "A Mejerxol'd Method? 'Love for Three Oranges' (1914–16)." *Slavic and East European Journal* 13 (Spring 1969): 23–41.

——. "Brecht's Soviet Connection: Tretiakov." *Brecht Heute* 3 (1973), in press.

——. "Nikolai Erdman: A Soviet Dramatist Rediscovered." *Russian Literature Triquarterly* 2 (1972): 413–34.

——. "V. E. Meyerhold: A Russian Predecessor of Avant-Garde Theater." *Comparative Literature* 17 (Summer 1965): 234–50.

Houghton, Norris. *Moscow Rehearsals.* New York, 1936.

——. *Return Engagement.* New York, 1962.

Huppert, Hugo, ed. *Mysterium buffo.* Reclams-Universalbibliothek 135. 3rd ed. Leipzig, 1969.

Il'inskii, Igor'. *Sam o sebe.* Moscow, 1962.

*Istoriia sovetskogo dramaticheskogo teatra v 6 tt.* Vol. 2, *1921–25,* edited by K. L. Rudnitskii. Moscow, 1966.

Iutkevich, Sergei. *Kontrapunkt rezhissera.* Moscow, 1960.

Iuzovskii, Iu. *Zachem liudi khodiat v teatr.* Moscow, 1964.

Jelagin, Juri. *Temnyi genii.* New York, 1955.

——. *Ukroshchenie iskusstv.* New York, 1952. Translated as *The Taming of the Arts.* New York, 1951.

Khersonskii, Khrisanf. *Stranitsy iunosti kino.* Moscow, 1965.

*Khudozniki teatra. See* Shifrina, A. N.

Kobrin, Iu. *Teatr im. Meierkhol'da i rabochii zritel'.* Introduction by A. V. Lunacharskii. Moscow, 1926.

Komissarzhevskaia. *See Vera Fedorovna Komissarzhevskaia.*

Kopelew, Lew. "Brecht und die russische Theaterrevolution." *Brecht Heute* 3 (1973), in press.

Kramer, Hilton. "Return to Modernism." In *Soviet Union: The Fifty Years.* Edited by Harrison Salisbury. New York, 1967.

Kryzhitskii, G. *Rezhisserskie portrety.* Moscow and Leningrad, 1938.

Kugel', A. R. *Profili teatra.* Edited by A. V. Lunacharskii. Moscow, 1929.

Küppers-Lissitzky, Sophie. *El Lissitzky.* London and Greenwich, Conn., 1968.

Lacis, Asja. *Revolutionär im Beruf.* Edited by Hildegard Brenner. Munich, 1972. *See also* Lazis

Lazis, Anna. "Das Programm eines proletarischen Kindertheaters." *Alternative* 59/60 (1968): 64–67. *See also* Lacis

Lebel, Jean-Jacques. "Happenings, Theory and Practice." *New Writers* 4 (1967): 13–45.

*Lef* (1923–25); *Novyi Lef* (1927–28). Reprint. *Slavische Propyläen,* no. 91, 4 vols. Munich, 1970.

Levitskii, A. A. "Portret Doriana Greia." In *Rasskazy o kinematografe,* pp. 78–106. Moscow, 1964.

Leyda, Jay. *Kino: A History of the Russian and Soviet Film.* London, 1960. Reprint. London, 1973.

*Literaturnoe nasledstvo. See* Lunacharskii, Polotskaia (Chekhov).

Lunacharskii, A. V. *Izbrannye stat'i v 2 tt.* Vol. 1. Moscow, 1958.

———. *Neizdannye materialy. Literaturnoe nasledstvo,* vol. 82. Moscow, 1970.

Magarshack, David. *Stanislavsky on the Art of the Stage.* London, 1950.

Maiakovskii, V. V. *Maiakovskii v vospominaniakh sovremennikov.* Moscow, 1963.

———. *Polnoe sobranie sochinenii v 13 tt.* Moscow, 1955–60.

*See also* Mayakovsky

Maksimova, V. " 'Dokhodnoe mesto' v Teatre revoliutsii." In *Voprosy teatra,* pp. 37–54. Moscow, 1967.

Markov, P. A. *Pravda teatra.* Moscow, 1965.

Martinek, Karel. *Mejerchold.* Prague, 1963.

Mayakovsky, Vladimir. *Complete Plays.* New York, 1968.

*See also* Maiakovskii

Merezhkovskii, D. S. *Gogol' i chort.* Moscow, 1906.

Meyerhold. *See Vstrechi.*

*Meyerhold. See* Hoffman, Ludwig.

Mgebrov, A. A. *Zhizn' v teatre.* Moscow and Leningrad, 1932.

Mic, Constant. *See* Miklashevskii.

Miklashevskii, Konstantin [Constant Mic]. *La commedia dell'arte.* St. Petersburg, 1914. Rev. ed. Paris, 1927.

*Moskovskii Teatr Revoliutsii (1921–32). See* Boiarskii, Ia. O.

Moussinac, Léon. *La décoration théâtrale.* Paris, 1922.

*Muzei im. Bakhrushina. See* Shifrina, A. N.

Nemirovich-Danchenko, Vladimir. *My Life in the Russian Theatre.* Translated by John Cournos. Boston, 1936.

Nezhnyi, Igor'. "Teatr Okhlopkova." *Teatr* (November 1961): 131–43.

Nikitina, E. F., ed. *Gogol' i Meierkhol'd.* Moscow, 1927.

Novitskii, Pavel. *Sovremennye teatral'nye sistemy.* Moscow, 1933.

*Novyi Lef. See Lef.*

Okhlopkov, N. "Ob uslovnosti." *Teatr* (November 1959): 58–77; (December 1959): 52–73.

Olesha, Iu. *P'esy.* Moscow, 1967.

Piast, V. *Vstrechi.* Moscow, 1929.

*50 let sovetskogo iskusstva: khudozhniki teatra. See* Shifrina, A. N.

Piscator, Erwin. *Schriften.* Edited by Ludwig Hoffmann. 2 vols. Berlin, 1968.

Polotskaia, E. A. "Chekhov i Meierkhol'd." In *Literaturnoe nasledstvo,* vol. 68, pp. 417–48. Moscow, 1960. Introduction to letters from Meyerhold to Chekhov.

Pluchek, V. *Na stsene Maiakovskii.* Moscow, 1962.

Raikh, B. *Brekht.* Moscow, 1960.

*See also* Reich

Reich, Bernhard. *Im Wettlauf mit der Zeit.* Berlin, 1970. Translated into Russian as Raikh, B. *Vena; Berlin; Moskva; Berlin.* Moscow, 1972.

*See also* Raikh

*"Revizor" v teatre im. Meierkhol'da.* Leningrad, 1927.

Rickey, George. *Constructivism.* New York, 1967.

Ripellino, Angelo Maria. *Il trucco e l'anima.* Turin, 1965.

———. *Majakovskij e il teatro russo*

*d'avanguardia.* Rome, 1959.

Rodina, T. M. *Aleksandr Blok i russkii teatr nachala XX-go veka.* Moscow, 1972.

Rostotskii, B. *O rezhisserskom tvorchestve V. E. Meierkhol'da.* Moscow, 1960.

Rouché, Jacques. *L'Art théâtral moderne.* Paris, 1910.

Rubinstein, Ida. "Spectacles de gala d'Ida Rubinstein 1913." In *Comoedia.* Collection des plus beaux numéros de *Comoedia* illustré et des programmes consacrés aux ballets et galas russes depuis le début à Paris (1900–21): 109–117.

Rudnitskii, K[onstantin Lazarevich]. " 'Revizor' u Meierkhol'da." *Teatr* (December 1967): 65–80.

———. *Rezhisser Meierkhol'd.* Moscow, 1969.

Rülicke-Weiler, Käthe. "Brecht in der USSR." *Neue Deutsche Literatur* (February 1968):7–28.

———. *Die Dramaturgie Brechts.* Berlin, 1968.

Sayler, Oliver. *Russian Theater Under the Revolution.* Boston, 1920.

Schlemmer, Oskar; Moholy-Nagy, Laszlo; and Molnar, Farkas. *Die Bühne im Bauhaus.* Bauhausbücher, vol. 4. Frankfurt, 1925. Reprint. Mainz and Berlin, 1965.

Shifrina, A. N., and Iasulovich, N. Iu., eds. *Muzei im. Bakhrushina.* Moscow, 1971.

———, and Kostina, E. M., eds. *50 let sovetskogo iskusstva: khudozhniki teatra.* Moscow, 1969.

Shklovskii, Viktor. *O Maiakovskom.* Moscow, 1940.

Simonov, Ruben. *Stanislavsky's Protégé Vakhtangov.* Translated by Miriam Goldina. New York, 1969.

Sitkovetskaia, M. M. "V. E. Meierkhol'd do oktiabria." In *Vstrechi s proshlym,* pp. 299–338. Moscow, 1970.

Slonim, Marc. *Russian Theater.* Cleveland, 1961; New York, 1962.

Smirnova, Vera. *Knigi i sud'by.* Moscow, 1968.

Solov'eva, Inna. "Radi chego?" Review of revival of Nikolai Erdman's *Mandate.* *Teatr* (March 1957): 70–81.

*Staatstheater W. Meyerhold.* Theater program of 1930 tour. Berlin, 1930.

Stanislavskii, K. S. *Sobranie sochinenii v 8 tt.* Moscow, 1954–61.

———. *Pisateli, artisty, rezhissery o velikom deiatele russkogo teatra (1863–1963).* Edited by S. V. Zakharev and Sh. Sh. Bogatyrev. Moscow, 1963.

*See also* Stanislavsky

Stanislavsky, K. S. *My Life in Art.* Boston, 1924. Translated into Russian as *Moia zhizn' v iskusstve.* Moscow, 1926.

*See also* Stanislavskii

Stark, E. A. *Starinnyi teatr.* Petersburg, 1912.

*Der Sturm.* Edited by Herwarth Walden. No. 129 (Berlin, 1912).

Symons, James M. *Meyerhold's Theatre of the Grotesque, 1920–32.* Books of the Theatre Series, 8. Coral Gables, Fla., 1971.

Tairov, A. Ia. "Fokusnichestvo v nauke teatral'nogo iskusstva." *Masterstvo teatra, vremennik Kamernogo teatra* 1 (December 1922): 25–30.

———. *Notes of a Director.* Translated by William Kuhlke. Books of the Theatre Series, 7. Coral Gables, Fla., 1969.

———. *Zapiski rezhissera; Stat'i; Besedy; Rechi; Pis'ma.* Moscow, 1970.

*See also* Hoffman, Ludwig

*Teatr im. Meierkhol'da; Muzei; Katalog vystavki 5 let (1920–25)* Moscow, 1926.

*Teatr revoliutsii. See* Boiarskii, Ia. O.

*Teatral'nyi oktiabr'.* Leningrad and Moscow, 1926.

Teliakovskii, V. A. *Vospominaniia.* Leningrad and Moscow, 1965.

Timé, E. *Dorogi iskusstva*. Moscow, 1967.

*Theater of the Bauhaus*. Middletown, Conn., 1961.

Tret'iakov, Sergei M. *Ich will ein Kind haben*. Translated by Bertolt Brecht. Mimeographed. Freiburg, n.d.

———. "Khochu rebenka." *Novyi Lef* (March 1927): 3–11.

———. *Slyshish' Moskva?!* Moscow, 1966.
See also Tretjakov

Tretjakov, Sergej. *Die Arbeit des Schriftstellers*. Edited by Heiner Boehncke. Reinbek, 1972.

*Tulane Drama Review* T 30 (Winter 1965). Special issue on Happenings.
See also *Drama Review*

Ul'ianov, N. "Kurmastsep." *Novyi Zhurnal*, no. 100 (New York, 1970): 222–44.

Vakhtangov, E. *Materialy i stat'i*. Edited by L. D. Vendrovskaia. Moscow, 1959.
See also Hoffman, Ludwig

van Gyseghem, André. *Theatre in Soviet Russia*. London, 1943.

*Vera Fedorovna Komissarzhevskaia: Pis'ma aktrisy, vospominaniia o nei, materialy*. Leningrad and Moscow, 1964. [Cited in the text as *Komissarzhevskaia*.]

Volkov, N[ikolai Dmitrievich]. *Aleksandr*

*Blok i teatr*. Moscow, 1926.

———. *Meierkhol'd*. 2 vols. Moscow and Leningrad, 1929.

———. *Teatral'nye vechera*. Moscow, 1966.

Vsevolodskii-Gerngross, V. *Istoriia russkogo teatra*. Leningrad and Moscow, 1929.

*Vstrechi s Meierkhol'dom* (Moscow, 1967). [Cited in the text as *Encounters*.]

Willett, John. *The Theatre of Bertolt Brecht*. London, 1959.

Wirth, Andrzej. "Brecht and Grotowski." *Brecht Heute* I (1971): 188–95.

Worrall, Nick. "Meyerhold directs Gogol's 'Government Inspector.'" *Theatre Quarterly* 2 (1972): 75–95.

———. "Meyerhold's 'The Magnificent Cuckold.'" *Drama Review* T 57 (Spring 1973): 14–34.

Yershov, Peter. *Comedy in the Soviet Theater*. New York, 1957.

Zakhava, B. *Sovremenniki: Vakhtangov, Meierkhol'd*. Moscow, 1969.

Zharov, Mikhail. *Zhizn', teatr, kino*. Moscow, 1966.

Zingerman, Boris I. *Zhan Vilar i drugie*. Moscow, 1964.

Znosko-Borovskii, Evgenii A. *Russkii teatr nachala XX-go veka*. Prague, 1923?.

# Index